Getting Out From Under

THE CONSUMER CREDIT FOUNDATION OF AMERICA

PRESENTS

Getting Out From Under

The Complete Guide to Controlling Your Finances, Negotiating Your Creditors, and Emerging Debt-Free

Kenneth Winter Bley
and Alvin R. Lewitas

DISCLAIMER

In accord with the Declaration of Principles, a statement jointly developed and ratified by a Committee of the American Bar Association and a Committee of Publishers and Associations, this book is written and published to provide editorial opinions not necessarily based on the laws of any particular state or states.

Neither the authors nor the publishers hold themselves out to be providing legal or accurate facts or engaging in the profession or practice of law by virtue of writing or publishing this book. The laws of individual states vary greatly. If the reader requires professional legal assistance, the service of an attorney should be immediately engaged. Names of appropriate attorneys can be obtained from any local Bar Association Referral Service.

WARNING

Written for non-lawyers, this book attempts to introduce readers to many of the laws and legal procedures that may affect them. This book **does not** prepare readers to fully understand, much less handle, legal matters without guidance by an attorney. The meaning, application and effect of every law and legal procedure depends on specific facts and circumstances, and no discussion contained in this book should be considered accurate or complete in respect to any particular circumstances. Before making any decision, taking any action, or refraining from taking any action in reliance on the meaning or application of any law or legal procedure, the reader should make every effort to consult with a qualified attorney.

ISBN 0-9629551-0-8
Library of Congress No. 91-072769

The Consumer's Press, Inc.
Chicago, Illinois

(312) 943-7495

AN ACKNOWLEDGEMENT FROM KENNETH WINTER BLEY

It often has been said that the main purpose of law school is to teach law students to forget how to write plain English. Another purpose of a legal education is to learn the rules, so you can spend the rest of your life searching for exceptions to those rules. Evidently, I learned well. My first manuscript contained more legalese than a law school text. The rules that the book was about were buried under pages and pages of discussions of technical exceptions.

This book owes its existence to Alvin Lewitas. His heavy cleaver, fine-tip pen, hundreds of hours, and countless revisions finally yielded a readable text. Our editor, Rosanne Ulman, brought the language to life and rectified the grammar. Susan Block's contributions and efforts continue to go far beyond the call of duty. Thanks, also, to Brierton Design of Chicago, Illinois, for the thoughtful cover design.

Debtor-creditor law is a vast topic that cannot be learned from law books. It has to be lived and there is always something new to learn. The real authors of this book are the lawyers and clients who taught me just about everything I know about this subject. Michael Cole, who patiently introduced me to the intricacies the Bankruptcy Code and the Uniform Commercial Code. Jerry Kalish, who never let me forget that laws are for people and not the reverse. Keevan Morgan, a modern era dragon slayer who is steadfastly guarding the honor of our profession. Finally, hundreds of clients who have educated me about the real-world workings of their businesses and financial affairs.

CONTENTS

GETTING OUT FROM UNDER

CONTENTS

C O N T E N T S

section three
ALL ABOUT YOUR CREDITORS

CONTENTS

section four CONSUMER WEAPONS

CONTENTS

section five
SPECIFIC KINDS OF DEBTS AND ASSETS

CONTENTS

CONTENTS

section six
HANDLING YOUR MONEY

CONTENTS

section seven
SOME HELPFUL TECHNIQUES

section ONE

PUTTING IT INTO PROPER PERSPECTIVE

RELAX AND CLEAR YOUR HEAD

CHAPTER ONE

It's not as bad as you fear.

You are probably reading this book because you can't pay all your bills and still keep a roof over your head and food on your table.

Tens of millions of Americans have financial problems. The vast majority of them are hard-working, decent, and honest men and women. Many have had the opportunity to cheat their way out of debt, but have chosen to maintain their integrity and self-respect. As you read this book, you will find many different but legal ways to handle, what may now seem to be, overwhelming debts. Before you read on -

1 **Take several deep breaths, clear your head, and relax.**

You can't solve your financial problems by worrying. You can get out from under your debts by carefully and calmly considering your situation and developing workable solutions.

2 **Don't berate yourself.**

You are not a villain just because you can't pay your bills. You have not committed a crime merely because you are in debt.

3 **Put your financial difficulties into proper perspective.**

Health, freedom, and loving personal relationships are far more important. Don't let your financial problems cost you your health or family. Financial problems are the leading cause of marital problems, but only if you allow them to get in your way.

4 **Your financial worries are only as bad as you let them be.**

Unless they are caused by medical, or other ONGOING catastrophic expenses, your financial problems are manageable. You can decide that your lifestyle, or whatever it is that's causing your financial problems, is not worth the ordeal of indebtedness.

DEBT IN AMERICA

Chapter Two

You're not alone.

We are all in debt and we will always be in debt. Every person, company, institution, and unit of government will always owe something to somebody. We owe many things other than money, including services, products, loyalty, honesty, and love.

But this book is about only one kind of debt - financial debt, which is the obligation to repay money legally owed - and this book is about only one kind of debtor - the individual consumer.

When most people talk about debts, they speak only of voluntary debts,

Voluntary Debts

Mortgage Loans
Automobile Loans
Utility Bills
Rent
Retail Charge Accounts
Credit Cards

Involuntary Debts

Taxes
Medical Expenses
User Fees
Alimony
Fines
Civil Liability

But many debts are loaded on us without our personal consent.

CHAPTER 2

Consumer borrowing *energizes* the economy by spreading money around and creating millions of new jobs and newly enriched consumers.

Consumers account for about 60% of American purchases, and about 40% of these purchases are made on credit. For better or for worse, modern American society and its economy could not function without personal financial debt. Try to imagine an America without consumer debt:

All purchases would be C.O.D. - cash on delivery. Everyone would carry bundles of cash to pay for goods and services the moment they are received.

All utilities would have to be coin-operated.

Only a handful of people would have enough cash to buy cars, and even fewer could buy homes.

The constant need for, and use of cash, would slow down and reduce sales and all other transactions.

Without reasonable amounts of consumer debt, the American economy would be far smaller than its current size. Far fewer goods and services would be sold. Many businesses would become obsolete and totally unnecessary, including all credit related businesses. Millions and millions of jobs would be lost forever.

It is estimated that consumer households owe $3.4 trillion. The transactions creating these debts could not possibly have been handled with cash. There is less than $290 billion of American currency in circulation.

In fact, reduction of overall consumer indebtedness is one of the most reliable indicators of an oncoming economic recession.

However, the American economy can pay a price for relying so heavily on consumer debt. Reasonable levels of consumer debt energizes our economy. When debts are not paid, however, energy is drained from the economy.

Fortunately, only a small percentage of consumer debts are not paid. Most of the time, about 10 out of every 1,000 debts owed to credit card companies are not paid. About 15 out of every 1,000 debts owed to banks are not paid. Losses from these bad debts are easily covered by the profits from those that are paid.

However, when the economy is bad, people lose jobs and bad debt rates increase. Even a modest increase in the bad debt rate can lead to a chain reaction, damaging lenders and the rest of the economy.

THE BUSINESS OF LENDING

CHAPTER THREE

Let us look at how lenders make and lose money:

When you deposit your paycheck into your bank account, you're, in essence, making a loan to your bank. Your bank earns its profit by taking your money and lending it to another person or business. Of course, the bank wouldn't make a profit unless it charges its borrowers more interest than it pays you.

Creditors get much of the money they lend from consumers. Sometimes, lenders get their money directly from consumers who deposit funds in savings and checking accounts. Often, lenders obtain money from pension plans and insurance companies who are holding and investing money that consumers have entrusted to them.

Here is the how and why of it:

Suppose a lender has $100 of its own money. If it lends that $100 and charges 10% interest, when the loan is repaid the lender will have made a profit of $10, or 10%.

The bank receives a 10% return on its $100 investment:

BANK	>> **$100 loaned** >> << **$110 repaid** <<	**BORROWER**

Now suppose that lender also obtains $900 from you (a depositor), agreeing to pay you 5% interest. The bank then turns around and lends its own $100 plus your $900, charging that borrower 10% interest. When the borrower repays the bank its $1,000 loan, the bank gets $100 interest. After your bank repays the $900 it obtained from you, plus the $45 interest it owes to you, the bank still has $55.

By borrowing money, the bank receives a 55% return on its $100 investment:

DEPOSITORS	>> **$900 loaned** >>	**BANK**	>> **$1000 loaned** >>	**BORROWER**
	<< **$945 repaid** <<		<< **$1100 repaid** <<	

On its face, borrowing and then relending the borrowed money seems like a license to steal. But a closer look shows that it's not always so easy:

If the money your bank lends to a borrower is not repaid, your bank still has to repay the money it borrowed from you, plus interest. The bank ends up losing its initial $100 and still owes you $900 plus $45 interest:

DEPOSITORS	>> **$900 loaned** >>	**BANK**	>> **$1000 loaned** >>	**BORROWER**
	<< **$945 repaid** <<		<< **$0 repaid** <<	

Of course, it would be foolish for a bank, or any lender, to put all its eggs in one basket by lending all of its money to one borrower. Instead, prudent lenders limit the amount they will lend to any one borrower.

Suppose this lender limits its loans to $50 each and makes twenty such loans, charging each borrower 10% interest. Then, if one of the $50 loans goes bad, the lender will not lose money. When the 19 good loans are repaid, the lender will get back $950 of its principal (19 x $50), plus $95 interest (19 x $5), for a total of $1,045. After repaying the $945 it owes to its depositors, the lender still has its original $100:

DEPOSITORS	>> **$900 loaned** >>	**BANK**	>> **$500 loaned** >>	**BORROWER 1**
	<< **$945 repaid** <<		<< **$550 repaid** <<	
			>> **$500 loaned** >>	**BORROWER 20**
			<< **$0 repaid** <<	

That's not as bad as losing all the money, but the lender still has not made any profit.

> So, the lender decides to limit it loans to $10 each, allowing it to make 100 of these smaller loans. Then, it will not hurt as much if one of the loans goes bad. When the 99 good loans are repaid, the lender gets back $990 principal (99 x $10) plus $99 interest (99 x $1), for a total of $1,089. After repaying the $900 it borrowed from you and the $45 interest it owes to you, the lender still has the $100 it started with, plus a profit of $44.
>
> Indeed, if the lender limits each loan it makes to no more than 1% of the total amount it lends, it will at least break even if no more than 5% of the loans go bad.

A lender's chance of making or losing money depends on many factors, including:

Quality of the borrowers
Proportion of good loans to bad loans
Amount of each loan relative to the total amount lent
Interest rates the lender pays
Interest rates the lender charges
Lender's operating expenses
Economy, in general

In a recession, many consumers and businesses are unable to pay their existing debts. Fewer eligible borrowers are willing to borrow money. Consequently, bad loans become a larger portion of the lender's total loan portfolio.

Inflation always helps borrowers and hurts lenders, except when the borrower has a floating interest rate loan. In order to make a profit, a lender has to charge a rate greater than the rate of inflation.

> Suppose the annual rate of inflation is 15%. At the end of a year, $1,000 buys only what $850 bought at the beginning of the year. If the lender makes a $1,000 loan, charging 10% interest, at the end of the year the lender will have $1,100. However that $1,100 buys only what $935 bought at the start of the year. In contrast, the borrower was able to buy $1,000 worth of goods but paid for them with money that is now worth only $935.

Lending is not an easy business, and each type of lender has its own problems and preferences as you will soon see.

DEBT AND MORALITY

Chapter Four

Don't feel guilty about owing money.

Debt has been around throughout recorded history but attitudes about it have varied a lot from time to time and culture to culture. Our Judeo-Christian heritage always has recognized the necessity for borrowing, but never has been totally comfortable with the idea of the resulting debt.

The Old Testament required that all slaves be freed, and all debts be forgiven, every seventh year. In modern times, the burden of debt itself can become a form of slavery.

Later, Catholic Canon Law rejected the Old Testament tolerance for debt. It discouraged all forms of borrowing and prohibited the charging of interest. Eventually, and out of economic necessity, relatively low rates of interest were permitted.

Around the time of the Protestant Reformation, attitudes toward debt markedly changed. Not only was the charging of interest proper, but borrowers who didn't pay their debts were thrown into "debtor's prison." There they would stay until relatives, or friends, paid their debts.

For many years, western society even tolerated "indentured servitude." This was a form of slavery where the debtor was forced to work for nothing, in order to pay off a debt. This debt could, very well, include the cost of travel from Europe to America.

Contemporary Western attitudes have pretty much returned to where they were some five thousand years ago. Debt is considered an economic necessity. Many laws have now been enacted to protect borrowers from predatory lenders. Indeed, bankruptcy laws are considered so important that the United States Constitution entrusted them only to the federal government, rather than to the whims of state and local governments.

Modern American society doesn't consider debt to be either evil or immoral. Although borrowing too much is considered imprudent, and sometimes irresponsible, it isn't a crime and few Americans view it as such.

Modern American society demands only that borrowing be done in *GOOD FAITH*, with a sincere intent to pay. Then, a subsequent inability to pay a debt isn't perceived as a sin. Most Americans understand that situations beyond a person's control can arise that prevent repayment of all debts.

However, *cheating* is rightfully viewed differently. Cheating is doing something that a person knows is *unfair* and is likely to *hurt another*. Cheating is immoral and, if it becomes too prevalent, can cause a collapse of our economic system.

Every voluntary debt arises from an exchange of promises. The creditor promises to give something in return for which the borrower promises to make future payments. The bargain is fair if:

Both parties are fully informed
Both parties have equal bargaining power
Both parties are honest

Otherwise, one party can reap a windfall at the expense of the other. Unfortunately, there are a number of borrowers and creditors who intentionally cheat. They are the:

Creditors

who deceive consumers about the actual costs of borrowing;

who exploit consumer confusion or ignorance to make unfairly high profits;

who extend credit knowing that the consumer didn't get a fair deal;

who offer credit knowing that the consumer is either over-extended or will have trouble paying the debt;

who use strong-arm tactics and deceitful practices to collect from consumers who are in legitimate financial trouble.

Borrowers

who lie about their income or assets to obtain credit;

who seek and accept credit with no intention of paying;

who are fully able, but refuse, to pay their legitimate debts.

section TWO

STEP BY STEP PROCEDURE FOR HANDLING YOUR DEBTS

INTRODUCTION TO SECTION TWO

Most consumers fail to overcome their financial problems and give up without a fight, or they just keep paying bills until they run out of money, time, and options. Unless you want your debts and creditors to rule your life, you have to take control over your financial situation.

> The worksheets prepared for this book (and located at the end of the book) will help you assemble and work with the information discussed throughout this section.

Don't worry if you are one of those people intimidated by mathematics and accounting. The worksheets do most of the work for you. Each worksheet has its own instructions.

All you have to do is collect the necessary information and perform some simple grammar school addition, subtraction, multiplication, and division.

The task of assembling and working with the information is almost as important as getting the right answers. Doing the worksheets requires you to think about how much money you have to spend, how you are spending it, and what is really important to you.

Be aware that your notes and working papers may have to be produced in court some day. Do not save any papers that contain information that can be used against you. Even if the information is just hypothetical, an unscrupulous opponent may try to twist it to show that you did something wrong, such as failing to report income or concealing assets. Destroy them as soon as you are finished with them - and before you are asked to produce them.

UNDERSTANDING YOUR SITUATION

CHAPTER FIVE

Most consumers do not understand their situation as well as they think they do.

Just knowing that you don't have enough money to pay your bills is not very useful. You also have to know why you are short of money, how short of money you are, and what you can do about it. Gut feelings and instincts do not give you reliable answers to these questions. Only proper information and careful thought will give you the answers. Save your feelings and gut instincts for the decisions you will make AFTER you have used your head.

Most financial problems are not as bad as consumers fear. As a rule of thumb:

> Your financial problems are MANAGEABLE if they arise from an inability to pay PAST debts.
>
> Your financial problems are SERIOUS if you will not be able to acquire essential items needed in the FUTURE, even if you do not have to pay any of your past debts.

In order to properly understand your financial situation, you should assemble and consider information about your

- CASH INCOME
- LIVING EXPENSES
- DEBTS
- ASSETS

After you assemble this information, you will use it to determine what alternatives are open to you.

CASH INCOME

Of course, your income determines how much you have to spend. Although non-cash income can help you reduce certain expenses, it rarely has a major effect on your financial condition.

Determine your CASH income for the past year and use that figure to estimate your cash income for the coming year. Be realistic! Include only income on which you can reasonably rely. Take into account any increases or decreases you truly expect to happen. If your estimate of future income greatly differs from last year's actual income, make sure you have sound reasons for the difference.

By examining all your past cash income and expected future sources of cash income, you can determine to what extent your expected income will meet your future living expenses, your future debt payments, and your past due debts. Finally, you also will determine whether it is practical for you to try to increase your cash income.

LIVING EXPENSES

Everyone knows what "living expenses" are, but no two people agree on what are NECESSARY living expenses. That's because no one is really sure what is really necessary, and no two people's needs are exactly the same.

Some people list necessary living expenses as the costs of those items needed to maintain life. Perhaps there was a time when it was enough just to have a roof, some fire wood, one set of clothing, and a loaf of bread. Life is not that simple any more. Few people living in modern America can survive on these minimum necessities. Indeed, about the only way for you to be certain as to whether something is necessary is to try to survive without it.

> It's neither fun nor useful to try to figure out your minimum necessary living expenses, so don't bother.

However, it is very important to understand each of your expenses and to decide how important each expense is to you. You need to list all of last year's expenses, determine how necessary each one was, and then estimate your expenses over the next twelve months.

> Do NOT include any past or future debt payments. Debt payments are different from other expenses because you are legally obligated to continue paying them. You can't just get rid of your liability for debts; you have to get the consent of your creditors, or take other carefully thought-out actions. Later you will examine each of your debt obligations separately.

You will find it useful to group your expenses into three categories:

Essential Expenses	unavoidable expenses you simply can't live without. Somehow or another, you must secure enough income to pay these expenses.
Important Expenses	expenses needed to maintain the same standard of living as you now enjoy, but which you can temporarily do without, if necessary.
Avoidable Expenses	expenses unnecessary to maintain your basic standard of living.

You are the only one who really knows what you need, so it's important that you be honest with yourself. It's easy to recognize that a vacation home, designer clothing, caviar, and laser disks fall into neither the essential nor the important category. However, it's harder to decide whether and when to spend money on a reliable car, a warm winter coat, or toys for a toddler.

It isn't possible, or even necessary, to assign every expense to its precise category. It's more important to get a good estimate of the total expenses within each group. After finding out what you can afford and when you can afford it, you may decide that some of your expenses are really more, or less, necessary than they may seem right now.

By carefully examining each of your expenses and their importance, you can determine whether it's possible to reduce your expenses; which expenses are least important to you and, therefore, most easily eliminated; and how much money you can free up to handle your debts.

DEBTS

When you incur a debt, you have chosen to defer payment for something you wish to obtain now. Unlike other expenses, though, a debt can take on a life all its own. Debts grow because of interest charges and late payment charges. This continuing growth can make it difficult, if not impossible, to reduce the original amount of the debt itself. Some debts can even cost you more to avoid than to pay. Nevertheless, by carefully examining each of your debts, and each of your creditors, you can determine:

which debts are most important and need to be paid first
which debts can be disputed
which debts can be reduced by means other than payment
how much money you will need to handle your debts
which creditors are dangerous
which creditors you can put off or ignore, and
how much time you have before creditors can start hurting you.

1ST, *group your debts by their FUTURE IMPORTANCE to you >*

Think of your future debt payments as expenses and group them in the same way that you group your cash expenses:

Essential Debts A debt is essential if it represents a critical living expense. For example, housing is a critical expense, and you probably have to pay mortgage payments or rent to keep a roof over your head. If it's impossible to sell your home and move, your mortgage payments are essential. But, if you can sell your house and buy or rent less expensive housing, or move in with parents, some or all of your mortgage debt is not essential.

Important Debts A debt is important if it's necessary to substantially maintain your present standard of living. Financing for a reliable recent model car may be important, but financing for a new luxury car probably is not.

Avoidable Debts A debt is avoidable if it's incurred for something that does not affect your basic lifestyle. For example, you don't need a country club membership in order to play golf. You always can play on a public course. Running up large bills for custom-tailored clothing at designer boutiques is probably an avoidable debt; perfectly acceptable clothing can be purchased at a department store.

2ND, *identify those creditors that are DANGEROUS to you >*

Assess how dangerous each creditor is to you. If you don't pay, what can the creditor do to you and how long will it take. Determine whether you need a product or service that you can obtain only from that creditor, such as electricity. If the creditor is secured, decide whether you want to keep the collateral or can afford to let it be repossessed. If the creditor is unsecured, estimate how long it will take the creditor to obtain a judgment against you. Take into account whether you have any defenses or counterclaims against the creditor.

Do not make the common mistake of confusing pushy creditors with important or dangerous creditors. Often, a creditor makes a lot of noise because there is nothing else it can do. Most likely, you will find your Essential Debts are owed to the most dangerous creditors and the avoidable debts to the least dangerous creditors.

ASSETS

Your assets, the property you own, are both your strength and your vulnerability. They permit you to live as well as you are living, and you can voluntarily use them to pay some of your debts. On the other hand, your creditors may be able to use some of your assets to FORCE you to pay your debts. Creditors rarely pursue used household goods and personal effects because they are not worth anything, and rarely can be sold for enough to justify the cost and effort.

List each asset you own that can be sold for enough to be worth the trouble, and then determine:

Its Value

One of two values most often applies to property:

Fair Market Value — the price an item will bring if sold by a willing seller to a willing buyer, if neither of them is under any pressure to buy or sell. This is the price you can expect to get if you have time to sell the asset to someone who wants it.

Liquidation Value — the price an asset will bring if it's sold quickly and under pressure, such as at a sale at public auction.

Whether it is collateral for a debt

If the asset already secures a debt, note how much you owe on that debt.

Equity in the property

Your equity equals the value remaining after you have paid off all debts secured by that asset. If the asset is not collateral, your equity is the same as the value. "Quick Equity" is your equity if the property is sold quickly for its Liquidation Value. "Full Equity" is your equity if the property is sold for its Fair Market Value.

How much of your equity is protected from creditors

All states exempt, or protect, certain property from creditors. Which property and how much varies from state to state. Generally, but not always, property is not exempt from secured creditors when they are given the property as collateral.

By carefully and honestly examining each of your assets, you can determine whether you have assets you don't need, and you can sell for cash, you can use as collateral for a loan, and you should protect from your creditors.

IDENTIFYING YOUR ALTERNATIVES

CHAPTER SIX

There are many different ways to handle any one particular debt.

But the way you handle that debt limits your options for handling other debts. Developing the "best" strategy for handling all of your debts is not as easy as deciding how to handle a single debt.

To simplify your planning, examine each possible alternative and eliminate those that are not practical for you. You can handle your financial problems in any of the following ways:

- **Pay your debts**
- **Ignore some or all of your debts**
- **Protect your income and assets from creditors**
- **Discharge your debts through legal procedures**
- **Combine two or more alternatives**

PAYING YOUR DEBTS

The first and most obvious alternative is to pay all of your debts. However, if you could pay all your debts right now, you wouldn't have any financial problems. Therefore, your more likely options are:

- Pay your debts over time
- Pay your debts by reducing them
- Pay your debts by selling property
- Pay your debts by borrowing money

DETERMINE WHETHER YOU CAN PAY ALL YOUR DEBTS OVER TIME

If your estimates of your income and expenses are reliable, you can determine, with some degree of certainty, whether it's possible for you to pay all your debts over time and what sacrifices you will have to make to do so. Earlier, you estimated your income and expenses for the coming 12 months and grouped both your living expenses and your debts into nine categories:

Essential	Expenses * Debts - future monthly payments * Debts - past due amounts
Important	Expenses Debts - future monthly payments * Debts - past due amounts
Avoidable	Expenses Debts - future monthly payments * Debts - past due amounts

Assuming you can't reduce any of your debts, then Important Expenses and Avoidable Expenses are the only two categories you will be able to reduce. However, you may be able to pay all past due amounts over time. So, add the remaining four categories (marked with asterisks * above) and deduct their total from your estimated monthly cash income:

	Your Estimated Monthly Cash Income
LESS	Essential Expenses and All Future Monthly Debt Payments (*)
EQUALS	Monthly Income Available to Pay Past Due Debts

Any money left over at the end of the month can go to pay your past due debts. Divide the total amount of your past due debts by your leftover monthly income to see how long it will take you to bring all of your debts current:

	Your Total Past Due Debts (Essential, Important and Avoidable)
DIVIDED BY	Monthly Income Available to Pay Past Due Debts
EQUALS	Number of Months to Bring Debts Current

The length of time it will take to bring your past due debts current is very important. During this time your creditors will be waiting to collect money that is already past due. Although most creditors will happily agree to let you bring your past due payments current over a few months, or even a year, most will resist if it is going to take much longer than that.

You may have difficulty persuading your creditors to give you more than a year without resorting to a Chapter 13 proceeding under the Bankruptcy Code. If it will take you more than three years to pay off your past due debts, forget it; paying all your debts isn't a viable alternative for you. Even under a Chapter 13 plan, five years is the maximum time allowed to pay your past due debts. Determine how long it will take to pay off your past debts, before adopting any approach.

Remember, during this time you will not be spending money on Important Expenses, and that affects your standard of living. If you think it is too much of a sacrifice to refrain from spending on such expenses, repeat the same calculations, except this time deduct both Essential Expenses and Important Expenses before paying past due debts. If you can pay your Essential and Important Debts and your Essential and Important Expenses, and bring your past due debts current within a reasonably short time, solving your financial problems should be easy.

Also remember that during this time you will not be spending on Avoidable Expenses. If you think that it is too much of a sacrifice to refrain from spending on such expenses while bringing your debts current, then you must find a way to increase your income.

DETERMINE WHETHER YOU CAN PAY YOUR DEBTS BY REDUCING THEM

If you cannot pay all your debts, or you can't make the sacrifices necessary to pay them, you still may be able to reduce some or all of your debts in one of two ways:

Enter into settlement agreements with one or more creditors >

Determine if this approach is practical by reviewing each of the debts you listed. Decide if it's likely that you can settle with any of your creditors. If you think that you can achieve one or more settlements, repeat your calculations to see if your income is sufficient to handle your reduced level of debts. Sometimes, a credible threat of proceedings under the Bankruptcy Code helps persuade a difficult, but rational, creditor to enter into a settlement. Unfortunately, though, difficult creditors often are not rational.

Seek relief under Chapter 13 of the Bankruptcy Code >

Under Chapter 13 proceedings, you can force unsecured creditors to accept much less than the full amounts of their claimed debts, and you have three or, in some cases, five years to bring current any past due secured debts. Reading the discussion of in Chapter 12 about bankruptcy will help you better understand this alternative.

DETERMINE WHETHER YOU CAN PAY YOUR DEBTS BY SELLING PROPERTY

If your cash income is not large enough to pay off your debts, you may be able to raise cash by selling some of your property. For the purposes of this analysis, selling property has the same effect as increasing your income. It produces cash that can be used to help handle your debts. In addition to real estate, types of property that often are valuable enough to sell include antiques, appliances, collections, electronic equipment, and motor vehicles.

The amount an asset will sell for depends on how it's sold. If you can take your time and find a buyer who isn't taking advantage of your financial problems, you should be able to sell the asset for its full fair market value. If you are under pressure, you probably will have to sell the asset quickly and get only its liquidation value. Both values vary with changing economic conditions. Generally, a depressed economy means lower values. However, sometimes, certain used items actually increase in value because people can't afford to buy new products.

Earlier, you made a list of all your valuable property and estimated each item's liquidation value and fair market value. You can use that information to decide whether selling assets can help you resolve your debts.

1ST, review your list of assets and your circumstances to decide which items, if any, are practical and worthwhile to sell. If you have only one refrigerator, you can't sell it unless you are moving somewhere that already has a refrigerator. If you have only one car and need it for work, you can't sell it unless you can replace it with a less expensive vehicle. If you have spent most of your life assembling a valued collection, the price it will fetch may not be worth its loss to you. On the other hand, you may not need that second car, fancy stereo, or vacation home.

2ND, list the items that are practical for you to sell along with their anticipated selling prices, and total their combined values. If you are under severe time pressure, use liquidation values. If you expect to have enough time, use fair market values.

3RD, treat the money you can get from selling assets as additional cash income. Take the combined value of the assets you can sell and divide that amount by twelve (because you are working with monthly figures). Add this monthly amount to your expected monthly cash income. Repeat the calculations you did before and see if your income, including the money from selling assets, will be sufficient to handle your debts.

DETERMINE WHETHER YOU CAN PAY YOUR DEBTS BY BORROWING

As is explained in Chapter 18 (Debt Payments and Debt Consolidations), it's rarely a good idea to borrow from a new creditor to pay old creditors, especially if the new creditor is a relative or a friend.

Borrowing new money to pay old debts makes sense only when you can obtain a long-term loan that reduces the total monthly debt payments YOU ACTUALLY ARE MAKING (versus what you are supposed to be paying) and solves ALL of your financial problems. Otherwise, you're just jumping from the frying pan into the fire.

You probably will not get a long-term loan to pay off old debts without putting up collateral. Real estate is about the only property that most consumers can use as collateral for a long-term loan. You can determine whether obtaining a long-term loan is practical:

1ST, determine whether your property has sufficient value to enable you to borrow as much as you need. Add up the fair market values of all your real estate and any other property that can be used as collateral. Then subtract your total debts.

If the total value of the property you can use as collateral isn't greater than your total debts, it's unlikely that borrowing money will be practical for you.

2ND, determine what your monthly payments will be. Your monthly payments depend on the amount of the loan (your total debts), plus loan transaction costs, interest rate, and length of the loan. Find out the new monthly payments from the proposed new creditor. If you know the interest rate, you can determine the exact monthly payments by using a financial calculator or a loan amortization table. The following table will give you a rough idea of your possible monthly payments:

INTEREST RATE	MONTHLY PAYMENT for each $1,000.00 borrowed		
	10 year loan	20 year loan	30 year loan
5.0 %	10.61	6.60	5.37
6.0 %	11.10	7.16	6.00
7.0 %	11.61	7.75	6.65
8.0 %	12.13	8.36	7.34
9.0 %	12.67	9.00	8.05
10.0 %	13.22	9.65	8.78
11.0 %	13.76	10.32	9.52
12.0 %	14.35	11.01	10.29
13.0 %	14.93	11.72	11.06
14.0 %	15.53	12.44	11.85
15.0 %	16.13	13.17	12.64
16.0 %	16.75	13.91	13.45
17.0 %	17.38	14.67	14.26
18.0 %	18.01	15.43	15.07
19.0 %	18.67	16.21	15.89
20.0 %	19.33	16.99	16.71

For example, if the lowest interest rate you can get is 10% and you need to borrow $50,000.00, your monthly payments on a thirty-year loan will be $8.78 x 50, or $439.00 per month.

3RD, determine whether you can make the payments. Take your expected monthly income, subtract your Essential Monthly Expenses, and then subtract the new monthly loan payments.

> *If your income is not sufficient to cover your Essential Expenses and the new monthly loan payments, borrowing the money is not a practical alternative for you.*

4TH, determine whether it is advantageous to borrow the money.

> *If your old monthly debt payments are lower than the new monthly loan payments, borrowing the money will make your financial situation worse.*
>
> *If your income is not sufficient to cover your Essential Monthly Expenses, your Important Monthly Expenses, and your new monthly loan payments, you will have to reduce your standard of living in order to make your new monthly loan payments.*

IGNORING SOME OR ALL OF YOUR DEBTS

If you are one of the millions of consumers who have no income, no assets, and no need for a good credit history, there is nothing that an unsecured creditor can do to you. At worst, the creditor can aggravate you for a while and, if a judgment is obtained, make you appear for an examination.

Even if you have some income and assets, you may be able to ignore some, or all, of your ordinary creditors. However, don't ignore your creditors just because it's the easiest thing to do. Before you ignore any creditor, determine:

- Whether the creditor poses a real danger to you
    - Whether the creditor will become dangerous if it obtains a judgment against you

You will find it helpful to read Chapters 10 (Creditors' Favorite Weapons) and Chapter 14 (Handling Specific Debts).

If you find that a particular creditor does not pose a danger to you, then your best course of action may be to ignore that debt, at least until you are in a position to do something about it. If you are able to ignore enough of your debts, you may be able to handle those debts that must be paid. Generally, it's much better to ignore a creditor than to make promises you cannot keep.

DETERMINING WHETHER A CREDITOR POSES A DANGER TO YOU

In order to determine whether ignoring a debt is practical, you must carefully consider whether that creditor poses a danger to you. You may find it helpful to group your creditors into the following four categories:

Creditors who cannot be ignored without risking serious legal consequences >

Obligations for child support, alimony, court-imposed fines and penalties, and court-ordered restitution for criminal conduct can't be ignored. They can be enforced in many unpleasant ways.

Creditors who cannot be ignored without risk of losing an essential service or product >

You'll only hurt yourself by ignoring debts owed to creditors whose services or products you will need. Failure to pay rent may result in an eviction. Failure to pay a utility bill may result in the loss of a essential service. However, if you are planning to move out of state, neither of these creditors poses a danger to you.

Secured creditors who cannot be ignored without losing the collateral >

Debts secured by your assets must be paid or you probably will lose the collateral. These include your mortgage and car loans. However, if you do not care about the collateral, the debt is no different from any other ordinary unsecured debt. Tax debts are secured by just about all of your earnings, real estate, and other assets you own. Debts on government-guaranteed educational loans should be considered secured by any and all of your future income tax refunds.

Ordinary unsecured creditors >

Most credit card bills, store charges, and similar debts cannot be enforced unless the creditor first obtains a judgment and then manages to successfully enforce that judgment.

DETERMINING WHETHER A JUDGMENT POSES A DANGER TO YOU

Eventually, though, any creditor may be able to obtain a judgment against you. Before you let that happen, you need to know how much of your Income and assets a judgment creditor can reach.

Don't worry about furniture, clothing, and other property that cannot easily be sold for enough to justify the effort. If an asset is not worth enough for you to take the trouble to sell, a judgment creditor won't want it either. Collection attorneys are not in the business of conducting garage sales.

If you have income, determine how much of it can be attached or garnished. Federal and state laws also protect much of your income and property from most creditors. State laws vary, and you need to check your own state's wage attachment or garnishment statute. Federal law protects Social Security benefits, federal retirement benefits, wages of federal employees, and benefit payments from federally approved and *bona fide* employer pension plans. Federal law also prevents creditors, other than the IRS, from taking more than 25% of a consumer's disposable earnings.

If you have property, determine how much of it is vulnerable to judgment creditors. Again, state laws vary, so check your own state's exemption statute. Federal law offers very little protection of property.

Even if you know how to use a law library, it's difficult for a non-lawyer to determine exactly what protections your state offers. These legal protections often appear under strange names. Sometimes, a protection is not written as a prohibition against doing something; instead it's merely omitted as a legal procedure. In those instances, it is the absence of legal authorization that protects consumers from a particular collection procedure.

> If you want to know exactly what income and property are protected from your creditors, you ought to consult a lawyer or check with the clerk of your county court. It's easier to find out if the particular type of income or property in which you have a particular interest, is protected than to obtain a complete list of all legal protections.

PROTECTING YOUR INCOME AND ASSETS

If you have enough time, you can take steps to protect some, or all, of your income and assets from your creditors. There is no simple rule of thumb for determining whether this approach is practical for you. Rather, you have to carefully go through a three step process:

1ST, identify all the income and property that are important to you.

2ND, determine which income and property are not legally protected, or exempt, from judgment creditors.

3RD, make it uneconomical, difficult, or impossible for a judgment creditor to seize that income and property. Many ways to do this are discussed at length in Chapter 12 (Important Consumer Strategies) and Chapter 15 (Protecting Specific Assets).

It's difficult to protect property from secured creditors who have liens on that property. Often, though, you can take steps to protect that property from other creditors.

DISCHARGING YOUR DEBTS

If all else fails, there is relief for you through a liquidation under Chapter 7 of the United States Bankruptcy Code. This alternative is discussed, at length, in Chapter 12 of this book.

If you are especially concerned about the publicity or formality of a Chapter 7 bankruptcy, you may be able to obtain relief through an Assignment for the Benefit of Creditors (ABC). An ABC operates much like an informal, out-of-court bankruptcy, but in many ways is not as effective as a proceeding under the Bankruptcy Code. ABCs are described in greater detail in Chapter 12 (Important Consumer Strategies).

COMBINING ALTERNATIVES

If you choose to solve your financial woes by combining alternatives, you can either:

> Use different approaches for different creditors. For example, you can pay one debt in full, settle a second debt, and ignore a third or,
>
> use a series of different approaches with the same creditor. For example, you can start by ignoring a creditor, then offer the creditor's lawyer a settlement, and finally seek relief under the Bankruptcy Code.

ADOPTING A STRATEGY

CHAPTER SEVEN

You need a strategy.

Your strategy, or overall plan, will be designed to achieve your final goal and must take into account ALL of your financial and personal circumstances. If you don't have a strategy, you won't know where you're going or how you got there. You will be at the mercy of your creditors and other forces that affect your life. There are countless ways to go about formulating your strategy, but all of them require careful attention to detail. Naturally, the simpler your circumstances, the easier the task.

This chapter sets forth our recommended method for developing a goal-driven strategy. This method enables you to base each choice on your overall objectives and to see the effect of each choice on your overall situation. If you carefully perform each of the following steps, you should end up with a workable strategy that will suit your needs.

1ST, *identify your goals and determine their relative importance >*

Everyone has different goals in life, but here are some common ones:

Peace of mind
Freedom from stress
Independence
Self respect
Enjoyable and fulfilling occupation
Providing quality education for children
Eating well
Living in a comfortable residence
Driving a reliable vehicle
Financial security for dependents
Dressing well
Moving to a warmer climate
Pursuing a hobby
Theater, film, or other cultural activities

Now, identify the goals that REQUIRE MONEY and assign each one a value in order of its importance. For example, if you have 15 goals, your most important goal has a value of 15 and your least important a value of 1. Don't include making money as a goal. Making money is not a goal in itself. Instead, list the things that money can get you.

2ND, *determine whether your anticipated spending is consistent with your goals >*

For each of your NON-essential expenses and NON-essential debts, make two lists:

GOALS THAT THE EXPENSE OR DEBT ENABLES YOU TO ACHIEVE	GOALS THAT THE EXPENSE OR DEBT PREVENTS YOU FROM ACHIEVING

Contrast the two lists to determine whether the expense or debt is in line with your goals. The simplest way to do this is to use the values you assigned to your goals. Subtract the total of the values on the second list from the total of values on the first list. The resulting numerical score of any one particular item is not important. Rather, the RELATIONSHIPS between all the scores are what is important - expenses and debts that have higher scores contribute more toward achieving your overall goals than those that have lower scores.

Assigning and tallying numerical values is a useful way to assess your priorities, but this approach has flaws that can produce some rather silly results. Don't mechanically follow the numbers. Apply some common sense.

3RD, *determine whether your income is sufficient to achieve your goals >*

See if your cash income will cover all the expenses that are consistent with your goals, plus future monthly payments for the debts that are consistent with your goals.

If your income isn't sufficient, eliminate the least important expenses and debts, until the remaining expenses and debt payments are low enough for you to afford.

4TH, *determine how to handle your other existing debts >*

You still have three other types of existing debt obligations that you need to handle:

Past due amounts owed for debts that help you achieve your goals.

Past due amounts for debts that prevent you from achieving your goals.

Obligations to make future payments on debts that prevent you from achieving your goals.

Review each remaining obligation and determine the best alternative for managing it. At this point, you may find that you do not have sufficient income to handle all your remaining debts. If so, revise your budget to free up more cash, or find ways to manage some of your remaining debts without paying cash.

5TH, *check your cash flow >*

So far, you have ignored the timing of your income, expenses, and debt payments. However, just having a large enough annual income is not always enough. You need to make sure you will have cash when you need it, especially if you intend to enter into a payment plan with one or more creditors. The only way to do this is to prepare a cash flow projection for the next 12 months. After you prepare your cash flow projection, you may find that you will have to adjust the timing of some of your expenses or payments.

6TH, *review your strategy and make sure all the parts fit together >*

Make sure that your approaches work together as an overall strategy. For example, it makes no sense to settle with one unimportant creditor if you're planning to file bankruptcy to discharge other debts.

7TH, *make sure your strategy is consistent with YOUR goals, values and personality >*

You are not likely to dramatically change your goals, values, and personality within the time you have to solve your financial problems. A strategy that doesn't suit you probably won't work. If you're a compulsive spender, don't kid yourself into believing that you're going to pay all your creditors by holding yourself to a bare-bones budget for the next two years. Be realistic!

IMPLEMENTING YOUR STRATEGY

CHAPTER EIGHT

Now you need to implement your strategy.

This involves little more than organizing yourself by making a chronological list of the things you need to do and then DOING them.

1ST, *determine the specific actions you need to take >*

You already have a budget and cash flow projection for handling your income and payments. You also have a list of debts and your general approach to dealing with them. Now you should list specific actions other than making payments. The easiest way to make this list is to examine each category of activity and note everything that you must remember to do. Use the following outline to help you get started.

GENERAL ACTIONS:

See a debt counselor
Look for a lender
See an accountant
See a lawyer

SPECIFIC ACTIONS:

For each source of income:

Actions needed to increase it
Actions needed to protect it from creditors

For each item of valuable property:

Actions needed to determine its value
Actions needed to sell it
Actions needed to use it as collateral
Actions needed to protect it from creditors

For each Debt:

Actions needed to compromise it
Actions needed to dispute it
Actions needed to discharge it
Actions needed to sell collateral
Actions needed to surrender collateral
Actions needed to protect collateral
Actions needed to obtain time
Actions needed to enter into a payment plan

For each expense:

Actions needed to reduce it

2ND, *prepare a schedule* >

After you have completed your "to do" list, determine when you need to do each of them. Put them in chronological order and prepare a schedule or time-table.

3RD, *follow your strategy* >

Unless it becomes clear that your strategy is not working, stick with it. You have put a lot of thought into your strategy and it's probably very good. A carefully considered plan has a much better chance to succeed than any hunches or impulses you may have later. When the unexpected happens, find a way to fit it into your strategy. If your circumstances change so much that you can't follow your strategy, don't just plunge ahead without thinking. Rather, go back and formulate a new strategy.

4TH, *be patient and persistent* >

It took you a while to get into your current financial situation. It's going to take time to get out of it. Be patient. Don't give up. Remember, if you have enough income to cover your essential expenses and future debt payments, it's almost certain that your financial problems are manageable. If you keep at them, you can, and WILL solve them.

section THREE

ALL ABOUT YOUR CREDITORS

UNDERSTANDING CREDITORS

CHAPTER NINE

You need to know as much about your creditors as they know about you.

WHY YOU NEED TO UNDERSTAND YOUR CREDITORS

You are in a battle for your financial survival. In this battle, your creditors are your adversaries. Your mission is to stop or at least delay your creditors from harassing you, taking your property and damaging your ability to put food on your family's table.

In order to succeed in this battle, you need to understand creditor psychology. You have to fathom how they think. You have to know what they want, what will satisfy them, what they can and will do to you. Finally, you must understand how they most likely will do it to you.

Understanding your creditors will do a lot to help you conquer your debts and protect yourself and your family from creditor tyranny.

TYPES OF BUSINESS CULTURES

By understanding creditors' attitudes toward you, you will be able to plan how to handle various situations as they arise. Creditors' attitudes toward their own businesses and customers vary from company to company and from individual to individual.

When you deal with a large institution, you will find that corporate attitude, or institutional culture, is more important than the personal feelings of individual employees. When dealing with small or decentralized lenders, the individual employee's attitudes usually count more.

Chapter 9

Many institutions have corporate cultures and organizational attitudes that are drilled into all employees and affect their every decision. The following is a useful over-simplification by which we categorize various corporate attitudes:

Highly Professional This is the decide-by-the-numbers approach, or "What's the bottom line?" Emotions, feelings, charity, morality, and ethics simply don't factor into corporate operations or decisions. Most large lenders fall into this category. When dealing with any of them, remember that you are talking to someone who invariably follows a strict set of rules and procedures.

Predatory Found among both large and small creditors, predators see the world as a battlefield. They view consumers as a resource to be exploited and will do almost anything to increase profits. Employees feel pressured to be aggressive because their effectiveness is measured by profits. When making decisions, they rely only on cost-benefit analyses. Surprisingly, these are often the easiest creditors to manage. When given opportunity and motive, predators are likely to do something that legally justifies your refusal to pay. They also may end up forgiving your debt so they can concentrate on victimizing others.

Fat and Content These lenders, who exist because some long-ago founders built successful businesses, tend to take their businesses for granted. Frequently, a single family owns the business and routinely think of it as a money machine. Many of the employees working for such companies have been with them for years. Everyone is making a comfortable living. Their attitudes toward you may, above all, depend on their perceptions of you. When dealing with these lenders, get them to like you. Ethnicity, mutual friends, mutual problems, partial payments, and a Christmas card all serve to strengthen your ties to them. Many are making such an assured good living that they care more about their affinity with clients than the bottom line. If you NEVER lie to them, they may work with you forever.

Insolvent or Anxious These lenders may themselves be in financial trouble. For whatever reasons, they are having trouble repaying their own creditors, who lent them the money that they have lent to you. Insolvent or anxious creditors sound very tough and aggressive on the phone, but will do almost anything for quick cash. If you can raise the money, and have the tenacity to demand a final settlement, this is the best time to cut a deal. They may take as little as twenty-five or fifty cents on the dollar just to feed their cash flow. However, don't delay. Once they are belly-up, the trustee or successor may not be in such a hurry to settle with you on the same terms.

GOOD GUYS Few and far between, these are almost always in smaller organizations. There is nothing worse for a consumer who intends to lie and cheat than to come up against a creditor who is really a good guy. Don't confuse good guys with predators who only pretend to care. Real good guys play straight. They do everything reasonably possible to help you. They listen and offer suggestions. If you have money to spare, pay them first. Many of these lenders become savage if you lie to them. They will try to bury you, if they can. They don't forget anything and might chase you for years if they think they have been duped. The only way to deal with these creditors is honestly and frequently. Many will not only work with you, but actually help you, as long as you don't try to take them for a ride.

LARGE VERSUS SMALL CREDITORS

Apart from a lender's cultural climate, size is probably its most telling characteristic. A local credit union and corporate giant differ in more ways than numbers alone. They are completely separate species because of their different sizes.

LARGE INSTITUTIONS

Large institutions usually have lots of money, equipment, and people. Such expansive resources enable them to do many more things than their smaller counterparts, but size also creates its own set of problems:

CONTROL AND MANAGEMENT Many large institutions spend almost as much time and energy on internal organization as on conducting business. In a highly centralized organization, where senior managers make almost all decisions, the staff has to endlessly generate written reports and numbers for senior management's use. In a decentralized organization, which contains a series of independently managed divisions or departments, middle and senior managers have to spend much of their time in meetings to make sure everybody is rowing in the same direction. In both situations, however, managing a large institution creates a demand for frequent meetings and a constant flow of paperwork.

Just knowing what's going on isn't enough; senior management has to control the institution's activities. The larger the institution is, the more people it requires. The more people, the greater the possibility of incompetence and dishonesty. Top management can't be peering over every employee's shoulder. All employees are required to follow standardized procedures, use standardized forms, and get prior managerial approval to do anything new or different.

Consequently, such institutions have trouble initiating new programs, deviating from established routines, and dealing with unusual problems. A large organization equipped with round holes often has no mechanism for handling a square peg. And if the peg is too small to attract the attention of senior management, it may be set aside and forgotten.

Large institutions are more likely than are their smaller counterparts to make procedural and clerical mistakes. For example, a letter or payment directed to the wrong department will be diligently recorded and kept, but it may take weeks, or longer, to find its way to the proper office.

RISK AVOIDANCE The larger and more successful an institution, the less likely it will take risks. Many of these institutions generate adequate profits as well as nice incomes for their mid-level and senior employees. No one wants to risk the goose that's producing the golden eggs. These institutions have armies of lawyers, accountants, and other professionals who tend to be inordinately conservative. They fear being wrong and try to avoid involving the institution in any sort of controversy. Unless the potential profits are huge, large organizations will not undertake an endeavor that poses any risk of causing significant damage to the organization.

> Consequently, large lenders generally make fewer substantive mistakes, such as violating the Truth in Lending Act. But they frequently make clerical mistakes that may provide you with certain opportunities.

PUBLIC IMAGE Most large lending institutions spend generously on public relations and advertising, hoping to make the institution appear stable, professional, honest, and humane. The large institution needs this image to attract enough customers and investment funds to maintain its success.

Sensitivity to adverse publicity makes large institutions vulnerable.

They don't want, but can handle, news coverage of a foreclosure on a family with six kids, charging higher interest rates to minorities and the poor, or any of the many other unpleasant things they do in the ordinary course of business. However, publicity about unlawful or unethical practices creates a more serious problem. Such publicity can lead to government inquiries and class action lawsuits.

SMALL VERSUS BIG PROBLEMS Large institutions prefer to dispose of small problems as quickly and cheaply as possible. As long as a problem is just a nuisance that merely interferes with the daily routine, the institution and its employees will look for ways to get rid of the matter, even if the institution has to take a loss.

However, if an institution believes that a problem is large enough to threaten its very survival, growth, or public image, it will use every possible means to protect itself. It will call on politicians it has financed, governmental appointees and bureaucrats thinking of future employment, judges seeking reelection contributions, powerful lawyers and accountants, law enforcement officials, and anyone else who can be persuaded, cajoled, coerced, or otherwise induced to help the institution fend off the threat.

DEALING WITH THEM As long as you, the consumer, makes regular payments, you probably will not receive any communications from a large institution, other than computer-generated bills and enclosed advertising and promotional materials. However, consumers frequently miss a monthly payment for any number of reasons. They may misplace the bill, go on vacation, misdirect the payment, forget to stamp the envelope, fall ill, or find themselves short of money that month. So when you miss a payment, the typical computer program does nothing other than generate another bill - until you miss or underpay two consecutive payments.

When the computer flags a problem account, it generates a notice asking the consumer to bring the account current or to call someone in the "Consumer Relations Department" (that's what we call "collections"). If the consumer doesn't pay or call as demanded, a series of collection notices begins, or the account is immediately assigned to an employee in the collections department who calls the consumer.

THE COLLECTIONS DEPARTMENT In a very real sense, collection employees who staff the telephones at large institutions are little more than a link between the consumer and the computer. They answer to one or more junior supervisors, who help the phone personnel handle complaints, hostile customers, and who screen problems for their boss, the department manager.

The department manager, the only person within the department with any real authority, is in charge of the collection operations. These managers tend to be very experienced and street-wise. They disbelieve everything customers have to say. Most managers spend years on the phones before being promoted.

Young, low-paid employees, just out of school usually man the telephones. In their few days of training, they learn to follow very precise collection procedures and carefully worded scripts. They sit in front of a computer monitor and keyboard, wearing telephone headsets, and making calls from a computer generated list of delinquent accounts.

They know nothing about an account except what appears on the computer screen. They record nothing except what they type into the computer. Their phone calls are often monitored by the junior supervisors. Their performance is measured by the number of calls, the length of their calls and the amount of money collected pursuant to their calls. Few companies reward their staff for being caring, compassionate or humane.

Well-trained collection personnel are firm but polite, persistent but patient. Don't be misled by their warm and friendly voices. These people are the creditor's front-line soldiers. Their jobs, incomes and promotions depend on how much money they collect from customers. They probably don't care about your personal problems, and even if they do, they have little or no power to help you. All they want to hear is that you have sent, or will send, a check before a certain date. If they hear that from a customer, they will enter it into the computer and go on to another account.

If the amount owed exceeds some pre-determined amount, or the account remains delinquent for a specified length of time, the computer will automatically include the account on a special list for the department manager's attention.

SMALL BUSINESSES

Small lenders differ markedly from large institutions. Typically, small lenders are staffed by a few people who know just about everything going on in the company. With small lenders, you are dealing with people more than with rigid policies or procedures. Small lenders don't have to handle large volumes of transactions, so there is no need for assembly line rules and procedures. Management of a small company is closer to the operations, has much more control over hiring and training personnel, and usually has the time to handle individual consumers on a case by case basis.

All this makes small lenders more likely to be guided by feelings about particular borrowers. Often, it will be to your advantage to develop a personal relationship with the small lender's key personnel. Little things like Christmas cards can help a lot. The dark side of such familiarity is that small lenders are more likely to pursue personal grudges. Unless you have a carefully considered plan to provoke an incompetent lender into making a mistake, never break a promise or be impolite to anyone who works for a small lender.

Small lenders don't fit neatly into categories because they vary so much in every respect. Some small lenders are extremely sophisticated; some are bunglers. Small lenders range from honorable to reprehensible. It can prove difficult to figure out whether you are dealing with an honest lender. They all have learned enough financial jargon to sound like they know what they are talking about, and the most reprehensible of this breed are skilled at conning consumers into trusting them.

> Until you are certain you know what kind of people you are dealing with, it's best to proceed very cautiously. Keep in mind that there is a strong possibility that the lender isn't very professional, has made mistakes, isn't honest, can't be trusted, and has violated one or more laws.

SPECIFIC TYPES OF CREDITORS

BANKS

Automatic teller machines reveal the true soul of most banks. They mindlessly process every transaction in accord with mysterious rules that no one really understands. Anything out of the ordinary is politely spit out of the machine; anything suggesting something wrong is quickly and quietly swallowed by the machine and is never seen nor heard from again.

When dealing with a bank, it's important to understand their internal workings. Generally, banks handle business credits very differently from consumer loans. Since consumer loans usually are not large enough to carry the costs of individualized attention, they must be processed through a paperwork production line.

Consumer loan departments of most banks operate through a rigid system of established routines. Although bankers like to glorify these routines by calling them "bank policies," they really are nothing more than a set of very detailed instructions that the bank staff is required to follow. These instructions are carefully designed to standardize all paperwork and eliminate any risk that a junior level employee will have to make a decision.

REASONS WHY BANKS NEED STANDARDIZED PROCEDURES

There are good reasons for processing consumer loans like so many identical widgets:

> **Costs -** It costs less to run a production line than a custom shop. A consumer loan rarely generates enough profit (interest and loan charges) to cover the costs of carefully analyzing the financial condition of any particular loan applicant, drafting and typing special papers for one transaction, and keeping in regular contact with the borrower.
>
> Banks approve or reject loan applications on the basis of borrower "profiles," compiled from historical statistics. Generally, people who are married, have two children, own a house, and have been employed at the same job for at least two years are more likely to pay their debts than people who are not married, rent an apartment or house and change jobs frequently. Of course, not all married people pay their debts and not all single people default, but the banks have to work within proven probabilities. They can't, or won't, spend the money to closely examine each individual loan applicant.

Consumer loan papers are standardized and are printed so that they can't be altered. Bank personnel are prohibited from changing a single word. Indeed, most bank personnel haven't the faintest idea what the loan papers say, much less what they mean.

Computers handle the billing. If payments are regularly and promptly made, no bank employee even thinks about a particular loan.

Consumer Protection Laws - Banks are heavily regulated, which means they are being watched. Banks aren't especially worried about the consumers they cheat. Consumers can be intimidated, coerced, or paid off. But banks fear regulators because bank regulators know what they are doing and honestly try to enforce the laws.

All of this regulation has forced most banks to TRY to obey the consumer protection laws. Many banks succeed at obeying these laws by having every consumer loan document, procedure and policy approved by a large law firm that is heavily insured against malpractice. Nevertheless, incompetence and greed continue to lead a lot of banks into trouble. NEVER ASSUME THAT A BANK HAS COMPLIED WITH THE LAW.

Employee Inadequacies - Until recently, banks gave their employees fancy titles and job security, but very low wages. Consequently, the banking industry tended to attract conventional, risk adverse, and unambitious employees.

They weren't expected to know much, and they fulfilled that expectation. They were discouraged from thinking for themselves. Over time, employees who had the social or other necessary relationships to generate business rose to upper management, where they were able to utilize their most valued skill - fraternizing with people who had, or controlled, lots of money.

Times have changed, though. Instead of relying primarily on social connections, banks now generate much of their business through advertising and ambitious "business development specialists," known elsewhere as salesmen.

Decades of bad loans to third-world countries, Wall Street financiers buying billion-dollar companies with junk bonds, and real estate developers who specialized in 100% financing have created huge losses for banks. Stiff competition for deposits and loans have forced a lot of banks to pay higher interest rates to their depositors and charge lower interest rates to their borrowers. The result has been a severe squeeze on bank profits, leading to cost-cutting. Naturally, bank managers doing the cost-cutting don't want to cut their own salaries, so they focus on the junior staff, such as tellers, clerks, and consumer loan personnel.

Consequently, many banks are staffed with junior employees who have minimal training, know next to nothing about banking, and are little more than well-dressed data processors. They have little, if any, loyalty to the bank, think of borrowers as annoyances, and eventually look for a decent paying job somewhere else.

CHAPTER 9

EFFECTS OF GOVERNMENT REGULATION ON A BANK'S FREEDOM TO WORK WITH A BORROWER

Intensive regulation of banks isn't always a good thing for consumers. Although the regulators protect consumers, they also limit a bank's freedom to adjust to the needs of particular consumers, especially consumers in financial difficulty.

One of the most important jobs of bank regulators is to make sure each bank's loan portfolio is sound. If a sizeable portion of a bank's loans are bad, the bank itself is in serious trouble. Examiners regularly analyze banks' loan files to determine whether the loans are sound.

When bank examiners look at a particular loan, they decide whether a loan is non-performing, which means that the consumer isn't current on interest payments; in jeopardy of being uncollectible, because the consumer isn't current and there isn't enough collateral to ensure that the bank can collect the full amount owed; or uncollectible, and treated as a total or partial loss.

These labels, or classifications, are extremely important to a bank. Non-performing loans threaten the bank's normal operations. Remember, a bank must collect interest from its borrowers to be able to pay interest to its depositors and to pay its own operating expenses.

Banks try very, very hard to make sure that its borrowers pay at least the monthly interest. A bank can carry a loan for a long time, if the loan is considered to be a performing loan - that is, a loan on which the borrower is paying interest.

When a loan stops performing, it attracts the attention of the bank examiners, and the bankers start feeling pressure to collect. Banks are required to keep certain levels of accounting and cash reserves to cover losses from bad loans and investments. Banks can't use these reserves to make loans to customers and, when loans go bad, banks are required to replenish their reserves. So, bad loans hit the bank twice: First, the loss from the loan and, second, the need to put additional funds into the reserve, which further limits their ability to lend to other borrowers.

Consequently, banks try very hard to avoid having a loan classified as a bad debt. Sometimes the bank will try to bury a problem loan and hope it goes unnoticed; other times it will race to collect the loan before the next visit from the examiners. Banks tend to panic when the examiners are scheduled to arrive. They make many of their mistakes between the onset of an actual loan problem and the classification of the loan by the bank examiners.

Generally, banks are less concerned about small consumer loans than large commercial loans. However, if a bank has serious cash flow problems, or the bank's entire consumer loan portfolio is going bad, the bank looks for the simplest way to solve its problems.

Often, consumers provide the easiest target, because they are the least likely to fight back. If a bank needs cash badly enough, it will look for excuses to call loans, especially good loans because they are the ones that will pay. A bank with a bad loan portfolio may try to convince the regulators that the portfolio isn't as bad as it appears. One way to do this is to look for excuses to call marginal loans, and use the good collection numbers from those loans to hide the bad collection numbers from other loans.

Banks have more freedom to work out a settlement with the borrower after classifying a loan as completely uncollectible, because it has nothing further to lose. A loan may be classified as partially uncollectible at any time after default, but probably will not be classified as completely uncollectible until all valuable collateral has been sold and all likely sources of collection have been pursued.

> A strategy to consider in dealing with banks is to surrender the collateral and ignore the bank's threats until it has charged-off your loan. This may take strong nerves on your part, but the rewards can be great.

CREDIT CARD COMPANIES

The credit card business is dominated by giant organizations and this business has been enormously profitable for them. In 1990, consumers charged almost $350 billion on their personal credit cards. Credit card issuers generate income by taking anywhere between 1.5% and 4.5% on each transaction from the merchant, charging high interest rates to consumers when their bills in are not paid in full **and** on time, charging cardholders an annual fee, taking a percentage of revenues made from the sales brochures that they enclose with their monthly statements, and selling their mailing lists. The credit card industry usually has a bad debt rate of less than 2.0%. Default rates increase whenever the economy is in a slowdown.

Mastercard and Visa are associations of member banks, each of which issues its own cards. The number of member banks is diminishing because many of the smaller banks that jumped on this bandwagon didn't know what they were doing or didn't have enough volume and lost their (silk) shirts. Specialty cards are really issued through the Mastercard or Visa systems in conjunction with a member bank.

Many of the banks that issue Mastercards and Visa cards are relatively poor at collecting bad accounts. All routinely write off any credit card debts that are less than some predetermined amount, sometimes as high as $5,000. Note, though, that some member banks are extremely aggressive and have special programs for pursuing cardholders who run up their bills just before filing bankruptcy.

American Express has its own collection department. It's very aggressive and, on occasion, has been known to skirt the limits of prudent collection practices. Sear's collection practices for its Discover Card are much more conservative, but this may change as the Discover Card becomes better established.

CREDIT UNIONS

Modern credit unions are a strange collection of creatures. They came into being for the sole benefit of their memberships, but today that isn't always the case. Some credit unions are extremely fine and honest lenders; some are basically unscrupulous; some are bunglers that survive only because they have a basically honest membership and honest borrowers. Traditionally, credit unions have been among the easiest creditors to handle. Now, though, credit unions vary so much in size, purpose, and make-up that no useful generalizations about them can be made, other than to say that these lenders are frequently the easiest from which to obtain credit.

FINANCE COMPANIES

As a general rule, finance companies are the best managed, most sophisticated and aggressive creditors of all. They are in business to make money by lending money, and they almost never forget it. Finance company loans usually involve more risk than do bank loans. Finance companies, therefore, charge higher interest rates than banks charge; they are more familiar with collecting bad debts than banks are; and their staffs, generally, have more real street smarts than do bankers. Finance companies focus on the bottom line.

The size of a finance company is extremely important. Large ones tend to know and obey the laws while following their own procedures very carefully. Larger companies often fear developing a reputation as a soft touch; hence, they may chase a borrower for years if he runs off with the collateral without paying the loan. Most large finance companies raise the capital they lend to consumers by selling their own stock to the general public or borrowing at relatively low rates of interest from other major lenders, such as insurance companies.

Smaller finance companies often try to get away with whatever they can. Especially notorious are finance companies that specialize in used cars and low-priced furniture loans. It pays to be wary of everything a small finance company does - the loan documentation, the resale of repossessed collateral, everything. There is a strong possibility that the finance company violated a law, or made some other serious error that will relieve you from all or part of your debt.

Most small finance companies must borrow the money that they lend to consumers. They can't borrow at the same low rates that large finance companies can. In fact, some small finance companies pay higher interest rates than you pay on your mortgage. These smaller companies can't make any profit at all unless they charge consumers very high interest rates.

LANDLORDS

Collecting the rent is the foremost concern of most landlords. They need the rent to pay their mortgages, property taxes, insurance and utilities. If you don't pay your rent, the landlord wants nothing more than to get you out and a paying tenant in.

Many landlords, especially smaller ones, will let a residential tenant walk away from a lease for the price of the security deposit because it's generally illegal for a landlord to actually throw you or lock you out. The landlord has to get a court order directing the sheriff or marshall to evict you. A landlord has to hire a lawyer to go to court and get you evicted. It can take months to get a court to evict a tenant. If the tenant has legitimate grievances, the process can take a year or more. Many courts will not evict a tenant in the middle of the winter and, if you file for relief under the Bankruptcy Code, the landlord's attorney may have to go to two courts to get you evicted.

HOSPITALS

Not-for-profit hospitals, clinics, and similar public interest institutions used to be the very easiest creditors with whom to negotiate. They understood that medical bills were not incurred voluntarily and that patients often had a host of other problems. More important, they were able to cover their operating costs with donations.

But times have changed and many hospitals and clinics are themselves going broke. Consumers still can work with most not-for-profit institutions but now the institutions usually require more than good-faith token payments. Medical bills tend to involve a great deal of money and are worth the cost of a collection attorney. However, collection agencies and attorneys handling these accounts are more inclined to empathize with consumers. They understand that injury and illness significantly diminish income and assets. When these accounts are not written off as uncollectible, reasonable monthly payments are usually agreed on. Some major hospitals also have made arrangements with local banks. These arrangements allow the bank to pay the hospital and give the consumer as long as four years to repay the bank.

PROFESSIONALS

Doctors, dentists, accountants and lawyers are typically the last to get paid. They like to think of themselves as professionals, and their professional codes of ethics won't normally allow them to abandon their patients or clients. Sometimes, they even have to provide services when they know they won't get paid. Often, professionals develop close personal relationships with their patients and clients. They will continue working because they value those relationships.

For these reasons, professionals have been extremely reluctant to suc their patients and clients. However, some professionals now have a hard time making ends meet. More and more of them are suing to collect fees, particularly when they are completely ignored in their collection efforts. There still are many professionals who will work with you, as long as you make some effort to pay **and** you let them know that you appreciate their services. Many will accept almost any payment plan you suggest.

RETAILERS

Most retailers are in business to sell. They extend credit in order to get more customers into their shops. They are extremely sensitive to public opinion.

> However, there are some so-called retailers who really are in the finance business. These barracudas peddle shoddy products to unsophisticated consumers. They charge very low prices for the merchandise but extract exorbitant interest rates for the credit.

Large retailers are far more inclined to write off bad debts than are small ones, who need the money. Although many retailers will eventually turn to collection agencies, most will bend over backward to avoid suing their customers. Regular token payments often will satisfy retailers. After all, the merchants still want you to continue shopping at the stores, even if you can longer use their store charge cards. They will still take your other credit cards, not to mention your cash.

SAVINGS AND LOAN ASSOCIATIONS

Savings and loan associations are a lot like banks, only friendlier and more understanding, or at least they used to be. Their lending goes primarily to home mortgages. Most of them also are very good at working with homeowners who have financial problems.

Government regulators rarely pressure an S&L to foreclose on a home loan. Recent problems encountered by so many S&L's are the result of loans they made that didn't involve home mortgages. Many of these institutions invested in risky deals, including purchasing large amounts of junk bonds and taking dangerous positions in real estate development and oil well deals.

TAX COLLECTORS

THE UNITED STATES INTERNAL REVENUE SERVICE

You can't just ignore your federal taxes. This is one of the few instances when time usually works against you. Interest and penalties on delinquent federal taxes often exceed the tax itself. Eventually the IRS will come after you and get you.

EVEN IF YOU DON'T HAVE THE MONEY TO PAY THE TAXES DUE, FILE ALL REQUIRED RETURNS ON TIME. It's a crime not to file your federal income tax returns when you are supposed to. Civil penalties for not filing a required return are enormous. If for no other reason, file the tax returns simply to start the statute of limitations running. This way, you'll avoid criminal charges for failure to file.

If you file a return without paying all the taxes you owe, the IRS computer will send you collection notices. The best way to deal with the IRS is to make sure your file never leaves the central computers. You don't want your file assigned to a local IRS office for collection. You can prevent local collection by responding to the notices and working out a payment plan with the IRS over the telephone. You never even have to go in to see them.

If you ignore the IRS notices, your file eventually will be sent to a local office for collection. Everyone knows how nasty the IRS can be - and it can be a nightmare if you are unfortunate enough to be assigned to a pit bull collection officer. Tired of hearing about many of the IRS abuses, Congress passed the Taxpayers' Bill of Rights. This prohibits the IRS from granting promotions on the basis of dollars collected and establishes other limited protection for consumers. Don't expect too much help from this so-called Bill of Rights.

IRS collection officers can always find you. Furthermore, almost none of your property is protected from them. Nearly all state and federal exemptions designed to protect your wages and property from other creditors simply don't apply to the IRS. Even bankruptcy will not discharge income tax obligations reportable within the three years prior to the filing of the petition for relief.

IRS officials will not compromise a tax obligation or interest unless there is little or no chance of collecting. Often, though, the IRS will forgive penalties if the taxpayer had a good reason for not paying.

STATE REVENUE DEPARTMENTS

Most state revenue officers aren't nearly as aggressive or powerful as IRS agents. However, time still works against you on state taxes, except when you move to another state. It's very difficult for one state's revenue officer to collect taxes from a consumer who has moved to another state.

If you're not planning to move to another state, it's best to work out a payment plan as early as possible. Most state revenue officers have the power to place a lien on your property, and many state exemption laws don't apply to state taxes. Just as with federal taxes, bankruptcy will not discharge state income tax obligations reportable within the three years prior to the filing of the petition for relief.

Many states have procedures for taxpayers to compromise their tax obligations. These procedures are worth pursuing. Some states offer tax amnesty programs in which all penalties and interest are waived. Be prepared to take advantage of these programs if your state adopts one.

UTILITIES

Most places heavily regulate utility companies, such as electric, water, natural gas, and telephone companies. State laws frequently require them to work with consumers who are having trouble paying their utility bills. For example, many states and municipalities don't allow utilities to cut off heat during the winter. Often, utilities must send a series of notices before shutting off service.

> Utility companies often fail to freely volunteer information about your legal rights. Press for information about any available payment plans, other arrangements or subsidies.

CREDITORS' FAVORITE WEAPONS

CHAPTER TEN

The arsenal of weapons available to creditors is much less effective in practice than it looks on paper:

- In-House Collections
- Credit Reporting Agencies
- Collection Agencies
- Repossessions and Foreclosures
- Lawsuits and Judgments
- Supplementary Proceedings

IN-HOUSE COLLECTION

Unless a debt is secured by collateral, a creditor cannot force a consumer to pay, without first obtaining a judgment. Therefore, a creditor, before turning the account over to a collection agency or attorney, tries one of these four tactics to persuade a consumer to voluntarily pay:

Appeal to your pride > Many creditors may say that if you were honest, you would pay the bill. Honesty, has nothing to do with your inability to pay a debt that you intended to pay when you first received, or applied for, the credit. Businesses extend credit in order to increase their sales. They know some bills will never be paid. If a business doesn't want to suffer that risk, it simply should not extend credit. Moreover, very few businesses pay their own bills on time. Even when they have available cash, many businesses delay paying their own bills until they absolutely must.

Try to make you feel guilty about not paying the bill > Don't feel guilty. Your first obligation is to yourself and your family. If you can't pay your own living expenses, you shouldn't be trying to pay your creditors. Also, if you have been a customer of the creditor for a long time, the creditor's profits from the your past business probably more than offsets the debt your creditor claims you owe.

Threaten you with cutting off further credit or submitting a bad credit report > If you don't want or need further credit from that creditor, then this is a hollow threat. If you can't pay your own living expenses, you probably won't get credit, even if the creditor doesn't submit a bad credit report. Moreover, such a report will not affect any credit you already have in place, as long as you keep those accounts current.

Turn your account over to a collection agency or lawyer > So what? All this means is that you don't have to pay your creditor now. Wait until the collection agency or attorney contacts you before you announce your plan of action.

Some large creditors have in-house collection departments that act about the same as do outside collection agencies. Almost invariably, these creditors first use the mails before turning to the telephone.

TYPICAL COLLECTION PROCEDURE

(1) Mail first bill.

(2) 30 days later, mail polite late payment/reminder notice.

(3) 30 days later, mail a letter politely asking consumer to make immediate payment or contact creditor to advise of any problem.

(4) 10-30 days later, telephone consumer to ask if there is a problem and politely request payment; or mail a mild warning that relationship will be hurt and consumer's credit standing will be damaged.

(5) 10-30 days later, telephone consumer to get a promise of payment by a specific date or to establish some sort of payment plan; or mail a firm demand for payment.

(6) 10-30 days later, mail firm demand and threaten account will be turned over to collection agency or attorney.

(7) 10-30 days later, mail final demand before turning account over to agency/attorney.

(8) Write off the account and make a note to refuse further credit.

(9) Report bad debt to a credit reporting service.

(10) Either forget the debt, especially if it's small, or turn the account over to a collection agency or attorney.

Each letter sent and phone call made costs the creditor time and money. Typically, it takes about five to six months before a merchant turns an account over to an outside collection agency or attorney.

Small creditors, such as a local retailer, often don't have any formal collection procedure. Instead, they call and emphasize that they are small businesses that can't afford to absorb unpaid accounts. This may or may not be true, but that shouldn't be your concern. Many small businesses choose to write off smaller debts they can't themselves collect, because they don't like to work with a collection agency. Unless the debt is large, they don't want to pay an attorney to try collect the account.

CREDIT REPORTING AGENCIES

There are credit-reporting agencies (CRAs) and trade associations that make their money by keeping computerized files on consumers. Businesses, and even some government agencies, pay fees to these CRAs, in return for access to these files. Businesses also pay them for their mailing lists. Information from these files are used in making decisions about giving consumer credit, providing insurance coverage, or offering employment to executives and others who are applying for jobs in sensitive positions.

After giving a consumer credit, most creditors rely on their own experience in the granting of additional credit. They rarely again check through a CRA. Sometimes, though, a creditor will order a credit report to confirm information provided by a consumer who is trying to settle a debt on the grounds of financial hardship.

A negative credit report is likely to prevent you from getting credit because a credit report is used by large volume lenders as a cheap screening device. Each lender follows its own particular set of guidelines for acceptance or rejection of credit. Generally,

> most lenders do not extend credit if a report shows pending criminal charges, a recent criminal conviction, a pending bankruptcy proceeding, unsatisfied judgments, or tax liens;
>
> few, if any, lenders extend credit if a report shows a recent bankruptcy, pending uninsured or underinsured lawsuits, or a "skip," meaning a consumer moved and the creditor couldn't find him;
>
> most lenders do not extend credit if a report shows a bankruptcy within 5 years, recent lawsuits, prior but settled judgments or tax liens, an unreliable payment history, disputed and unpaid bills from several creditors, or no credit history at all; and
>
> some lenders extend credit, even if a report shows a history of late payments, provided that payments aren't missed, are not more than 30 days late, and that disputed bills are limited to no more than one or two creditors.

A CRA opens a consumer file when a business requests, or submits, information about that consumer. Many CRAs do no independent investigation. They get all their information from their member businesses, and from consumers themselves. Large CRAs also get information from public records that show judgments, bankruptcy filings, felony convictions, pending lawsuits, and pending criminal charges. Investigations involve interviews with neighbors and employers and this is too expensive for ordinary credit transactions.

The history of the credit reporting industry was so bad that Congress enacted the Federal Fair Credit Reporting Act. Your many rights under this act are discussed in Chapter 13.

COLLECTION AGENCIES

Collection agencies are outside bill collectors, used by creditors who have given up trying to collect by themselves. Once an account is turned over to a collection agency, you should never again hear directly from the creditor.

Creditors are willing to pay relatively large contingency fees to debt collection agencies because they figure that getting part of something is better than keeping all of nothing. Collection agencies make no money unless they induce the consumer to pay. Debt collection firms generally keep between 25% and 50% of what they collect. Collection agencies are more successful at collecting bad or hard to collect debts than are creditors because:

> creditors are busy with other things, and have neither the time nor the inclination to collect bad debts;
>
> creditors don't have the training or disposition to effectively dun a consumer;
>
> creditors are reluctant to antagonize consumers, and are afraid of adverse publicity;
>
> creditors are unable and unwilling to engage in abusive practices frequently used by debt collectors.

When a creditor turns a file over to a collection agency, the agency receives certain information about the consumer. This information includes, when available, name, address, phone number, name and phone number of employer, social security number, spouse's name and social security number, name and address of nearest living relative, and, once-in-a-while, a brief description about how the debt was incurred. If these items sound familiar, that's because they generally appear on credit applications.

Debt collectors look at a number of factors when deciding how much time and effort to invest in collecting a particular debt:

1st, they look at the amount of money in question. It's just not worth very much of their time or effort to collect a debt of a few hundred dollars.

2nd, they note if the creditor is a particularly important customer of the agency and, if so, whether the creditor wants this particular account targeted.

3rd, they calculate how hard it will be to collect. A debt collector's ideal collection target is married, has 2 or 3 children, is a blue collar worker, has a mortgage on his house, is white, and is a high school graduate. If squeezed long or hard enough, this consumer will probably come up with the money.

The history of collection agencies is filled with tales of horror. Debt collectors think of consumers as targets and as "deadbeats." They don't care if the money they are trying to squeeze out of you is needed to feed the kids. To collect money from consumers, debt collectors have been known to:

Repeatedly telephone consumers at work, at home, and at all hours of the early morning and night;

directly call or write to employers, using the threat of job loss to coerce payment;

repeatedly call parents, children, and other family members as a way of intimidating consumers;

call neighbors and friends to embarrass the consumer; and

impersonate police, immigration officials, internal revenue agents, other law enforcement officials, lawyers, hospital emergency room personnel, doctors, relatives, undertakers, and a host of other fictitious persons in their attempt to gather collection information about consumers.

Debt collection abuses became so rampant that Congress passed the Fair Debt Collection Practices Act. Nevertheless, many debt collectors still do many of these things. Read Chapter 13 of this book to learn your rights under the law.

CHAPTER 10

REPOSSESSING AND FORECLOSING COLLATERAL

Secured creditors have more power over consumers than do unsecured creditors, but not nearly as much as most people think.

When talking about collateral, precise language is very important. It's misleading when you say that your house or car "belongs to" the bank or finance company. They belong to you, the consumer.

Collateral is security for the payment of a debt. If the debt isn't paid, the lender can look to the collateral to get paid. Ownership remains with the borrower, until the borrower's rights are terminated by a foreclosure conducted in accordance with the law.

A creditor's right to repossess and foreclose collateral are granted in a document called a "security agreement." Mortgages and trust deeds are examples of security agreements used for real estate. The security agreement must be signed by the person, usually the borrower, who owns the collateral. The security agreement must have language giving a security interest to the creditor. The security agreement is extremely difficult to enforce if it does not have language giving the creditor the right to repossess and sell the property if the borrower defaults. Sometimes, security agreements incorporate these rights by stating that the creditor shall have all rights under the Uniform Commercial Code.

In order to get cash out of the collateral, a creditor has to get possession of the collateral, in accordance with the law, and foreclose the borrower's rights in the collateral, also in accordance with the law. Sometimes, creditors first get possession of the collateral and then foreclose. Typically, this happens with cars and trucks. Sometimes, creditors foreclose before getting possession. Typically, this happens with real estate.

REPOSSESSION

Usually, physical repossession of the collateral matters more to a consumer than the legalities of a foreclosure.

> IF YOU POSSESS THE COLLATERAL, THE CREDITOR HAS TO GO TO COURT TO GET IT FROM YOU.
>
> IF THE CREDITOR IS IN POSSESSION OF THE COLLATERAL, YOU HAVE TO PAY THE DEBT, OR GO TO COURT TO GET THE COLLATERAL BACK.

A creditor can't just grab the collateral from you and sell it; certain Constitutional procedures, as well as various local, state, and federal statutes must first be followed.

A creditor CANNOT use force to repossess collateral > Generally, if you have possession of the collateral, you can simply tell the creditor to go away. The creditor must then go to court, and this takes the creditor time and costs money.

A creditor CANNOT enter your house or apartment without permission of a person who controls the premises, such as you or your spouse > This means that a creditor can't break into your home to repossess collateral. Even the landlord can't let the creditor into your home. The creditor has to go to court, which, again, takes time and costs money.

A creditor CANNOT sell or keep collateral without giving you prior notice > This means that, even if the collateral is repossessed, you almost certainly will have a chance to get it back. You must be given the opportunity to pay the debt, so you can get your collateral back, or you must be given the opportunity to see if you can get a better price for the collateral.

On the other hand, there are some things a creditor usually can do that many consumers don't know can happen:

A creditor CAN keep property that already is in its possession > For example, most states permit mechanics and repairmen to hold property they have fixed until they are paid. If you don't pay the repair bill, they can follow certain legal procedures and sell the property they repaired. However, they can't sell property they didn't repair and, once they return the property to you, they can't come and get it back.

A creditor CAN take peaceful possession of collateral located on public property > For example, a finance company can repossess a car that is sitting on property open to the public, such as a street, your employer's parking lot, or a shopping center.

A creditor CAN deduct your debt from a debt it owes to you > Called "off-set" or "set-off", this typically happens when a consumer has an account at a bank. When the consumer doesn't pay the loan, the bank grabs whatever money the consumer has in a checking, savings, or certificate of deposit account.

FORECLOSURE

Foreclosure is a complicated legal concept. It is the process by which a creditor can dispose of property that secures payment of a debt, or other legal obligation, when that debt or obligation is in default. Usually the collateral is sold, though sometimes it is kept by the creditor in satisfaction of the debt. In both cases, the owner's interests in the foreclosed property is terminated. Junior liens in favor of other creditors also are terminated. If the collateral is sold, the net proceeds of the sale are applied towards the debt. Any sale proceeds in excess of the debt must be turned over to the owner or any junior lien holders.

It is important to understand exactly what it is the creditor is selling, (or keeping in satisfaction of the debt). The creditor is NOT selling its own interest in the property because it does not own the property; the creditor has only the right to sell the owner's interests in the property. Moreover, the creditor can only sell the owner's rights, whatever they may be, and nothing more. If there are liens or other claims against the property that have priority over the foreclosing creditor's rights, those liens and interests remain unaffected by the foreclosure.

State laws always require that certain procedures be followed when property is foreclosed. Foreclosure procedures vary from state to state and depend on the type of collateral involved. Some foreclosures must be processed through court proceedings; others may be conducted privately. All foreclosure proceedings REQUIRE PRIOR NOTICE to the borrower and the owner of the collateral, if the owner is different from the borrower. The borrower almost always has the chance to redeem the collateral by paying off the debt. Sometimes, the borrower has the right to bring the obligation current.

Creditors have their lawyers handle foreclosures. IF YOU WANT TO KEEP PROPERTY THAT MAY BE FORECLOSED, CONSULT WITH A LAWYER AS SOON AS POSSIBLE.

DEFICIENCIES

Usually, creditors don't sell collateral for a price high enough to cover the amount owed. This leaves a "deficiency," which the creditor can attempt to collect from the consumer. But, creditors often commit errors when selling the collateral. ERRORS MADE BY CREDITORS CAN RELIEVE YOU FROM PAYING SOME, OR EVEN ALL, OF THE DEFICIENCY CLAIMED. The most common errors are:

Failure to give you prior notice of a sale of the collateral > Creditors must send you notice before selling, or otherwise disposing of, most kinds of collateral. This right cannot be relinquished by you before default, but can be after default. If you default, DO NOT SIGN AWAY ANY RIGHT TO BE GIVEN NOTICE, unless you receive a full and unconditional release for any deficiency.

Failure to sell the collateral in a "commercially reasonable" manner > Creditors must make a reasonable effort to recover a good price for collateral. Whenever possible, write the creditor a letter giving your suggestions about how the collateral can be sold for the best price. If you have any objections to the manner in which a creditor proposes to sell collateral, immediately send the creditor written notice of your objections, and include any suggestions you may have.

Keeping collateral too long before selling it > Creditors are always required to dispose of collateral within a reasonable time. If a creditor holds collateral too long, which can be only a couple of days for perishable items, the creditor may be judged to have taken the collateral in full satisfaction of the debt. This is especially true if the creditor uses the collateral. At the very least, the creditor may lose some interest for the time it should not have been holding the collateral. If a creditor holds collateral for a long time, consider writing a letter demanding that the creditor dispose of the collateral. But, be aware that the creditor may have forgotten about the collateral. If so, you will have blown the opportunity to argue that the creditor took the collateral in full satisfaction of the debt.

LAWSUITS AND JUDGMENTS

LAWSUITS

Being sued isn't much fun; it can be a time consuming and expensive burden. But, being sued hurts less than a tooth ache. Unlike physical pain, a lawsuit can be ignored, if you don't care whether a judgment is entered against you. Unless a creditor has collateral in hand, you can't legally be forced to pay a debt before first losing a lawsuit. You will understand why creditors don't like to sue, when you see what a creditor's lawsuit actually involves.

1st, the creditor has to retain a lawyer > Corporate creditors usually must be represented by an attorney. Individuals, though, have a Constitutional right to represent themselves.

2nd, the creditor has to pay filing costs and often legal fees > Many collection attorneys will work on a contingency basis. That is, the attorney keeps only a portion of what he or she actually collects from you. Smaller creditors who do not regularly employ collection attorneys often have trouble finding one who will work for a contingency fee. If the creditor can't find an attorney who will accept such a fee arrangement, the creditor has to pay legal fees of anywhere between $75 to $250 an hour.

Even when there is a contingency fee arrangement, the creditor pays all out-of-pocket costs. The costs for a routine collection lawsuit usually are between fifty and a hundred dollars a case. It can be a lot higher, if there is any difficulty serving the defendant with a summons. It can run into the thousands of dollars, if the lawsuit is actively defended. Costs to a creditor for a judicial mortgage foreclosure are rarely less than $500, but can run well into the thousands.

3rd, the creditor has to prepare its records for the lawyer > The creditor must collect all information and documents the lawyer needs before he can file the case. Sometimes, there isn't much to collect; occasionally, the file is so full of correspondence and grievances that the creditor must spend hours, or even days, to assemble it. Sometimes, creditors can't locate important documents, such as a signed disclosure statement signed by the consumer. Lenders also have been known to lose essential evidence, such as the signed promissory note.

4th, a lawyer must review the file > A responsible lawyer will read the file, make sure that everything needed is there, and look for any possible problems that might come out in court. This takes time and time costs money. Many attorneys let their paralegal assistants or secretaries handle the entire file and do the file review. Collection mills often use clerical assistants to do virtually everything, except appear in court.

5th, the attorney or clerk, has to prepare the paperwork > Filing a lawsuit requires someone to prepare the complaint, the summons, and usually one or two other legal papers that various courts require. At least two copies of each complaint and summons have to be prepared.

Lawyers usually rely on the creditor to supply the consumer's address for the summons. If the creditor has the wrong address, the summons will not be served. The creditor's attorney will not know he has the wrong address on file until the sheriff, or process server, reports that the defendant is not at the address listed on the summons. The attorney then has to try to find out where the consumer can be served.

These delays can take weeks or months. Sometimes, a creditor's attorney fails to follow-up. In some cases, failure to properly serve the consumer can bar the creditor's claim, before you even learn you've been sued. If you expect trouble with a creditor, don't disclose a new address or phone number.

6th, the papers have to be filed with the court > The papers are taken to the court clerk who opens a case file and returns stamped copies. Usually, it's the court clerk who issues the summons. The summons, a copy of the summons, and the complaint are then taken to the sheriff's office (or its local equivalent) for service of process.

7th, the defendant must be served > A sheriff's deputy, or other official process server, will try to deliver the summons and complaint to the named defendant. Usually, the deputy tries to serve the papers at the defendant's home. The papers can be served on the defendant or any member of the defendant's household over a reasonable age, typically about 13 years old. Except for extraordinary circumstances, the papers can't just be dropped on a doorstep. Some states permit creditors to use private process servers.

In some cases, the summons can be served by certified or registered mail. You have no legal or moral obligation to help your creditor serve you with summons. There is no law that says you have to answer your door to a process server, or accept registered or certified mail. Make sure that everyone working and living in your house clearly understands that they should not accept certified or registered mail, or accept any papers on your behalf.

8th, the defendant must be given reasonable time to appear and defend > Defendants are usually given 20 to 30 days to appear. Just filing an appearance with a court clerk gives a you about an additional month to file an answer. Filing an answer denying the complaint can give you another 30 to 60 days, and may delay the case for years, especially if you ask for a jury trial.

If you intend to seriously defend a lawsuit, consult an attorney as soon as you are served. If you aren't able to consult with an attorney, and you run out of time, you should:

> Get an appearance form from the clerk of the court and complete it. On the face of the form, write "SPECIAL AND LIMITED APPEARANCE". This will preserve your right to contend that the service of summons wasn't proper. Also, get a jury demand form and complete it. If there is no such form, on the appearance form write "JURY TRIAL DEMANDED". This can insure your right to a jury trial, rather than a trial before a judge.

File both forms with the court clerk and be sure to pay any required fees. If you can't afford the fees, ask the clerk for forms to have the fees waived.

9th, you have the right to be represented > If you're going to get a lawyer, get one as soon as possible. But, if you need time, most judges will give consumers at least 2 to 4 weeks to find a lawyer. Unless it's the day before trial, courts also will give a consumer time to replace a lawyer.

In civil cases, the court will not appoint a lawyer for you if you can't afford to hire one yourself. That right is reserved for criminal defendants only. There are a number of public service and not-for-profit law groups that may represent you for a nominal, if any, fee. TO GET A DELAY, YOU OR YOUR LAWYER MUST APPEAR IN COURT TO ASK FOR ONE.

10th, counterclaims > It's never much fun for a creditor to go to court claiming it is owed money and leave court paying money. Creditors make mistakes, and many of those mistakes give consumers the right to strike back. Violations of Truth in Lending laws, and other consumer protection laws can cost a creditor huge fines, judgments, attorneys's fees for both sides, class action suits, and even criminal investigations.

Mistakes are less likely to be noticed if no one is looking too closely. Few creditors relish the thought of a knowledgeable consumer's attorney scrutinizing the creditor's procedures and activities in search of a counterclaim. The larger the creditor, the less sure it is that nobody along the way made a mistake. The smaller the creditor, the more likely someone did make a mistake. Most creditors have much more to lose than do consumers. No knowledgeable collection lawyer ever tells a client that there is no chance it will lose a case. If there is any reasonable possibility that a consumer can win an important counter-claim, a creditor will feel intense pressure to settle the case.

11th, all kinds of "motions" > If the consumer files an answer denying the creditor's complaint, the creditor can't win, unless its attorney files and argues at least one court motion. Of course, you get the right to respond to that motion. Each motion usually takes at least two weeks.

12th, "discovery" > If there are any disputed facts, you can demand all kinds of discovery that requires the creditor to produce papers, testify, and answer written questions. Discovery is always a pain in the neck, and can be costly and time consuming for the creditor's staff and attorney.

13th, trial > A trial can be anything from a one hour hearing to weeks of complicated testimony and exhibits. Trials are very expensive. In many states, the courts are so burdened that the creditor have to wait five, or more, years before a case can be tried by a jury. In some places, it even takes years to get a case tried by a judge.

14th, appeals > Winning at the trial level isn't necessarily thc end. You very well may have grounds for an appeal, adding years more to the process.

15th, enforcing the judgment > Even if the creditor wins the case, so what! It still may not be able to collect, as you will soon see.

Most lawsuits are won by collection attorneys because the consumer ignores the suit and the creditor gets a default judgment. The last thing a creditor, or its attorney, wants is an actively defended lawsuit. If just 5% of consumers vigorously asserted their legal rights, collection mills would grind to a halt, and creditors would find their profits consumed by legal fees.

Many attorneys who specialize in consumer representation are expert at inexpensively asserting your legal rights to thwart, wear down, and often defeat unreasonable and dishonest creditors. If you actively defend a collection lawsuit, the creditor almost always agrees to a reasonable settlement, even if it's the day of trial.

JUDGMENTS

The entry of a judgment isn't the end of the world. After a judgment is entered, the underlying debt ceases to exist. It is replaced by the judgment itself. The consumer is then referred to as a "judgment debtor." The judgment itself is worthless to a creditor, unless it can be used to collect the debt.

One way a judgment creditor can try to enforce a judgment is by obtaining a judgment lien on the judgment debtor's real estate by recording a "memorandum of judgment." The purpose of the lien is to prevent the debtor from selling the real estate without paying the creditor. In most states, the creditor gets a lien only on real estate located in the counties within the state where a memorandum of the judgment is recorded.

As a general rule, a judgment creditor cannot get a judgment lien on personal property without using the powers of the court to enforce the judgment. Judgments are enforced through supplementary proceedings.

SUPPLEMENTARY PROCEEDINGS

If you don't have a regular income, or any property of value, you are "judgment proof." However, if you have regular income or property, the judgment creditor can ask the court to take them and use them to pay your debt. Most states protect some property from creditors by making it "exempt from execution."

CITATION PROCEEDINGS

The purpose of the proceedings is to help the judgment creditor discover income and assets that belong to the judgment debtor, and can be used to pay the debt. If property belonging to the consumer is found, the court has the power to issue an order to obtain and sell the property. The most common type of such order is a "turnover order" requiring the judgment debtor to deliver some particular property to the court clerk or sheriff.

A creditor can begin citation proceedings any time after being awarded a final judgment. If property belonging to the consumer is found, the court can order the property turned over to the creditor. Normally, a creditor can use citation proceedings against you only once.

A judgment creditor starts a citation proceeding by having the judgment debtor served with a citation summons. A citation summons does three things:

Prohibits you from transferring assets > This doesn't mean that you can't pay usual and ordinary living expenses. Its purpose is to prevent you from selling or hiding valuable property, such as a vacation home. Theoretically, a person who violates such an injunction can be held in contempt of court. As a practical matter, it's very difficult and expensive to enforce a citation injunction against the transferring of property. It usually takes a really flagrant violation involving a very valuable asset to provoke a court to take any real action.

Requires you to come to court and answer questions about your income and property > This is the most important part of the citation proceeding. A creditor can't enforce a judgment unless the creditor knows what property a debtor has and where that property is located.

The Examination A citation examination isn't particularly unpleasant. You are asked questions and you answer them, under oath. You can help prepare yourself to answer the questions by reading "Giving Testimony Under Oath" in Chapter 22. When you go to a citation examination, NEVER bring more than a few dollars, credit cards, or any valuable property with you. Don't wear an expensive watch, fur coat, or valuable jewelry. Don't even bring your car. The creditor's attorney may ask the court to order you to surrender any or all of these things.

IF YOU HAVE REASON TO BELIEVE YOU COMMITTED A CRIME, AND YOUR ANSWERS IN THE CITATION PROCEEDING MAY BE USED TO IMPLICATE OR CONVICT YOU OF THAT CRIME, IMMEDIATELY CONSULT WITH AN EXPERIENCED CRIMINAL ATTORNEY. DON'T ATTEMPT TO HANDLE THIS MATTER BY YOURSELF. Your attorney will not advise you to ignore the citation summons. Even if he believes that is the best thing for you to do, as an officer of the court, he can only advise you to appear in court and assert your rights under the Fifth Amendment.

Appearing for the Examination If you are properly served with the citation summons, go to court. If you received the summons, more likely than not, you have been properly served. Many judges are angered when consumers fail to appear for a citation examination. Remember, a judicial order to appear is easier to enforce than is a prohibition against selling your assets.

If you don't appear, some judges will immediately issue a warrant for your arrest. Most judges, however, will first serve you with a "rule to show cause." This orders you to appear before the court and explain why you shouldn't be held in contempt for failing to appear the first time. If you are properly served with the rule to show cause and still don't appear, a warrant for your arrest almost certainly will be issued.

The first time you are arrested, you probably will be given a new date to appear and be released, if an appearance bond is posted. Usually, this bond must be in cash. If after being arrested once, you don't appear a second time, you will forfeit the bond and the court will issue another warrant. Some judges will order that, when you are arrested the second time, you be held without bond and physically brought before the court. Other judges will just increase the amount of the cash bond.

Frequently, courts order that bond money be turned over to the judgment creditor on the theory that the bond money is the judgment debtor's property and that the creditor has a right to seize such property. Indeed, this is one of the ways that judgment creditors collect their debts. Every time the consumer doesn't appear and then gets arrested, he has to deposit a higher bond, and eventually the creditor collects a lot of money.

Often, orders to turn bond money over to a creditor are improper, but there are judges who do it anyway. The purpose of the bond is to insure that you appear in court. Much like collateral, the bond money belongs to the person who posted it, until the court enters an order that the bond be forfeited. If the judgment debtor appears in court and if the bond was posted by someone else, the court has no right to take any part of the bond. The court has no power to order the bond forfeited. It must order the bond money be returned to the person who posted it. It doesn't belong to the court, the creditor, or the judgment debtor.

If you are arrested, try to have someone, other than your spouse or a minor child, post the bond and make sure the receipt is issued in that person's name, not in your name. When a cash bond is posted for you, and the person posting it wants it returned, he or she should go to the court with you when you appear, show the receipt to the judge or court clerk and ask that the bond be discharged and the money returned. If the court refuses, something is very wrong. Notify the Office of the United States Attorney.

Even if you have to post the bond money for yourself, you may be able to get it back. When you appear in court ask that the bond be discharged, and claim the bond money as exempt property. Most states allow consumers to protect some cash from creditors.

As you can see, if you are properly served with a citation summons, it's easiest to appear the first time. If you really can't appear on the specified date, call the attorney and try to arrange for another date. Make written note of the date and time of the conversation, the names of the persons with whom you spoke, and the agreement that is reached. If you have time, confirm the agreement in a letter.

If you can't reach the attorney, or if he is unreasonable, call the court clerk. Be prepared to give a good reason, such as illness or accident. Make a written note of that conversation and, if time permits, confirm the conversation in a letter.

If you would rather not go to court, many attorneys will be happy to conduct the examination in their offices. The danger of this is that an attorney is likely to conduct a more thorough examination in the comfort of his office than in a crowded courtroom hallway.

Requires you to produce all records of your income and property > Few consumers keep financial records, other than their checkbooks and a copy of last year's tax return. Whatever financial records you have are supposed to be brought with you to the examination. If you have records, but don't bring them, the creditors' attorney may make a big fuss and ask the court to make you come back with them on another date.

PAYMENT PLANS

Most collection attorneys hope that the citation summons will prompt you to call them and arrange to make payments. If you have a regular job or property the creditor can reach, it may be a good idea to INFORMALLY agree to a payment plan you can handle.

Usually, the lawyer will agree to extend the citation proceedings while you make the payments. Sometimes, though, the lawyer will ask you to agree to a court ordered payment plan. Agreeing to a court ordered payment plan can put you in a difficult position. By agreeing to a plan, you admit that you are able to make the payments, subjecting yourself to the continuing supervision of the court, and taking on the burden of explaining any missed payments.

Agree to a court ordered payment plan ONLY if you have more to lose by not agreeing to the plan. You may want to agree to a court ordered payment plan if you intend to continue in your current job and there is an unacceptable risk that a wage attachment will cause your employer to fire you; or, the creditor can find and get property that you want to keep; or, the plan provides for payments that are substantially less than the creditor could get from a wage garnishment.

WAGE SEIZURES

The court can order that a judgment debtor's employer set aside some of your wages and pay them to the judgment creditor. Under federal law, this portion can't exceed about 25% of your take-home earnings, and must leave you with at least the federal minimum hourly wage. These limitations don't apply to debts for child support, to payments made in a Chapter 13 wage earner's bankruptcy proceedings, or to debts due for any federal or state tax. Many states have even smaller limits on the portion of your wages that can be garnished.

A creditor goes after your wages by having the court send a wage attachment summons to your employer. Responding to a wage attachment summons is time-consuming for the employer. If the employer doesn't properly respond to the summons, the employer may end up paying the creditor with its own money. The employer has to figure out how much of what the employee earns is subject to garnishment, and then try to make sense out of the enclosed legal blather to determine how much to send to the court.

Employers are legally prohibited from firing employees just because their wages are attached. Many employers violate this law. The best way to prevent your employer from firing you is to stay on good terms with your employer. If necessary, offer to reimburse the company for the costs of complying with the wage attachment order.

> If you are fired because your wages have been attached, consult with an attorney, the U.S. Department of Labor, your state labor department, and, if you have one, your union representative.

Wages of federal employees usually cannot be seized to satisfy debts. Congress did not do this to give federal employees special protection; rather, Congress was protecting federal agencies from the burden of dealing with a multitude of wage attachment summonses.

Chapter 10

SEIZURES OF PROPERTY OTHER THAN WAGES

Creditors can ask the court to order the seizure of almost any kind of property, even debts owed to you by third parties. The legal term for such seizures is "attachment," "garnishment," and "levy." Technically, these actions aren't the same, but all have the same effect of taking your property. Possible targets of such seizures are:

Cash and Cash Equivalents

When a judgment creditor wants to go after your cash, the court issues a summons or order to your bank. The bank is then required to tell the creditor how much of your money it is holding. The summons also orders the bank to hold the money until it receives a second order from the court. This second order directs the bank to pay all funds, up the amount of the judgment, to the court clerk or sheriff.

AVOID MAINTAINING ANY KIND OF ACCOUNT WITH YOUR NAME OR SOCIAL SECURITY NUMBER ON IT. This includes joint bank accounts and accounts naming you as "custodian" or "trustee" for a child. If your name or social security number is on an account, the account probably will, at least, be temporarily frozen and possibly used to pay your creditor. Further, a court can determine that the money in an account is really your money. It all depends on how it got into the account. Handling your cash is discussed in greater detail in Chapter 17.

Bank Deposits and Other Cash Accounts - Creditors almost always look first to your bank account. If there is money in the account there is nothing more to do than get a court order that the money be paid over.

Cash Equivalents - After cash, next best is property that can easily be converted to cash, such as certificates of deposit and publicly traded stocks and bonds. Seizing and selling such stocks and bonds can be a bother but is still a relatively good source of recovery for a creditor. But stocks, bonds and partnership interests in small, closely held companies are very difficult to sell and usually are ignored by creditors.

Retirement Funds - Some retirement funds can be reached by creditors, some cannot. Generally, but not always, federally approved pension plan funds cannot be reached by creditors, unless the consumer is in proceedings under the U.S. Bankruptcy Code. Often, IRAs and KEOGHS can be reached by creditors but many states are passing laws to protect them. The more control the consumer has over the retirement fund, the more likely that creditors can reach it.

Real Estate

Seizing and selling real estate to enforce a judgment is much more complicated and quite different than an ordinary mortgage foreclosure. And seizing and selling homes can be extraordinarily difficult. Some states do not permit judgment creditors to pursue a consumer's home. Several states do not permit creditors to go after a home that is co-owned by the consumer's spouse, unless the creditor also has a judgment against the spouse. Most judges despise taking homes, especially if children are involved. These judges will make the creditor's attorney cross every "t" and dot every "i" before issuing such an order.

It is unlikely a court will authorize the sale of a consumer's real estate, unless the sale will produce enough money to pay a meaningful amount to the judgment creditor. Surprisingly, real estate often is not worth enough to generate any money for the creditor.

Judicial sales of real estate bring notoriously low prices. Usually, the buyer has to pay cash, and it can be very difficult to arrange financing for a home that will be purchased at auction. Typically, these auctions attract only professional bone pickers, who make their living from other people's problems. Usually, there is at least one mortgage on the real estate. Unless the real estate is worth a lot more than the mortgage, there probably won't be enough equity for the creditor to recover very much money. It is hard to sell property subject to a mortgage, because the mortgage lender can exercise its right to accelerate the loan and declare the entire amount immediately due.

Selling real estate is expensive for a creditor. It involves at least one appraisal, several weeks of publication in a newspaper, at least one title search, and a sheriff's fee. And often, there are co-owners of the real estate. As you will soon see, this can be an enormous problem for the creditor. Moreover, almost every state gives consumers a homestead exemption. This means that the consumer has the right to be paid the amount of the exemption before anyone else receives a cent. If the sales price is not high enough to cover the amount of the homestead exemption, the sale will be neither approved nor confirmed. Most states require that the property be appraised to determine that it will sell for enough to cover, at least, the homestead exemption and the costs of the sale.

If a judgment creditor wants to pursue real estate, it asks the court to order the clerk or sheriff to "constructively" seize the property and conduct a public auction. Usually, the sheriff constructively seizes the property by recording a copy of the court order with the county recorder. The sheriff does not take physical possession of the premises, unless there is a special court order. Those orders are extremely rare and will be issued only if it is clear that the property is abandoned, or in immediate danger of serious damage.

The auction is solely for the purpose of raising cash to satisfy the judgment. Typically, the auction has to be advertised for two to four weeks. The auction is conducted by a court clerk, or a sheriff's deputy. It is important to understand that the actual real estate is not being sold. Rather, it is the consumer's "right, title and interest" in the real estate that is being sold. The successful bidder gets only the rights the consumer had, and no more. If there is a co-owner, usually a spouse, the sale will not affect the co-owner's rights, unless the creditor also has an enforceable judgment against all the co-owners.

If the property is owned in "joint tenancy," usually the consumer and spouse, and the creditor does not have a judgment against the spouse, it's almost impossible to find anyone willing to bid at the auction. The creditor gains nothing from such an auction, unless the creditor itself bids. If the creditor bids, it will have to use up some of the amount of its judgment, and probably will find itself in the unpleasant position of paying the consumer the amount of the consumer's homestead exemption. Even then, the creditor will not be able to do anything with what it bought, unless it can convince a court to order "partition" of the property.

Partition means physically dividing the real estate or selling the real estate and dividing the proceeds. Many states won't permit a court to order the partition of property owned by two or more "joint tenants" and most states make it very difficult. A separate lawsuit for partition must be brought by the creditor against the non-judgment co-owner. But, the creditor has no legal right to bring such a suit, unless it already has purchased the judgment debtor's ownership interests at the auction.

The sale does not even give the buyer possession of the real estate. If the property is leased prior to the recording of a judgment lien against the property, the tenant has the right to remain on premises until the lease expires. If the consumer does not voluntarily surrender the premises, the buyer has to go back to court and ask for another order, often called a "writ of assistance," directing the sheriff to evict the consumer. Most judges will give the consumer some time, and many judges will not issue such orders in the middle of a cold winter, especially if there are children involved. When they are given such orders, most sheriffs will call first, remind the consumer the order has been issued, and ask him to voluntarily leave within the time permitted by the order.

Unless a creditor has judgments against all of the owners, and the property is worth a lot more than the first mortgage, it is highly unlikely that the creditor will seriously try to use real estate, especially a home, to enforce a judgment. Remember, however, a judgment creditor is very likely to record a lien against the property that will restrict your ability to sell the property.

TANGIBLE PERSONAL PROPERTY

Seizing and selling tangible personal property is somewhat complicated:

TYPICAL ATTACHMENT PROCEDURE

(1) The creditor finds the property.

(2) The creditor asks the court to order the sheriff to take possession of the property.

(3) The creditor is required to post a bond in an amount that will be one and one-half to two times the estimated value of the property to be seized. If the property is being improperly seized, or is harmed, the bond will used to pay for the damages.

(4) The sheriff takes possession of the property.

(5) The creditor has to arrange and pay for storage of the property pending the auction.

(6) Many states require that certain types of property be appraised before it can be sold to make sure that it will sell for enough to cover any exemption and the costs of sale.

(7) The court orders the sheriff to advertise and conduct a public auction.

(8) The property is sold at public auction. Anyone can bid for the property, including the creditor and the consumer. Everyone except the creditor must pay cash. The creditor can bid all or any part of the amount of its judgment.

(9) The amount recovered from the auction, less all costs of storage and sale, are paid to the creditor and the judgment is satisfied by that amount. If the judgment is satisfied in full and any sale proceeds remain, they are paid to the consumer.

(10) Usually, if the consumer is the successful bidder, that creditor cannot go after the same property again even if there is a deficiency. However, other judgment creditors probably can.

HOUSEHOLD GOODS

Unless you are a collector, it's unlikely that a creditor will go after your household furniture, or even the sterling silver tea set inherited from your grandmother. Such belongings are a pain to seize, and virtually impossible to sell. Moreover, almost every state protects much of the value of household goods, and no sane creditor wants to ask a court to have the sheriff cart off your bedroom set.

PERSONAL BELONGINGS

Much like household goods, your personal belongings probably are of almost no interest to a creditor. Valuable jewelry is a notable exception, but many states protect wedding bands from creditors. Also, keep in mind that jewelry you bought from a retail store almost certainly is worth only fraction of what you paid. Small gems and lightweight gold pieces are almost impossible to resell for more than a few cents on the dollar.

VEHICLES

Creditors threaten to go after cars much more often than they actually do. Why? Because, it's unlikely that a creditor will be able to recover any money from the car. Typically, the consumer owes the finance company as much or more than the car is worth, and many states protect from creditors a portion of a car's value. However, if your car does have equity (the value of the car less the amount you owe to the finance company), the creditor may go after it. Moreover, you can be temporarily inconvenienced if a creditor convinces a court to order you to turn over the keys to a car you have driven to a citation examination.

RECOVERY OF TRANSFERRED PROPERTY

Sometimes, consumers, who expect to have a creditor chase them, try to hide property by putting it in someone else's name and secretly retaining ownership. This method of hiding assets is known as a "fraudulent transfer." If a consumer tries to hide property this way, and the creditor discovers it, the creditor may try to "avoid the fraudulent transfer" and recover the property from the person who received it.

To avoid a fraudulent transfer, the creditor first has to discover the transfer occurred, then sue the person who received the property - not the consumer who parted with the property. Discovering a fraudulent transfer can be very difficult, unless the creditor knows that the consumer once owned the property that was transferred. During citation proceedings, creditors' attorneys often routinely ask if the consumer has recently "sold anything" or "made any gifts." The typical answer, which the creditor's attorney has no reason to question, is: "Nothing other than the usual holiday and birthday gifts." However, if the consumer previously provided the creditor with a financial statement, the consumer should be prepared for questions about any property included in the financial statement.

Even if a creditor discovers a transfer, proving that it was fraudulent can involve some very technical and complicated legal problems. If the property is worth enough, and the creditor is owed enough, the creditor may try to convince the court there has been a fraudulent transfer.

There are two different theories a court can rely upon to find there has been a fraudulent transfer. Overlooking what often are important legal technicalities, they are in essence:

The Consumer Does Not Receive Enough For The Property

The gist of this doctrine is that a person who owes money should not be giving away his property. This doctrine can be applied by a court when two factors are BOTH present:

The consumer parts with the property, but does not receive adequate value from the person who receives the property >

For these purposes, adequate value means that the consumer must be paid something that has REAL FINANCIAL VALUE to the consumer. Love, sympathy, and loyalty are not sufficient. Payment for past services, promises of future services, and forgiveness of questionable liabilities are closely scrutinized. Hard cash, marketable property, and valid promissory notes and mortgages usually pass muster. Also, the consumer must receive ENOUGH real financial value. How much is enough depends upon the value of the property that was transferred at the time it was transferred. For example, if a consumer sells his undamaged late model Mercedes-Benz to his brother for $500, it probably is not enough. However, $500 may be enough for a house that is in foreclosure, burdened with lots of delinquent property taxes, and needs tens of thousands of dollars of repairs. As a general rule, if the amount is at all reasonable, it will be deemed enough.

AND, at the time the property is transferred, the consumer is (or is about to become), unable to pay his debts >

In many states, and in federal bankruptcy court, it is enough if the consumer owed money to anyone when he transferred the property. It is not necessary for the consumer to have owed the money to any particular creditor.

The Transfer is Intended to Prevent Creditors From Reaching The Property

The gist of this doctrine is that property cannot be deliberately put beyond a creditor's reach. This doctrine can be applied when EITHER of two factors is present.

The consumer transfers the property with intent to delay or hinder creditors >

As a practical matter, it is extremely difficult to prove intent, unless either (a) the consumer outright admits that he was trying to hide assets from his creditors, or (b) the consumer transfers extremely valuable property, or (c) the consumer engages in a pattern of transferring a large portion of his property.

OR, the person who receives the property is not purchasing in good faith >

This means that the person getting the property has to reasonably believe that the sale is genuine and not a sham. If the person receiving the property does not pay adequate value, it is likely that a court will find that the purchaser could not reasonably believe the sale was genuine. If the purchaser is related to the consumer, the court will closely examine the transaction.

UNDERSTANDING INTEREST AND OTHER CHARGES

CHAPTER ELEVEN

Determining true interest rates is very hard.

Competent creditors understand interest rates very well, but few consumers do. Creditors take advantage of this knowledge gap by focusing attention on the amount of the monthly payments rather than the true interest rate.

- Simple Interest
- Compound Interest
- Discount Interest
- Add-On Interest
- Variable Rates
- Late Payment Charges
- Prepayment Penalties
- Hidden Charges

GENERAL

An entire book is needed to cover the subject of interest rates. Even then, only a mathematician would understand everything. But thanks to the federal Truth in Lending Act, consumers now need to grasp only a few basic concepts. Even if you can't understand the following discussion of interest rates, at least remember two things:

CHAPTER 11

INTEREST PAYMENTS TAKE HARD EARNED DOLLARS OUT OF YOUR POCKET AND PUT THEM INTO THE POCKETS OF YOUR CREDITORS.

"ANNUAL PERCENTAGE RATE," OR "APR," IS THE ONLY RELIABLE INDICATOR OF THE ACTUAL INTEREST YOU HAVE TO PAY. Do not believe any other "interest rate" quoted by a creditor. When it comes to true interest rates, almost all lenders will lie.

Creditors compute interest in many different ways, but they all boil down to one, or some combination, of the following methods: Simple interest, compound interest, discount interest, add-on interest, and variable rate interest. Although technically not "interest," late payment charges and prepayment penalties can have about the same effect as increasing the rate of interest. APR is very close to the simple interest discussed below. Federal law requires creditors to tell consumers the actual APR.

The problem for consumers, and what ends up costing them so much money, is that most lenders hide several different kinds of interest charges within the same loan. They do this by calling them such things as closing points, application fees, and other fancy names.

The key to understanding interest rates is determining who gets to use the cash.

Assume a creditor lends you $1,000. You deposit all the money in a bank that pays you 5% simple interest:

If you pay all $1,000 back after one year, you've gotten the use of $1,000 for a year,

and you've collected $50.00 interest from your bank.

If you pay back $500 after six months and $500 after twelve months, then you've gotten the use of $1,000 for six months and the use of $500 for six months. This is the same as getting the use of $750 for one year,

and you've collected $37.50 interest from your bank.

If you pay back the $1,000 in twelve equal monthly installments of $83.33 each, it's the same as getting the use of $500 for a year,

and you've collected $25.00 interest from your bank.

If you pay the $1,000 back immediately, you haven't got the use of any of the money,

and you've collected no interest from your bank.

The longer you have the use of the money, the more interest you earn. Not having the use of the money you borrowed costs you interest. This is known as the "time value" of money and is the essence of all interest rates.

SIMPLE INTEREST

Simple interest is straightforward. The borrower does not make any installment payments, but pays the loan in full, when it's due. The interest is computed by dividing the amount of interest paid by the amount borrowed. The resulting percentage is then divided by the number of years, months or days.

> If you borrow $1,000, and at the end of one year pay the creditor $1,100, you have paid simple interest at the rate of 10% per year. [$100 / $1000 = .10 or 10%]
>
> If you borrow $1,000, and at the end of two years pay the creditor $1,200, you still have paid simple interest at the rate of 10% per year. [$200 / $1000 = .20 and then .20 / 2 years = .10]

COMPOUND INTEREST

Compounding interest increases the amount of interest you pay because you end up paying interest on the interest you owe. The amount of additional interest depends on the starting interest rate, how frequently the interest is compounded, and how often you make payments.

> Assume you borrow $1,000 for one year and agree to repay the loan plus 10% interest, compounded every six months. After 6 months, you will owe $50 interest for the use of $1,000 for 6 months. If you pay the $50 interest, it will not have a chance to compound. If, instead, you wait until the end of the year, then you will owe interest totalling $102.50:
>
> $50.00 for the use of $1,000 during the first six months
>
> $50.00 for the use of $1,000 during the second six months
>
> $ 2.50 for the use of the unpaid $50 interest during the second six months
>
> Daily compounding would increase the true interest rate to 10.5% per year, and the interest charges for the year would total $105. If the starting interest rate were 18%, daily compounding would increase the true interest rate to 19.7% per year, and the interest charges would total $197.

These days, most lenders charge interest that is compounded daily.

CHAPTER 11

DISCOUNT INTEREST

Imagine going to the bank to borrow $1,000. Instead of charging you interest at the end of the loan, the bank lends you $1,000 but keeps $100 of the loan proceeds. You get only $900. You're not paying 10% interest. Rather, you're paying $100 for the use of only $900. You will, in reality, be paying an interest rate of about 11% per year.

You would think that no one would lend money to consumers at a discount anymore, because Truth in Lending laws make lenders disclose the true interest rate. Technically, few consumer lenders lend at a discount today, but the law still permits creditors, especially mortgage lenders, to mislead consumers by disguising the discount as "points," "loan application fees," and "credit check fees."

These charges are supposed to be included in the final Truth in Lending Law disclosure of the APR. Many consumers just don't realize that they are being charged higher interest than they were originally quoted. And when they do realize it, most consumers just bite their tongues and pay.

ADD-ON INTEREST

Add-on interest is a favorite device of companies that finance car and van purchases. Interest is not charged periodically. Instead, it is added on to the principal amount of the loan.

Assume you want to borrow $1,000 for a year and pay 12 equal monthly installments. The finance company says it will charge you 10% interest and adds it on to the loan. You sign a promissory note for $1100. You will make twelve monthly payments of $91.67. Each month you reduce the amount of the loan, decrease the amount of money you get to use, and increase the amount of money the finance company has available to use for other loans. Constantly paying down the loan is the same as getting the use of less than $500 for that year.

Ten percent add-on interest is same as 20.5% simple interest. If you think that is outrageous, take a few moments to compute how much more it will cost if the add-on interest is compounded!

VARIABLE INTEREST RATES

Almost everyone has heard of variable or "floating" interest rates. In fact, many people have variable rate mortgage loans, but few people really understand them.

These variable rate loans became quite common after savings and loan banks realized how much money they were losing on low, fixed rate mortgages. This happened in the late 1970's, at a time when interest rates were skyrocketing. Although there was a good reason for introducing this new type of loan, many lenders misused variable rate loans to fleece borrowers. These abuses became so flagrant that the federal government imposed important restrictions on these lenders.

Typically, variable rate loans provide for increasing and decreasing the interest rate in accordance with, or "pegged to," some sort of an indicator. The choice of indicator is extremely important. In the past, many loans were pegged to some large bank's "prime rate." Prime rate has no real meaning and can be adjusted at a bank's will. All banks raise their prime rates as often and as high as they possibly can. Some banks even have made loans pegged to their own prime rate, then proceeded to create an artificial rate.

> It's dangerous to agree to a variable rate pegged to any indicator within the lender's control, especially a "prime rate." Fortunately, the federal government now prohibits the use of such indicators.
>
> Be wary of the initial or starting rate. Not long ago, many banks quoted artificially low rates as an inducement to get you to make the original loan. These rates frequently were below the bank's own indicators. Consequently, even if the indicator did not go up at all, there was a built-in increase in the loan's variable rate. Again, the federal government now prohibits the use of fake initial rates.

Another important feature of a variable rate loan is how often and how much the rate can change. Typically, the rate is adjusted once a year and cannot move by more than about a point each time. However, one percentage point can add a lot to your monthly payment. For example, if the rate on a $75,000, 30 year mortgage loan increases from 10% to 11% per year, the monthly payments will increase 8%, from $658 per month to $714 per month, totalling $672 over one year alone. Unless your income also increases by 8%, the mortgage loan payments will consume a bigger portion of your budget, leaving you less to save or to spend on other things. If your income does not increase, or the rate of inflation exceeds the increase of your income, the increased mortgage payments will compel you to reduce your standard of living.

Don't assume that the variable rate can go down as much as it can go up. Most variable rate loan documents permit the rates to rise a lot more than they can fall. Variable rate loans always put the lender in a no lose position and places you in a no win situation. That's why lenders urge you to use this form of financing.

LATE PAYMENT CHARGES

Late payment charges and "penalty" interest are very expensive for consumers and extremely profitable for creditors.

Assume you owe $75,000 on a 30 year mortgage with a 10% APR, and your monthly payments are about $658. If you are late every month for a year, it will cost you $240 in late payments. The bank may complain that your payments are late, but it will love you because it is making a fortune.

Now assume that your very first loan payment is a month late and you have to pay a $20 late payment charge. Of the $658 loan payment, about $625 is interest and $33 is repayment of principal. You can look at the late payment charge in either of two ways:

> The bank collected $20 for the use of $658 for one month, which is the same as compound interest at the rate of 36% per year, or
>
> The bank collected $20 for the use of $33 for one month, which is the same as simple interest at the rate of 727% per year.

If you were the bank, would you want your borrowers to pay on time, or would you prefer that they consistently pay one day late? Most states limit how much a creditor can charge for late payments. Depending on the type of loan, the limit is either a fixed amount or a percentage of the overdue amount.

Often, creditors try to impose late payment charges or interest that the consumer never agreed to pay. Don't pay these charges unless the creditor can produce your written agreement to pay them. Often, you will discover that there is no such agreement or that the agreement reflects lower charges than you are actually being billed. If ever a creditor claims that "the law allows" it to assess the charges, demand to see a copy of that law. Most likely, the law permits the creditor to assess charges if you agree to pay them. Rarely does the law impose such charges without your prior agreement.

PREPAYMENT PENALTIES

A prepayment penalty is an extra charge imposed for paying off a loan before it is due. Although federal and state laws prohibit prepayment penalties for many kinds of loans, particularly variable rate home loans, they still exist.

Sometimes, prepayment penalties are fair and reasonable. For example, interest rates are very high, but a lender believes that in the long run they will come way down. The lender may agree to lend money at a rate that is lower than current interest rates but higher than the projected future interest rates. In other words, the lender accepts a lower short term return in exchange for a possibly higher long term return. If the borrower pays off the loan as soon as interest rates fall, the lender ends up losing money.

The most inexcusable prepayment penalty is not even called a penalty and once was a common feature of car loans. The prepayment penalty is built into the interest computation. Assume you borrow $10,000 to buy a car and agree to pay 10% simple add-on interest over four years. The promissory note you sign will say that you owe $14,000. For some reason (perhaps your car gets stolen), you have to pay off the loan after only two years. You already will have paid $7,000 and would like to think that you could pay off the loan for $5,000, making a total of $12,000. After all, you used the money for only two years. That's $10,000 plus half the $4,000 interest. Unfortunately, you will discover that the interest is being computed in accordance with "the sum of the digits method," sometimes called the "rule of 78." Under this formula, you will have to come up with $5,980 to pay off the loan.

> In effect, you will be paying $6,480 interest for the use of $6,500 for two years.
> That is the same as a simple interest rate of just under 50% per year.

Often, the "sum of the digits method" is prohibited by law - and higher quality finance companies usually provide for a less extortionate prepayment penalty.

Sometimes, creditors try to collect a prepayment penalty after the consumer has defaulted, the collateral has been destroyed, or the creditor has called the loan. Don't let a creditor get away with this scam. The creditor is forcing the prepayment. If the creditor doesn't want its money, it doesn't have to call the entire loan.

HIDDEN CHARGES

Over the years, lenders have found ways to create all sorts of additional charges. Few are clearly disclosed until the borrower receives a Truth in Lending Disclosure Statement, and some are not even shown there. Some charges are more reasonable than others, but all cost you money and they add up fast. They include:

Loan Application Fees - Loan application fees range up to hundreds of dollars - up front - and usually are not refundable even if the loan is declined. Lenders claim that these fees cover their costs of processing the application, but they usually have no relationship to the lender's actual expenses. As often as not, loan application fees are just an excuse for extracting money from consumers anxious to buy a home. Some abusive companies have even been known to accept fees without any intention of making a loan.

Loan Insurance - Frequently, lenders require borrowers to purchase loan insurance, most often in conjunction with mortgages. The insurance is purchased from a third party, usually a federal agency such as the Federal National Mortgage Association, but sometimes from private companies. If the borrower does not pay, the insurer is required to purchase the loan from the lender. The insurance relieves the lender of most the risk. So far, this is reasonable.

However, all interests rates are computed to include a portion to cover bad loans. Recalling the discussion in Chapter 3 (The Business of Lending), lenders spread their losses from bad loans among the good loans. In theory, if the lender has little or no risk of loss, the interest rate should be somewhat lower. Indeed, most federal programs limit interest rates when there is federal mortgage insurance.

Unlike government agencies, private mortgage insurers usually do not impose the same limitations on interest rates and lenders often do not voluntarily reduce their rates. Consequently, the borrower not only pays for the mortgage insurance, but continues to pay an interest rate that includes a portion for a risk of loss that does not exist. When this happens, the borrower is being overcharged.

Escrows - Many mortgage lenders require borrowers to make monthly deposits into an escrow account earmarked for property taxes and sometimes property insurance. The purpose of the escrow to make sure there will be sufficient funds to cover these admittedly important expenses of protecting the collateral. Once or twice a year, the lender pays the taxes and insurance.

However, many lenders do not pay the borrower any interest on the funds sitting in the escrow account. These lenders claim that it costs them so much to administer the accounts that they would lose money if they paid interest. Consider how much time it takes to mail two to four checks in a year, and then decide for yourself whether the lenders could afford to pay at least some interest on the escrow funds.

Documentation Fees - Many loan documentation fees are appropriate. Lenders should be able to recover fees charged by government agencies for recording mortgages, automobile title liens, and other out-of-pocket expenses.

However, lenders are beginning to charge fees for document "preparation." Mortgage lenders charge as much as fifty dollars for issuing a release of mortgage after the loan has been paid off. The so-called preparation consists of having a secretary fill in the blanks on a form and finding a bank officer to sign and seal the paper.

Cash Advances - Everyone knows that taking a cash advance on a credit card is expensive. Interest rates are high and there is a minimum charge, even when the money is paid back the next day. Many consumers do not know that with many credit cards, drawing a cash advance also triggers interest charges on regular purchases.

When a cash advance is drawn, the credit card company goes back to the date each purchase was made and charges interest from that day forward. Some companies even start charging a higher interest rate once a cash advance is drawn. Most credit card companies forgive the interest charges on the purchases if the entire balance, including the cash advance, is paid when the next bill is due.

> If you must take a cash advance from a credit card company, and will not be able to repay it all with the next bill, save money by drawing the advance on a different card than you use for purchases. That way, you can pay-off your purchases on one card and only incur interest on the cash advance taken on the other card.

section

FOUR

CONSUMER WEAPONS

IMPORTANT CONSUMER STRATEGIES

Chapter Twelve

ASSIGNMENTS FOR THE BENEFIT OF CREDITORS

Assignment for the benefit of creditors, "ABC," is a legal device rarely used by lawyers in consumer cases. ABCs traditionally have been used for defunct corporations. Some states don't even permit them. Other states govern them by specific statute, while still others by "common law," or court decisions.

Few people even know what they are. But in certain instances, an ABC is a better alternative than seeking relief under the Bankruptcy Code.

> NEVER attempt an ABC on your own. ALWAYS consult with a qualified lawyer before proceeding with an ABC.

An ABC consists of assigning all the consumer's property to an "assignee." This assignee liquidates the property and distributes the cash among the creditors. The consumer keeps all exempt property. An ABC operates to bar the creditors from taking legal action against the consumer.

An assignee can be any disinterested adult, but most assignments are made to specialists in this field. The assignee is a fiduciary, or trustee, for the creditors and is paid a percentage of the proceeds recovered from the liquidation.

Some states have statutes that specify how to distribute the proceeds; in other states, the assignee follows the distribution scheme outlined in Chapter 7 of the United States Bankruptcy Code. In all cases, federal law gives the federal government highest priority.

There are several advantages of ABCs:

They are not court proceedings and often go unnoticed by the public and many credit reporting agencies.

ABCs are quick and easy to start, often requiring nothing more than a one-page document accompanied by a list of creditors. Soon afterwards, the assignee will require you to complete lists of all assets and liabilities.

Assignees usually are not able to closely examine your prior activities. Unlike proceedings under the Bankruptcy Code, with ABCs you usually do not have the same affirmative duties to make disclosures to the assignee. This benefits you if you're concerned, for example, about disclosing something such as a transfer of property. Some assignees, however, take their tasks very seriously and perform more thorough investigations than do Chapter 7 trustees.

Preferential payments cannot be recovered. Assignees have no power to recover preferential payments to certain creditors over others creditors. You may choose to pay your brother-in-law in full before you pay Diners Club anything. That is a preferential payment that an assignee may not be able to recover.

Fraudulent transfers may be more difficult to recover because assignees operate under state law, not federal law. In some states, it's more difficult to recover fraudulent conveyances than it is under the Bankruptcy Code. Also, assignees may confront the same out-of-state jurisdictional problems as do creditors.

Federal taxes get paid first. Federal law gives U.S. government debts priority over all other unsecured debts. This can be a big advantage to the consumer if the taxes are of a type that cannot be discharged under the Bankruptcy Code.

Assignees usually recover more for creditors than do Chapter 7 trustees. Most assignees are allowed more freedom, confront less red tape, and have more practical experience than most Chapter 7 trustees.

ABCs also have disadvantages:

Assignees won't accept ABCs unless they can make money. If there aren't sufficient assets from which an assignee's fee can be recovered, you will have to pay the assignee's fee.

An ABC may not be recognized in another state. Proceedings under the Bankruptcy Code protect a consumer in every state. An ABC in one state may not be fully recognized in another state.

Creditors often distrust ABCs. Some assignees have been known to be less than honest. They have been known to take kickbacks from auctioneers and even render false accountings. But then again, so have Chapter 7 trustees.

Assignees aren't as free to deal with collateral because they must obtain the creditor's consent before selling collateral for less than the total amount owed to the creditor. Technically, Chapter 7 trustees have the same limitation, but the Bankruptcy Code gives Chapter 7 trustees more tools to work with when dealing with secured creditors.

An ABC can hasten the start of involuntary bankruptcy proceedings because you're basically admitting that you are insolvent. If one or more creditors decide to file an involuntary petition within 120 days of your ABC, it is likely that the Bankruptcy Court will grant it.

Debts discharged through an ABC can be taxed as income. Debts discharged through proceedings under the Bankruptcy Code generally cannot be taxed as income.

BUYING TIME

HOW TIME HELPS THE CONSUMER

EVENTUALLY, EVERY DEBT BECOMES UNCOLLECTIBLE

Time may not heal all wounds, but it usually works to a consumer's advantage. If a debt can't be paid right away, the consumer might want to look for ways to hinder the creditor's collection processes and activities. With the passage of time, many things can happen and very few of them hurt the consumer:

A debt may become legally unenforceable due to a statute of limitations or even a change in the law. Statutes of limitations can be as short as two years or as long as twenty years, depending on the kind of debt, federal law, laws of the particular state, or the consumer's actions.

A creditor may give up trying to collect the debt and write it off. This is a fairly common practice, particularly when the debt is not too large.

A creditor may be distracted by a newer, more pressing problem.

A creditor's records may be misfiled, lost, or destroyed.

A creditor may get into legal trouble for doing something wrong that the consumer didn't know about at the time but can use as a defense after the error is disclosed.

A creditor may mishandle the collateral, relieving the consumer from any further obligation to pay.

A creditor may attempt to bring a lawsuit but not prosecute it because of oversight or the costs involved. When this happens, the court dismisses the case.

A creditor may go out of business.

The claimed debt may no longer be reportable by a credit reporting agency. Bankruptcies cannot be reported after 10 years. Suits and judgments cannot be reported after 7 years, or the applicable statute of limitations, whichever is longer. Accounts placed for collection, arrests and other adverse information can't be reported after 7 years. Exceptions to these time limitations include reports prepared for transactions involving more than $50,000, life insurance of $50,000 or more, and employment at a job that pays $20,000 per year or more.

WHEN TIME DOESN'T HELP THE CONSUMER

Time doesn't always help the consumer. For example, time hurts a consumer who continues to make mortgage payments. Eventually, the mortgage gets low enough, or the value of the house high enough, to make it worthwhile for a creditor to go after the equity in the house. Meanwhile, interest has continued to accumulate, making the debt even larger.

The I.R.S., in particular, is infamous for using this wait-and-collect approach, sometimes known as "sandbagging." Statutory penalties and interest can inflate even a modest tax obligation into a blimp.

DON'T ACCUMULATE PROPERTY THAT A CREDITOR CAN SEIZE LATER. If this is likely to happen, it may be better for you to go through a bankruptcy when you have the least to lose. Or you may choose to acquire property in the name of someone else, a person you completely trust.

TECHNIQUES FOR GAINING TIME

Most creditors display patience if they believe that waiting will get them paid. They lose their patience when they think the consumer is stalling without any real intention of paying. There are three ways to gain time:

Ask The Creditor For Time > Simply asking for time is usually easiest, but you have to give a good reason. Most creditors will agree to wait 60 days. You also have to promise to make a payment at the end of that time. If you don't honor this promise, the creditor frequently will target you.

As a general rule, don't ask a creditor for time unless you are confident you can perform or are sure you will make good use of the extra time to achieve some objective. Just delaying your creditor for no good reason will achieve nothing and may motivate the creditor to target you.

Temporarily Satisfy The Creditor > Although you can't give the creditor everything he wants, you may be able to give him enough to convince him not to take any further action against you for a while. Sometimes, it's enough to return a credit card so the company doesn't have to worry about your running up more bills. Often, you can obtain a lot of time by surrendering collateral you don't need. This means a lot to automobile finance companies.

Making one or more payments is the most common way to satisfy a creditor. However, making just one payment, even if it's large, will not hold a creditor off for long. It's more effective to make small, but regular, monthly payments. The creditor is unlikely to take any further action for fear of ending the stream of payments.

Some creditors even remove an account from the collection department if a consumer makes three or four monthly payments. They go through the entire collection process all over again if the consumer stops making payments. The size of payments necessary varies, depending on the creditor and the type of debt. Negotiating payment plans is discussed in more detail below.

Manufacture Time By Disrupting A Creditor's Collection Efforts > With some planning and a little effort, a consumer can obtain a lot of time by confounding or disrupting a creditor's routine collection procedures. The immediate objectives are to:

Slow down the creditor's collection machinery.

Force the creditor to do additional work.

Create opportunities for the creditor to lose or forget your file.

Create opportunities for the creditor to make a mistake that will excuse you from making payments.

Create valid reasons for your own failure to make payments or other inaction.

There are two general approaches to disrupting a creditor's collection efforts:

Burden the Creditor with Trivial but Unusual Tasks > Repeatedly do things that force the creditor to abandon the normal routine. Force the creditor to spend the time, energy and thought dealing with trivial but abnormal account activities. Trivial, unusual tasks are more likely to fall between the cracks, and sometimes cause files to become lost or forgotten.

It's essential that the task not be important, otherwise it will attract special attention. This approach will more likely succeed with a large creditor than a small one who is not as dependent on formal procedures. Some of the actions you can take include:

Directing your payments and/or correspondence to branch offices or departments that aren't accustomed to receiving such things. Often, a payment or letter will not be forwarded at all, or will be forwarded to the wrong place.

Sending several partial payments for odd amounts at frequent but irregular intervals. Often, errors are made when computers or bookkeepers recompute the account balance. Payments hand delivered on the last possible day often don't get entered in time for the next statement.

Sending the creditor change of address/telephone notices. A post office box can be very useful as a new address. And sometimes, the new address will be incorrectly entered into the creditor's computer or books.

Telephone tag. (See Chapter 19.)

Responding to a creditor with numerous lengthy letters politely asking questions or detailing grievances but never flat out refusing to pay. Possible grievances are discussed in the next section.

QUESTIONS THAT OFTEN NEED TO BE ASKED

How was the interest calculated?

When and how did you agree to pay interest or that interest rate?

Why weren't you credited for a payment or partial payment?

Why weren't you given credit for returned goods?

Why aren't your statements being sent to your new address?

Why are your statements being mailed X number of days after they are dated, leaving you insufficient time to pay the bill?

It's best NOT to complain about why your calls or letters haven't been returned. Such a complaint is likely to prompt the creditor to pay special attention to you. Instead, use the creditor's failure to respond as a reason why you didn't make a payment or do something else that was awaiting the creditor's response.

Create a Major Problem for the Creditor > If the creditor (or collection agency) appears to have done something wrong or made a serious mistake, a consumer can put the creditor on the defensive and force the creditor to proceed very carefully and possibly even abandon collection efforts. Some of the most common major errors committed by creditors include:

Violating the Truth in Lending Act by misstating the "**A**nnual **P**ercentage **R**ate" in advertising literature or telephone conversations.

Improperly computing or charging interest or late payment charges.

Improperly disposing of repossessed collateral.

Never obtaining, or losing, essential documents such as signed Truth in Lending Disclosure Statements and Notices of Rights of Rescission.

Once the consumer raises the problem, the creditor is likely to spend considerably more time and effort reading and preparing correspondence, computing balances, and planning action. Often, the creditor will seek legal or other professional advice.

If you file a complaint with a government agency or get the attention of the news media or a consumer advocacy group, the creditor will have to spend a lot of time, energy and money dealing with the problem. Sometimes, the creditor may even decide that collecting the account isn't worth the trouble, expense or risk.

However, this approach involves a substantial risk of making a serious enemy out of the creditor, especially if you file a complaint with a government agency. Take this approach only if you are quite confident you are in the right, or if you have nothing to lose by provoking the creditor to aggressively target you.

GRIEVANCES

Every debt represents just one side of a transaction. In return for incurring that debt, you are supposed to get something of about equal value. If you don't get everything you are promised or you reasonably expected, a creditor deserves to collect only a part or none of the debt.

IDENTIFYING GRIEVANCES

It's impossible to list every possible type of complaint, but some of the most common ones include:

Defective or incomplete goods that don't work as advertised, injure someone, or damage something.

Inadequate, unprofessional, or incomplete services.

Late delivery or performance.

Prices or interest charges higher than advertised, usually in the form of undisclosed additional charges or charges that are buried in the small print.

"Bait and switch" - a bargain is advertised but the merchant really intends to convince you to buy a more expensive product. Typically, the merchant claims to be out of the advertised product, or the salesperson immediately tells the consumer that the advertised product isn't much good and the consumer should buy a different product.

False advertising - it's best if the false advertising is in print, but false claims about a product or service made orally by a salesperson can be raised as a valid defense.

Failure to honor a written or verbal warranty. Salespeople often make promises that you may be able to enforce even though they aren't in writing.

Violations of consumer protection laws, especially the Truth in Lending and Truth in Leasing Acts.

ASSERTING GRIEVANCES

It's important that you promptly inform the creditor of every complaint you have, especially if you don't intend to, or can't, pay the debt in full. If you don't complain within a reasonable time, the creditor will have the right to assume that you are satisfied with the transaction.

State laws sometimes provide that you can't assert a complaint after a certain period of time. That period depends on the laws of the particular state, the nature of the transaction and the specific circumstances. Complaints about credit card charges are always subject to federal law and are discussed under Truth in Lending in Chapter 13 of this book.

Always complain as soon as you learn about a problem, even if you think it's too late or don't believe that complaining will get any results. Whenever possible, put your complaint in writing so you can prove you made it. Include the time and the person to whom you spoke, and save these notes.

Never tell your creditor that you don't have any complaints or any more complaints. You may have forgotten something or not yet know you have a complaint. If asked, just say that you have listed all of the complaints that you could think of at the time.

Many consumers mistakenly believe that, once they accept and agree to pay for an unsatisfactory product or a service, there isn't anything they can do about the bill. For example, your car breaks down far away from home. The mechanic won't give you your car back unless you pay twice his estimated bill. You obviously need your car, so what can you do? Sign whatever it is you must sign to get your car, but protect your rights by adding the words "under protest" wherever you sign your name, especially on the charge slip. These magic words are less likely to be noticed and less likely to perpetuate the argument if you quietly write them next to your signature. Even if you don't write those magic words, you still can argue that you were compelled to sign under "duress." Your agreement may not be binding on you because it was not voluntary.

REPORTING GRIEVANCES AND GETTING ASSISTANCE

If you believe that a creditor is doing something wrong, or if your financial problems are overwhelming, seek immediate assistance. In addition to private lawyers, many government and public agencies can give you advice and take action of their own.

If the authority you initially reach can't do anything, ask them for help finding the correct authority. Don't give up. Keep at it and you will reach someone who can give you good advice and has the power to provide appropriate help. A lot of people out there are paid to help you.

Even if your complaint seems trivial in amount, it may be legally important. For example, many mortgage lenders used to require consumers to make their first installment payment immediately, rather than after the first month. Borrowers believed that the actual amount involved wasn't enough to fight over. However, shifting payments from the end of the month to the beginning of the month has a significant impact on the actual interest rate. Aside from being fraudulent, this practice often led to a Truth in Lending disclosure violation because the APR was wrong. Some lenders still try to use this trick. Consumers who catch them at it have a very important weapon to use against the lender.

Although slow to move, government agencies can be extremely powerful allies. Sometimes, you have to keep reminding them of your problems without becoming a nuisance. Do NOT misuse any government agency to pursue imaginary grievances or to harass a creditor. More likely than not, such misconduct will come back to haunt you.

MOBILITY

If a creditor knows where to find a consumer, he can try to do all sorts of things to pressure him to pay. But, if a consumer can't be located, there is nothing a creditor can do except submit a bad credit report and foreclose on whatever collateral the creditor manages to find.

Creditors start to worry when their mail to the consumer is returned or the consumer's phone is disconnected. They will first re-check the consumer's last known residence and place of work. If the consumer isn't there, a creditor will do one or more of the following to locate the consumer:

Contact the relatives and friends whose names appear on the credit application.

Contact the former landlord and employer for forwarding information.

Request a mail tracer from the post office, hoping the consumer left a forwarding address.

Obtain one or more credit reports to look for a new address or particular location where the consumer is still using charge cards.

Look through telephone directories and call neighbors and people with the same last name.

Check with the state's Motor Vehicle Bureau.

Check with the county and the voting district.

Check with the local library.

Try to persuade an employee of a local school or the Social Security Administration to illegally disclose a new address or place of work.

It takes time and money to find someone. Depending on the type and amount of the debt, most creditors stop looking after one or two tries. This usually takes from six months to two years after the creditor starts collection activity.

The larger the amount and the more the creditor feels intentionally wronged, the longer and more vigorously the creditor will pursue the consumer. Creditors owed only small amounts usually give up quickly and often don't even try to find a consumer.

Some creditors rarely give up. For example, the IRS almost invariably can find the taxpayer through the taxpayer's own return or someone else's tax return, such as an employer's withholding tax return, a bank's 1099 return, or any number of other reports filed with the government. Government-guaranteed student loan programs are persistent, have been known to keep looking for ten or more years, and ultimately are very successful at finding - though not collecting from - former student borrowers. Finance companies that specialize in vehicle loans usually will not write off a debt until they recover at least the vehicle.

If your creditors don't have your current home address or place of employment, you are in a good position to take certain precautions to delay and stop creditor harassment:

> If possible, don't leave a forwarding address with the post office. If you must receive your mail, have it forwarded to a close friend or relative. Better yet, have it forwarded to a post office box that isn't near your home. When corresponding with anyone your creditors may contact, don't provide a return address. Don't make any payments to the creditor with a check, or money order from your new bank.
>
> Tell as few people as possible where you are living and working. Alert those few people not to tell anyone else of your new address or place of work. Advise them that the people who are looking for you will use all sorts of tricks to get the address, including fabricating family illnesses and accidents, non-existent prizes and inheritances, fake police and insurance investigations, and fake friendships and class reunions.
>
> Make sure the phone company doesn't provide your new number when the old number is called. Use a completely unlisted telephone number at the new address or take the phone in another person's name at the same address. When you call people your creditors are likely to contact, don't leave a return telephone number - always call again.
>
> Don't apply for credit or insurance from any store, bank, or insurer that will check with a credit reporting agency. Your creditors will get all this new information from the agency and you are back where you started.

If the creditor cannot find you, sooner or later, the creditor will quit looking. Usually, time works to your advantage so, as a general rule, it's helpful to delay the creditor as long as possible.

PAYMENT PLANS AND SETTLEMENTS

DESCRIPTION

Payment plans and settlements alter the originally agreed upon payment terms of a debt. This is often called "restructuring a debt." Payment plans and settlements aren't the same thing.

> A PAYMENT PLAN is merely an arrangement to make one or more payments over time. A SETTLEMENT is an agreement where the debt is satisfied by payment of less than the full amount claimed by the creditor. Often, settlements include some sort of a payment plan.

Obviously, negotiating a settlement is a lot trickier than negotiating a payment plan.

PAYMENT PLANS A payment plan can be nothing more than an arrangement to pay the entire debt by rescheduling payments. A payment plan also can be part of a settlement providing for less than full payment of the amount claimed by the creditor. You might choose to enter into a payment plan for either of two reasons:

> As a part of a carefully considered overall strategy to pay your debts, or
>
> to gain additional time as part of your overall strategy.

It's a bad idea to enter into a payment plan just to keep one particular creditor quiet. There are less expensive ways to get one creditor off your back. Unless your overall strategy requires that you gain time, do not enter into a payment plan unless you are confident you will be able make the payments. If the creditor will not accept a payment plan that you can manage, you probably are better off making no promises and keeping your cash.

If you blow a payment plan, some creditors will give you a second chance, particularly if you call to tell them about it before their computer tells them. Many creditors no longer will trust you and will make a note of it in your file. But so what. If your account gets turned over to a collection agency or attorney, you'll have little trouble arranging another payment plan.

Payment plans don't necessarily consist of regular level monthly payments. They can be scheduled in any number of creative ways. For example:

> A grace period relieving you from making payments for a while. You should be able to get 30 to 60 days without too much effort.
>
> No payments or minimum payments during certain periods and higher payments during other periods. Keep your monthly payments low by promising a larger payment when you get your Christmas bonus or your income tax refund. If your work is seasonal, arrange to make minimal payments during your off-season and more sizeable payments during busy seasons.

Payments that begin small and increase over time.

Weekly payments, semi-monthly payments, bi-monthly payments, or even quarterly payments.

Payments tied to specific events, such as the sale of some particular piece of property, or the receipt of a sales commission.

SETTLEMENTS It's important to distinguish between two kinds of settlements. The first kind of settlement consists of compromising a dispute. In legalese, this is called an "accord and satisfaction" and only can occur if a genuine disagreement arises over how much, if anything, is owed.

A compromise requires each side to give up something in consideration for what it's getting. This built-in exchange of "consideration" helps make a compromise legally binding on both sides.

The other kind of settlement consists of the creditor agreeing to modify the consumer's obligations even though the two agree on the real amount owed. This kind of settlement is often called an "accommodation." Unlike a compromise, an accommodation doesn't automatically include an exchange of consideration. A creditor may be able to back out of an accommodation unless:

the consumer gives the creditor something of value in consideration for the accommodation,

the creditor is aware that the consumer will do something important or take certain actions based on the accommodation; or

the creditor goes along with the accommodation for a period of time before trying to back out of it.

Many people mistakenly think that a settlement is always a lump-sum cash payment. But settlements can also involve modifying any one or more of a consumer's obligations, including:

Reducing the principal amount of the debt.

Forgiving past due interest.

Reducing the interest rate.

Releasing a consumer from all or part of a debt in exchange for surrendering collateral to the creditor.

Releasing a guarantor or co-signer of the debt in exchange for something else the creditor is seeking from the consumer.

Releasing a consumer from a debt in exchange for a release from a counterclaim against the creditor.

NEGOTIATING A PLAN OR SETTLEMENT

Creditors generally want to be paid in full and on time. The exception are those creditors who make their real money from interest and late payment charges. Creditors don't voluntarily agree to payment plans or settlements without good reasons. It's your job to help the creditor find the reasons to agree.

WHY CREDITORS AGREE TO PLANS AND SETTLEMENTS Creditors agree to payment plans and settlements when they believe it's to their advantage to do so, or when they believe they won't recover more money without spending more time and effort than any added recovery would be worth. Some of the reasons creditors agree to payment plans and settlements include:

The consumer is "judgment proof" > The consumer has so little income and property that the creditor won't recover any more by obtaining and enforcing a judgment. If your creditor is convinced that it won't even recover the costs of collection, it will agree to a payment plan and even accept a significantly reduced cash settlement.

However, some creditors, notably utility companies, have policies of pursuing collection even if the consumer is unable to pay anything. These creditors usually have huge numbers of delinquent accounts. They believe it's more cost effective to mass process a lot of lawsuits than it is to try to distinguish between consumers who can't pay and consumers who can pay but say they can't.

Utilities have the added advantage of knowing that consumers must come back to them for essential services. Unless the consumer files for bankruptcy, the utility can refuse services if there is a previous amount still owed. It's a waste of breath to plead poverty to these creditors. In many places, though, state and local laws require utilities to agree to at least one payment plan.

The collateral is worth less than the consumer is offering to pay, and the consumer is otherwise judgment proof > Many creditors find themselves compelled to agree to payment plans and settlements because they can't recover enough by repossessing, foreclosing, and selling the collateral because:

It's expensive to dispose of collateral, especially real estate.

Collateral doesn't sell for its full value. Aware that creditors are anxious to get rid of repossessed property, potential buyers take advantage of these opportunities to get bargains.

Collateral value has diminished due to wear and tear, damage, obsolescence, or market conditions. Cars and electronic equipment quickly lose value. Real estate loses value during recessions and when interest rates are high.

The consumer has a potential defense or counterclaim > If a consumer has a defense to a creditor's claim or a counterclaim against the creditor, the creditor usually will not proceed unless it believes the chances of winning seem far greater than the risk of losing. Several factors enter into the creditor's thinking:

FACTORS CREDITORS CONSIDER WHEN EVALUATING CONTESTED LITIGATION

What are the chances of winning a lawsuit against the consumer?

Does the consumer have access to a good lawyer?

Is the defense or counterclaim based on clear facts?

Is the defense or counterclaim based on clear law or uncertain law?

Can the defense or counterclaim lead to a class action suit or other lawsuits against the creditor?

Can the defense or counterclaim cause the creditor problems with a government agency or the news media?

How much will it cost to bring a lawsuit against the consumer?

How much can the creditor collect if it wins?

How much will the creditor lose if the consumer wins?

How much can the creditor collect if it agrees to a payment plan or settlement?

The creditor itself needs cash > It's sometimes worth a little time and effort to find out if the creditor is under pressure to bring in cash, especially during a recession or when banks themselves are a little shaky. The creditor may be in desperate need of cash and may settle on very lenient terms.

The creditor is too busy with other matters > If a creditor, particularly a small one, is occupied with other more important matters, the creditor may be willing to enter into a payment plan or settlement just so it will not have to spend any more time on your account.

The debt isn't not large enough > Even though computers mindlessly generate bills for almost any amount, no creditor is going to let an employee spend any time trying to collect a $2 debt. Although a few creditors won't even try to collect a $5,000 debt, most draw the line somewhere in between. Remember that collection agencies keep only a portion of what they collect, and it usually costs at least $50 just to file a lawsuit. On the other hand, a nasty creditor may prefer to file a negative credit report rather than settle for a few cents on the dollar.

The consumer has been good customer > Sometimes, a creditor is willing to help a loyal customer from whom it has made a lot of money over the years. The creditor may feel that it has benefitted from doing business with the customer, the customer's good character has been established, and the customer has earned a break. A small creditor that knows its costumers is much more likely to show such loyalty than a large one.

ESTIMATING HOW MUCH TO OFFER A CREDITOR Unless you are just trying to gain time, your first task is to decide how much you can afford to pay and when you can pay it. Next, try to find reasons that will persuade the creditor to accept less than it ordinarily would want. Finally, try to estimate what the creditor will want and more importantly, what it will accept.

Never assume that you have to offer anything near what the creditor wants. Make your first offer as low as possible without sounding unreasonable. What is reasonable or unreasonable depends on the circumstances.

> If you owe $75,000 on a mortgage, offering $100 a month for two years would be unreasonable - unless you have a great defense or counterclaim. If you owe $10,000 on a credit card but are out of work and judgment proof, an offer of $50 a month until you get a job might be reasonable.

If your initial offer is rejected, DON'T BID AGAINST YOURSELF by immediately raising your offer. Instead, ask your creditor to think about the points you have made and to let you know what it wants. The creditor's counter-proposal will tell you the general ball-park area for any settlement. If the creditor asks for far more than you can manage, you know that you probably can't reach an agreement. However, the creditor most likely will ask for somewhat more than it's willing to accept. Tell the creditor that you understand its position but you simply can't manage that amount.

Your creditor may say he has to get back to you. That's fine. It gives you time to think about the creditor's counter-proposal. Unless you have specific reason for hurrying the matter, be patient. Time is on your side.

Payment Plans Creditors want a payment plan that at least covers the accruing interest.

> If the debt is a home mortgage with fewer than two-thirds of the payments made, interest probably is all but a few dollars of the original payment.
>
> If the debt is a car loan with fewer than one-third of the payments made, the interest probably is all but a few cents of the original payment.
>
> Interest on most other debts is a relatively small portion of the original payment.

Creditors usually want any overdue principal payments paid as soon as possible. To make up back principal payments, most will give you at least three months, and many will give you a year. Lenders are accustomed to accepting double payments for as long as it takes to catch up on the principal portion of your debt.

> Remember, though, do not offer what the creditor wants and NEVER offer more than you can afford to pay.

Settlements Creditors want to collect as much as possible. That's fair; after all, you want to pay as little as possible. Since you can't pay the entire debt, the amount owed is a relatively meaningless figure. Instead, your offer should be computed on the basis of the amount that actually can be collected:

COMPUTING A SETTLEMENT OFFER

1 Start with zero.

2 If you plan to defend against their lawsuit, add your anticipated legal fees and other costs of litigation.

3 Subtract the creditor's legal fees and costs of litigation.

4 If you have a valid counterclaim, subtract the amount you could recover.

5 If you have a valid defense to the entire claim, stop. (Ignore items 6-9.)

6 Add the liquidation value of any remaining collateral.

7 Subtract the creditor's costs of selling the collateral.

8 If you are willing to seek relief under the Bankruptcy Code, stop. (Ignore item 9.)

9 Add the amount the creditor could collect from you by enforcing a judgment. (That is, the liquidation value of all of your property, net of your exemptions, that the creditor could reach plus the attachable portion of your income, if any, for as long as you intend to remain employed where you are now working.)

Of course, you only can guess at many of the numbers, but try to be realistic. If your numbers are accurate, then your calculations should produce the objectively correct amount of a settlement. If it's a negative number, the creditor should pay you that amount, less your expected attorneys' fees and costs of litigation. If there is a good chance your lawsuit would burden the creditor with a class action lawsuit, regulatory problems, or adverse publicity, the creditor should pay you more.

PROVIDING A CREDITOR WITH INFORMATION It isn't hard to convince a creditor that you are judgment proof if you are unemployed and don't own a house or other substantial property. It's even easier to convince collection agencies and attorneys who will be wasting their time if they don't collect.

Some creditors believe you when you say you are broke if they have no reason to believe otherwise. Others automatically run a credit check to confirm your financial problems. Many careful creditors will ask you to answer some questions and may even require you to submit a financial statement.

When you prepare a financial statement, you will need to estimate the value of any property you own, such as a house or car. It's perfectly proper to use the lowest reasonable value. Two kinds of valuations are commonly used in financial statements prepared for payment plans or settlements:

> "**Fair market value**" is the value a willing buyer would pay to an unrelated willing seller, if neither were under any pressure.

"**Liquidation value**" is the price that can be obtained by selling the property quickly, or "under the hammer" at auction.

Both types of valuations are simultaneously fiction and fact. It's generally assumed you're applying fair market value. But, if you benefit more by using liquidation value, note that on the statement. Also, it's wise to note on the statement that all stated values are "estimated." If a listed value is a lot lower than the price you paid, it's wise to get an appraisal supporting your figures. You can get an estimate of the value of almost anything at very little or no cost. For example, local realtors are often willing to provide a free estimate of the market value of a home.

If a creditor asks you for proof of your financial condition, beware. The creditor may only be feigning interest in a payment plan or settlement. Its real interest may be to get information to help it garnish your wages, seize you bank account, or go after other property you own.

If the creditor already has a judgment against you, it probably can get this information from a citation proceeding, but you may be speeding up the process. If the creditor doesn't have a judgment, it probably won't be able to use the information right away, but may be able to use it later.

If you give the creditor a false financial statement, and you know or should know it's false, the creditor later may be able to get out of a settlement agreement. Also, giving a materially false financial statement to a federally chartered financial institution may be a crime, even if the institution doesn't agree to a payment plan or settlement.

A financial statement isn't usually considered false just because it contains a few small errors, omits some property, or the numbers are off a little. It really has to be a deliberate and consequential lie that is intended to mislead the creditor.

ATTITUDES The creditor mentality tends to see a glass as "half empty" instead of "half full." Many creditors think they are losing the difference between the original amount of the debt and the amount of the settlement. Some creditors become so caught up in this skewed thinking that they can't abide the idea of settling with a consumer who is left owning anything of value. This mentality may explain why it usually is easier to get a creditor to settle with an insolvent consumer than with a consumer who has a strong defense or counterclaim.

Be very careful how you deal with employees of large institutional lenders, especially banks. Often, these employees earn little more than titles, have no financial stake in your account, and will sacrifice their employers' financial interests for the sake of their egos. You don't have to sacrifice your dignity, but showing them respect and acting a little humble is likely to help your negotiations a lot more than you might expect.

Above all, remain quietly confident with the knowledge that your creditor wants something from you - not the reverse. Be it your money or your property, the creditor cannot get it without your cooperation or the time and expense of stumbling through the legal system. You have it within your power to withhold your cooperation unless you get something for it.

CHAPTER 12

IMPOSING A PAYMENT PLAN OR SETTLEMENT

Some payment plans and settlements do not result from negotiation. It is possible to impose a payment plan and a settlement on an unknowing and unwilling creditor. There are two ways to do this: Don't give the creditor any practical alternative, or induce the creditor to carelessly or inadvertently bind itself to the plan or settlement.

IMPOSING A PAYMENT PLAN You can convert almost any debt into a payment plan simply by refraining from paying the entire debt and, instead, making periodic, usually monthly, payments. For example, you owe a creditor $500 but you need time to pay it off. Simply start paying $50 or $100 a month. Unless it has an ax to grind, the creditor isn't going to send your account to a collection agency or attorney. Rather, the creditor will accept your payments, because it has a chance of collecting everything. Suing will take longer and likely will net a smaller recovery.

Sending $5 a month may not dissuade that creditor from taking collection action because the creditor probably can collect more money more quickly by suing. In order to impose a $5 per month payment plan, you most likely will have to induce the creditor to carelessly or inadvertently bind itself to the plan. Merely sending the $5 for one or two months will not achieve this. Instead, you have to either get the creditor to take the $5 a month for a long time, thereby establishing an agreement through the creditor's actual CONDUCT; or get the creditor to take the $5 knowing that taking the money will constitute agreement to the plan. This is most often successful when you manage to get the sympathy of a creditor.

IMPOSING A SETTLEMENT Imposing a settlement is much more difficult than imposing a payment plan, especially if there is not a *bona fide* dispute over some or all of the debt. You must induce the creditor to accept a smaller amount than is claimed. The difficulty is that the creditor must be aware that accepting the reduced payment constitutes agreement or the settlement probably won't be binding.

For a long time, consumers sent checks with restrictive endorsements that said something like, "Payee accepts this check in full satisfaction of all debts of maker." If the creditor cashed the check, it was out of luck. Large creditors who processed checks automatically and never saw the endorsements convinced state legislatures and courts that this was not fair to them. They got the laws changed in many states. In fact, under federal law, this technique does not work at all for charge cards if the check is sent to the same address where payments are usually processed. It is extremely unlikely you can successfully impose a legally binding settlement merely by sending a check with a restrictive endorsement.

GIVING NOTICE THAT ACCEPTING YOUR MONEY WILL BIND THE CREDITOR It's very difficult to induce a creditor to consent to a plan or a settlement without the creditor's help. However, that help does not have to be deliberate or even voluntary. Your objective is to give written notice that you are sending a payment as part of a proposed plan or settlement and hope the creditor's ignorance, size, or bureaucracy allows it to automatically accept the payment.

First, the consumer has to lay the groundwork by communicating with the creditor and setting forth reasons for a plan or settlement. The communication can be verbal or in writing, and the reasons can be grievances, legal defenses, or inability to pay.

If the creditor agrees to the plan or settlement, nothing further needs to be done except to put it in writing. If the creditor does not respond or needs time to consider the proposal, the consumer still can proceed with the same proposal. If the creditor rejects the proposal, the consumer can proceed with a slightly different proposal. The consumer sends the creditor a short, handwritten letter.

CONTENTS OF LETTER IMPOSING SETTLEMENT

States it is a follow-up to the earlier communication (including, if possible, the name of the employee with whom the consumer communicated);

Repeats the reasons for the plan or settlement;

Sets forth the terms of the proposed plan or settlement;

Mentions that you will be RELYING on the plan or settlement for some reason or another; and

Includes a check or money order that either has restrictive endorsement language on the back, saying something like "Payment pursuant to letter of agreement dated ..." or is securely stapled to the letter.

Keep a copy of the letter. If the check is merely stapled to the letter, keep a photocopy of the letter with the check stapled to it and keep the cancelled check when it is returned after it is cashed. If the debt is for a credit or charge card, the letter must NOT be sent to the address where payments normally are made. Instead, the letter must be sent to some other department, preferably not the same one the consumer communicated with in the first place.

If the creditor accepts the payment, and many creditors will, the odds are good that it will be legally bound to the plan or settlement. At the very least, you will have a strong bargaining position and an excuse for not making the usual payments.

OTHER TERMS AND DOCUMENTATION

In addition to amounts and dates, other terms of a plan or settlement that consumers should write into any agreement, when applicable, include:

A creditor's agreement not to submit a bad credit report and to respond to any credit inquiries positively.

Forgiveness of any late charges, penalty interest, and/or costs of collection.

Release of some collateral or the creditor's agreement not to pursue certain collateral or other property.

Release from any deficiency remaining after the sale of collateral.

Release of a co-signor or guarantor.

Application of payments first to principal then to collection costs, then to interest, and finally to late charges.

Reapplication of prior payments to principal.

Acknowledgement of a *bona fide* dispute between the consumer and creditor.

Acknowledgement that there has been a compromise, not a forgiveness of debt.

MAKE SURE any agreement is in writing and clearly states every provision that is important to you. In a negotiated agreement, the written document can be as formal and complete as the consumer and creditor want it to be. If you are trying to impose the agreement on the creditor, you may have to forego clarity and completeness. If the letter containing the agreement looks too formal or is too long, it will be more likely to catch someone's attention.

TAX RAMIFICATIONS

You can end up owing income taxes on a debt that is forgiven because the IRS treats the forgiven amount as income to the consumer. When you think about it, this makes sense. If you borrow $100, but only have to repay $90, you have gotten $10 income.

Debts discharged in bankruptcy proceedings are not taxed as income. Undisputed debts that are forgiven, outside of bankruptcy proceedings, are taxed as income.

However, a compromise of a DISPUTED debt is NOT the same as forgiveness of a debt. For example, a store sells you a $100 product. You find a defect and the store reduces the price to $90. You haven't gotten $10 of income. The product was really worth only $90. Or, assume a bank lends you $100 and, later, improperly freezes your account that results in damages to you. When the debt is compromised for $90, it may be reasonable to allocate the $10 to the damages the bank caused. It may also be appropriate to retroactively reduce the interest rate for the current year, reallocate a portion of the interest payments to principal, and treat the loan as paid in full.

Banks are required to inform the IRS of the forgiveness of debts. Other creditors are not, but they may anyway, just for the spite of it.

PROTECTING INCOME AND ASSETS

A creditor has only two rational reasons to go after a consumer's income or property; to coerce the consumer to pay all the money owed, or to recover some part of the money owed to it. If a creditor cannot attain either of these two objectives, the creditor is wasting time, effort, and money. Also, the creditor will fail unless the consumer cares about the property in question and responds to the pressure.

> Never let a creditor know that you care about any particular property. A creditor who cannot identify a pressure point is limited to conventional collection methods.

A creditor cannot recover money from property unless the property sells for more than the total of all debts (mortgages and other liens) secured by the property, plus the amount of the legal exemption, plus the actual costs of seizing and selling the property. To tip this equation in your favor, either:

> increase the amount you must pay others before the seizing creditor can recover anything, or
>
> reduce the value of the property.

The following techniques employ one or both of these methods to protect income and property from creditors.

> Before using some of these techniques, remember that if you seek relief under the United States Bankruptcy Code, you may be denied a discharge if it is proven that you transferred, concealed, or damaged property with intent to hinder or delay a creditor within the previous year. It's far less likely that you will be denied a discharge if you can demonstrate other valid reasons for your actions.

LEGAL EXEMPTIONS

Legal exemptions provide the greatest protection to consumers from unsecured judgment creditors. "Exempt" is shorthand for "exempt from execution." Exempt property is protected and cannot be reached by judgment creditors. Exemptions can be waived when a consumer gives a creditor collateral, but some legal exemptions cannot. Some states exempt large amounts of property, while others are quite miserly. Some states give special protection to homes while others give special protection to life insurance policies, trade tools, or retirement funds.

Although the United States Bankruptcy Code adopted a national set of exemptions, it applies only in bankruptcy proceedings and even then, only if your state has not enacted its own set of exemptions. Many states have enacted their own, but the exemptions included in the Bankruptcy Code are widely followed and give you an idea of how exemptions work:

U.S. Bankruptcy Code Exemptions

Bodily injury recoveries:	
Injury and related losses	Up to $7,500.
Loss of future earnings	To the extent necessary to support debtor and dependents.
Wrongful death	To the extent necessary to support debtor and dependents.
Crime victim reparations	All.
Disability Benefits	All.
Employee stock, bonus, profit sharing, welfare and retirement plans	To the extent reasonably necessary to support debtor and dependents. (Courts disagree whether retirement benefits under private pension and welfare plans are exempted.)
Health Aids	All professionally prescribed health aids.
Homestead	Up to $7,500 of the value of a consumer's home (The consumer must live there) Up to $3,750 of any unused portion of this exemption may be used to exempt other property.
Household Goods Personal Effects	Up to $200 of the value of any one item, $4,000 total.
Jewelry	Up to $500.
Life Insurance	Any life insurance policy and up to $4,000 of the cash value. Proceeds of insurance on the life of another to the extent reasonably necessary to support debtor and dependents.
Other Property	Up to $400 for any property.
Public Assistance	All.
Social Security	All.
Tools and books used for occupation	Up to $750.
Unemployment Compensation	All.
Vehicle	Up to $1,200 of the value of one motor vehicle .
Veterans' Benefits	All.

Under federal and almost every state law, most of your wages CANNOT be attached by a creditor. This is not because wages are "exempt." Rather, the laws limit the portion of a consumer's wages that can be attached.

The value of exemptions to a consumer depends in large measure on the type of income and property the consumer has. An effective strategy is to shift as much income and property as possible from non-exempt to exempt classifications. For example, most states exempt all life insurance policies and its cash value - provided the policy covers the life of the consumer and names one or more legal dependents as named beneficiary. Consumers in those states can quickly put cash savings into whole life insurance policies. If you need cash, you can easily and cheaply borrow against the exempt policy, and the money you borrow is also exempt.

Other states exempt all of the consumer's home. Consumers in those states can invest savings in home repairs and improvements. However, you probably waived this exemption when you borrowed the money to purchase the home. It will do you no good to improve the home if the mortgage can be foreclosed. However, if your mortgage is current, but you're behind on other bills, this is a viable option.

Almost all states require that the court or the sheriff inform you of your right to select and list exempt property. Sheriffs' offices are relatively diligent, but judges have been known to forget about exemptions when ordering that property be turned over during citation proceedings. Be aware of your exemption rights and be prepared to assert them at any citation proceeding and when the sheriff attempts to seize property you want to protect.

Sometimes, personal property, especially a bank account, is seized before you can assert your exemptions. You may, therefore, lose the use of the property for a short while. To prevent this type of problem, prepare a signed list of exemptions and file it with the court as soon as you learn a creditor is attempting to execute its judgment against you. The danger in doing this, though, is that your list may give the creditor information it otherwise might not discover, so be careful as to what you divulge.

TRANSFERRING ALL OR SOME OWNERSHIP

Generally, judgment creditors can reach property only if a consumer owns the property or has rights in the property.

> If a consumer completely divests (transfers or sells) property, unsecured creditors cannot reach that property.
>
> If a consumer divests a partial interest in property, he may reduce the amount the creditor can recover from the property. This may be enough to discourage the creditor from pursuing the property.

All transfers of a consumer's interests will help protect the transferred property from creditors, and all transfers become increasingly effective as time passes.

Ownership of almost anything can be divided. A significant advantage of selling a partial interest in property is that partial interests are usually worth disproportionately less. For example, you own a car that has a fair market value of $10,000. The car is not collateral for any loan. You sell a 1/2 interest in the car to your brother. Make sure to get a new title showing the co-ownership. "Adequate value" for that 1/2 interest is much less than $5,000, because re-selling half a car is hard to do. It's extremely unlikely a stranger would pay very much for the right to share the use of your car.

The same reasoning applies to almost every kind of property, including real estate, stocks, and even ownership of a small business. The key elements of an effective transfer are:

Timing — Transfer the property as early as possible but not while there is an injunction, such as a citation proceeding, in effect.

Adequate Value The more financial value you receive, the more effective the transfer. It doesn't matter if, after the sale, you go out and recklessly spend the money received. Your release from a valid prior debt can be considered adequate value, although it may be considered a preference if you seek relief under the Bankruptcy Code too soon after the transfer.

Arm's Length A transfer will be less vulnerable to attack if it is not to an "insider," such as a relative or business partner. However, even transfers to insiders can be protected if you carefully cover all the other elements.

Formality Formal papers, especially publicly recorded documents, can be very important. Papers often are essential to effect the transfer. Formality tends to lend the transfer authenticity, showing time, effort and sincere intent.

If all of these elements are covered, a transfer will not look like, nor be treated as, a sham. However, a creditor or bankruptcy trustee can pursue, and possibly recover, transferred property if:

The property is fraudulently transferred > Avoid this by receiving adequate value for the property or by completing the transfer before you get into financial difficulties. Value does not have to be paid immediately. A reasonable down payment and a valid and binding promissory note are good enough, even if the payment terms are very favorable to the purchaser. However, keep in mind that your creditors can then attach the promissory note.

The property is transferred while you are under an injunction, such as a citation proceeding, prohibiting the transfer > Avoid this by transferring the property either before or after the citation proceedings. However, if you wait until after the citation proceedings, the creditor may already have grabbed the property.

You are in proceedings under the Bankruptcy Code, and the transfer is a preference > Avoid this by making sure the transfer is completed at least 91 days prior to the start of the proceedings. If the transfer is to an insider, it must be completed at least a year and a day before the start of the proceedings. A transfer will not be treated as a preference if you receive adequate value for the property. In this case, though, adequate value CANNOT be the satisfaction of a pre-existing debt.

The creditor has a lien against the property > If the property is collateral for a debt and the creditor has a valid lien, you cannot lawfully transfer the property without the creditors consent. The easiest way to avoid problems with a tax or judgment lien is by transferring the property before the lien arises. Even if there already is a judgment or tax lien, you still may be able to transfer the property. Most judgment liens are good only against real estate located in counties where a memorandum of the judgment is recorded. Most tax liens are effective only against property while it is located in the state where a notice of lien is filed.

However, it may be useful to transfer property, even if the transfer may later appear to be a sham. Transfers slow down creditors and make it harder for them to reach property. Remember, time usually is on your side, and creditors often are will not expend the time, effort, and money it takes to pursue property that has been transferred.

If you need to gain time, you can transfer property in any number of creative ways. For example, form a small corporation, and contribute the property to the corporation in exchange for shares of stock. Creditors then have to go after the shares of stock before they can reach the property. While a creditor chases the stock, the corporation can use, and even transfer, the property.

ALTERING YOUR OWNERSHIP RIGHTS

You do not have to actually transfer property to another legal entity to alter your ownership rights. You can enter into agreements with other people that alter your ownership rights in ways that will make it more difficult for a judgment creditor to reach or sell the property. Some possibilities include:

Selling Options to Purchase > You can sell someone an option to purchase property at a specified price. As long as you are given adequate value for the option, the option price is reasonable, and the option is effective for a reasonable length of time, the creditor must honor the option.

Prohibiting or Restricting Rights to Sell > Owners of small corporations and partnerships often enter into agreements that restrict or prohibit sales of ownership interests to outside parties. People who own small business simply do not want to find themselves in business with a stranger. Usually, these agreements enable the owners to force each other to buy out their interests, but such forced sales often are at low prices and provide for payment over a long period of time. Co-owners of real estate use similar agreements.

Waivers of Partition Rights > In many states, it is unclear exactly when co-owners of real estate can force partition and sale of the property. It may be in the owners' best interests to enter into an agreement that waives all rights to seek partition of the property. If one of the owners is in financial difficulty, he also should receive something of tangible adequate value in addition to the waiver. If the property is in joint tenancy, the waiver agreement should clearly state that the joint tenancy is not being terminated. The agreement should be publicly recorded, because it may not be effective otherwise and recording establishes its age and authenticity.

Leases > Almost any kind of property, even seats on stock exchanges, can be leased to someone else. If the lease provides for a reasonable rent and is for a reasonable duration, it will have to be honored, and the property will be harder to sell. Leased personal property is almost impossible to sell. Be careful with real estate though, because a lease may make it more valuable. But remember, the creditor may be able to reach the lease payments.

ENCUMBERING PROPERTY WITH SECURED DEBT

Sometimes, you cannot, or do not want to, transfer ownership of property. Instead, you can burden the property with liens or other security interests that give a friendly creditor first claim on the property. Property burdened with a lot of debt doesn't leave enough equity for a creditor to pursue.

Liens that protect property are subject to the same limitations as outright transfers of ownership. Timing, adequate value, arm's length and formality are key elements. Another problem with using liens to protect property is that an effective lien will carry with it a real debt. Using liens to protect property may merely delay, or even aggravate, your financial problems.

If you have carefully assessed your situation and developed your strategy, then you may want to try to use essential but unsecured or undersecured debts to protect your income or property.

SECOND AND THIRD MORTGAGES Consumers must sometimes choose to take second, or even a third mortgage on their homes. Usually, these junior mortgages consist of a long term debt with manageable monthly payments. These mortgages reduce the equity in the home to the point that there is nothing left for other creditors to pursue. Be aware, though, that there may be some problems with doing this.

A judgment creditor can record a lien against the property. In some states, that lien remains effective for 20 years and can be renewed. Even though the creditor can't force the sale of the property, the creditor will be able to collect if and when the consumer sells the property. Every mortgage payment increases the amount of equity available to a patient creditor.

Some first mortgages prohibit junior mortgages. Although such provisions are hard to make stick and are rarely enforced, you should consider consulting with a lawyer before breaching such an agreement.

WAGE ATTACHMENTS AND ASSIGNMENTS In most states, only one wage attachment can be enforced at any given time, and no state permits total wage attachments to exceed the maximum permitted by federal law. For example, if you assign part of your earnings to someone else, a new wage attachment order must await completion of the existing wage assignment. What is the practical meaning of this?

Well, you can arrange to have wage assignments filed ahead of the post-judgment wage garnishment order obtained by your creditor. Your creditor can wait a long time before his order is of any value, and such an order often is good for no more than 90 days. The creditor is then forced to go back to court to seek a new order. This can encourage a creditor to settle a dispute reasonably.

Now, imagine that among your other debts, you are paying your brother $100 a week for the money he lent you to buy your car. Rather than paying him directly, you and he might agree that he will be repaid through a wage assignment. Your gross weekly salary is $500 and your net, after taxes is $400. Your employer writes one check to your brother for $100 and writes you another check for $300. The $100 paid to your brother under the wage assignment is 25% of your disposable (take-home) earnings. No other creditor can garnish your wages until this first wage assignment is paid off, or otherwise expires.

Or, if you are having trouble making mortgage or auto payments, you may want to offer one or both of those creditors a wage assignment as additional security that your payments will arrive on time. For reasons previously explained, an arm's length agreement with an unrelated creditor will be much more difficult for a judgment creditor to attack.

Your employer will be less troubled by a voluntary wage assignment than a court ordered wage attachment. However, before you make a wage assignment, make sure your employer will not hold it against you.

REDUCING VALUE

Most creditors look at property in its existing condition. Except for finance companies that specialize in automobile loans, few creditors even consider how much more could be recovered if a few dollars were spent on repairing or improving the property. You can take advantage of this tendency to reduce the likelihood that a creditor will pursue some particular piece of property.

The aim is to discourage creditors from pursuing property by reducing the amount the creditor could recover from a sale of the property. This can be done by:

Reducing the apparent value of the property > Typically, this means refraining from normal cleaning and maintenance. Don't wash or tune up the car. Don't mow the lawn. Don't paint the house.

Temporarily reducing the actual value of the property > Remove any enhancements that were not originally part of the collateral, such as a car tape deck or the house window-dressings.

Reduce the value of the property in such a way that it will cost the creditor a lot to restore the property, but will cost YOU very little because of your special skills > If you're a carpenter, remove all the interior doors, so that you can properly plane and sand them. Perhaps, you may decide to send out the door hinges for plating. If you're a mechanic, remove the carburetor or air conditioner and thoroughly clean them.

These techniques have certain risks:

The creditor may not even be interested in the property, and you will have wasted your time and effort.

If the creditor takes the property anyway, the property will bring less at a foreclosure auction, and you may be left with an even larger deficiency. But, if you or a friend bid at the foreclosure auction, your savings may be worth more than the increased deficiency will cost you, particularly if you're judgment proof and the creditor can't collect the deficiency.

If the creditor takes the property from which you removed a part, and you aren't going to bid for the property at auction, it's probably in your best interest to voluntarily surrender the part to the creditor.

Finally, you may get carried away by your anger or frustration and damage the property just to hurt your creditor. You can get into serious legal trouble if you maliciously destroy a creditor's collateral. Moreover, you will just be hurting yourself if it turns out that the creditor never really intended to pursue that property.

PLACING PROPERTY BEYOND CREDITORS' REACH

Everyone has heard about big corporate embezzlers and drug lords who deposit their ill-gotten gains in numbered Swiss accounts. They do this because it's difficult to find that money. Even if the money is discovered, courts in the United States have little or no power over banks in foreign countries.

Foreign bank accounts simply are not practical for most of us. However, the same technique can be used almost as effectively within the United States or just across the Canadian and Mexican borders. It is very difficult for a court in one state to help a creditor recover property located in another state. Often, it's even difficult for a court in one county to exercise power over property in another county within the same state.

Even if a creditor obtains a judgment in one state, the creditor will have difficulty seizing property in a second state unless the creditor "registers" the judgment in the second state. This is a time-consuming and sometimes costly nuisance that most creditors will not bother with because, by the time the creditor can register the judgment, the property can be sold or moved to a third state. Furthermore, the creditor may register the judgment in the second state only to find that the second state exempts that kind of property.

A judgment creditor can try to convince a judge to order a consumer to sign documents that will enable the creditor to obtain property in another jurisdiction. A consumer who doesn't obey can be held in contempt of court and fined or jailed until he signs the papers. This is an extraordinary and extreme measure that is unlikely to arise unless the judge is furious at the consumer, and the property is extremely valuable. Furthermore, this measure is completely ineffective if anyone, other than the consumer, has a valid interest in the property.

USING LEGAL ENTITIES

The law treats some entities, such as corporations and trusts, as if they were individuals. The law considers them to be separate from the people who own, control, or manage them. As a general rule, shareholders and officers of a corporation are not personally liable for corporation's debts, and corporations are not liable for the debts of their officers and shareholders. Similarly, trustees and beneficiaries of trusts are not personally liable for the trust's debts, and the trust is not liable for the debts of its trustees and beneficiaries.

An obstacle to using legal entities to protect assets is the need for a good lawyer. Often, such a lawyer will cost more than the income and assets are worth.

CORPORATIONS Shareholders of a corporation own stock of the corporation - NOT the assets of the corporation. Beneficiaries of a trust do NOT own the assets of the trust. The legal distinctions between a corporation and its shareholders, and between a trust and its beneficiaries, are very important.

Assume that you are the majority shareholder of a corporation, and a creditor gets a judgment against you. The creditor cannot reach the assets of the corporation unless and until it obtains your stock. If you're the only shareholder, the creditor can use the stock to liquidate the corporation and sell its assets. However, if you aren't the only shareholder, it may be impossible for the creditor to get hold of the corporation's assets.

Typically, people think of using a corporation to shield shareholders from liability. However, a corporation can also be used to shield your income and assets from your personal creditors. For example, a creditor obtains a judgment against you. You happen to be a salesman. Before the creditor obtained the judgment, you formed XYZ Corporation. You bought half the stock of XYZ and your non-liable spouse bought the other half. Your sales are made through XYZ and all commissions are paid directly to the corporation. You and your spouse control the timing, nature, and amounts of all cash distributions made by the corporation. If the creditor attempts to garnish your wages, XYZ can reduce your salary to nothing. If the creditor attempts to seize your stock, XYZ can pay out all corporate income in the form of salaries or bonuses to you or your spouse. If all else fails, you can abandon the corporation. The creditor is rendered helpless while you and your spouse proceed to form a new corporation.

TRUSTS Trusts are more flexible, but also trickier, than corporations. Trusts are not very effective unless they are created before you get into financial trouble. The idea is to put assets into a trust, appoint at least one trustee other than you, and structure the trust in such a way that creditors cannot reach the trust's income or assets. Protecting the trust from creditors usually involves one of two techniques:

Including a "spendthrift clause" > This prohibits the beneficiary of the trust from anticipating the right to receive income or assets from the trust, and prohibits income and assets of the trust from being used to pay the beneficiary's creditors. However, most states don't permit people to create spendthrift trusts for themselves. A major exception is the federal Employment Retirement Income Security Act (ERISA) which requires certain retirement trusts to include a spendthrift clause.

Naming more than one beneficiary and giving the trustee complete discretion as to when and how much each beneficiary receives > This can be very effective if the trust is created and funded early enough that contributions to the trust cannot be recovered as "fraudulent conveyances."

With a little creativity, a trust can include many other provisions that make it difficult or impossible for a creditor to get hold of the trust's income or assets.

Other problems with trusts often can be overcome but must be considered. If the person who creates the trust, the "settlor," is not one of the trustees, the income of the trust will be taxed at a higher rate than individual tax rates. Also, contributions to a trust that have beneficiaries other than the settlor may be subject to gift taxes. Finally, many states disregard spendthrift clauses if the consumer owes alimony or support.

SELLING AND SPENDING PROCEEDS

Cash is more portable and flexible than any other property. You have the right to sell any property unless it is collateral. After selling the property, you can spend the cash on living expenses or use it to acquire exempt property.

Some collateral can be almost impossible to sell without the secured creditor's consent. Transferring ownership of real estate and motor vehicles involves recording a document of title with some public office. Most automobile lenders keep possession of automobile titles until their loans are paid off. Moreover, if a creditor's lien has been properly recorded, any sale of the real estate or automobile will be subject to the lien. It is surprising, though, how many creditors fail to properly record their liens. In some states, it's a misdemeanor to deliberately sell a creditor's collateral, but these laws are often violated and almost never enforced.

RELIEF UNDER THE U.S. BANKRUPTCY CODE

The right to relief from the burdens of debt was considered so important by the Founding Fathers that the U.S. Constitution gives to the federal government the power to enact bankruptcy laws. Every year, hundreds of thousands of Americans and tens of thousands of businesses are compelled to seek help from the United States Bankruptcy Code.

THE BANKRUPTCY CODE OFFERS MOST CONSUMERS THE ULTIMATE RELIEF FROM OVERWHELMING DEBTS.

CONSULTING WITH A LAWYER

Some self-help books assure consumers that they can handle their own bankruptcies. But you will maximize the chance for success, particularly if property of any value is involved, if you hire an experienced lawyer.

This discussion gives you only enough information to see that relief under the Bankruptcy Code may be a good solution for you. Do not seek relief under the Bankruptcy Code without consulting with an experienced bankruptcy lawyer if:

You have valuable property you do not want to lose.

You owe delinquent taxes.

You have used a credit card within 40 days.

You owe money for a government-guaranteed educational loan that you want discharged.

You have transferred valuable property within the last year.

You have used a written financial statement to get credit and you still owe money to that creditor.

You have sought relief under the Code within the last 6 years.

You want to avoid part, or all, of a secured claim.

You want to make minimum payments under a Chapter 13 plan.

You are seeking relief under Chapter 11.

You are under investigation for a crime or you have reason to believe that you might disclose something that could be used to convict you of a crime.

If any of these circumstances apply to you, or you have any other reason to think that a lawyer could be of assistance, you probably will find that the lawyer's fees are well worth the benefits. If you are at all uncertain, at least consult with a lawyer. Usually an initial consultation carries no charge. If nothing else, having an attorney can insulate you from stress and aggravation.

Attorneys' fees for handling simple cases range anywhere from about $300 in rural areas to as much as $1,000 in large cities. Complicated and difficult cases cost more. However, attorney's fees for consumer cases rarely get out of hand because a judge must approve them.

BASIC CONCEPTS

A consumer seeking relief from debts under the Bankruptcy Code need not necessarily be bankrupt. The Code itself avoids using the word "bankrupt." People and businesses that seek relief under the Code are called "debtors," not bankrupts.

TYPES OF RELIEF The Bankruptcy Code is divided into various Chapters. Three Chapters provide different kinds of relief for consumers:

Chapter 7 (liquidation) Chapter 7 provides relief commonly known as "bankruptcy." This allows the consumer, in effect, to get a fresh start. As a general rule, it's easier and better to file for relief under Chapter 7 than under Chapter 11 or 13. With a Chapter 7 filing, you get it over with quickly, and you aren't burdened with payments for several years.

With some important exceptions, discussed below, all of the consumer's debts are discharged with creditors prohibited from collecting them. The THEORETICAL price for this fresh start is conceding to the creditors all non-exempt property.

The court appoints an interim trustee - "interim" because the creditors have the right to elect a replacement. Most often a lawyer, the trustee administers, or controls, the debtor's property. He is supposed to liquidate, or sell, the property and give the cash to creditors. The trustee also is supposed to look for hidden assets and fraudulent transfers of property.

In practice, the trustee receives only a token fee from the court unless he liquidates a lot of property or otherwise recovers a lot of money for the creditors. Few trustees find it profitable to chase a relatively few dollars, or even a lot of dollars if it's too time consuming or the outcome is questionable. Very few Chapter 7 trustees want to make life hard for consumers. Even if they stumble across a family heirloom that might be worth selling, most trustees will file a "no asset report" and go on to the next case. However, if a consumer has a lot of equity in his home or other property, the Chapter 7 trustee is likely to try to get the property - even if it is jointly owned by a spouse or someone else.

Unlike a creditor trying to enforce a state court judgment, a trustee doesn't need to obtain a "partition" order. A trustee has little trouble reaching property in other states. It's also very easy for a trustee to convince a bankruptcy court to order the sale of valuable property.

Chapter 11 (reorganization) Although available to individuals, Chapter 11 was designed to give a business some protection from its creditors while it reorganizes its affairs. However, Chapter 11 reorganizations are complicated and relatively expensive.

The debtor, referred to in the Bankruptcy Code as a debtor-in-possession (DIP), keeps possession and control over all its property and continues operating its business or personal affairs. In theory, the DIP is a trustee under an obligation to protect creditors. Also in theory, the DIP is supervised by the United States Trustee. A representative of the Trustee conducts an examination of the debtor.

The DIP proposes a plan of reorganization that can be approved by the judge alone, but usually must be accepted by a majority of the creditors. In theory, the DIP and creditors negotiate with each other to develop a program that will satisfy as many of the players as possible.

Under the plan, which can take years to implement, the DIP pays off some or all of its debts while continuing to operate its own affairs. Often, such plans provide for the orderly liquidation of the assets because the DIP is better able to handle the liquidation than is a Chapter 7 trustee.

Some Chapter 11 cases succeed just as the designers of the Code had hoped. A great many do not:

> Chapter 11 debtors sometimes fool themselves into thinking they can successfully reorganize. They would have been better off going straight into a Chapter 7 filing.
>
> Many Chapter 11 cases fail because one or more of the players is incompetent, dishonest, or irrational.

Sometimes, unsophisticated creditors or debtors become too adversarial. Their fighting essentially destroys any chance of reorganization and any hope of paying its creditors.

Some debtors exploit the Code to enrich themselves at the creditors' expense.

Often, attorneys, trustees, and accountants bury the debtor under a mountain of professional fees.

Sometimes, the debtor can't fulfill the Code's requirements regarding taxes and the government refuses to forego any of its legal rights. This will force a liquidation.

Chapter 13 (adjustment of debts) Chapter 13 provides a means for consumers to pay off some or all of their debts through a rather simple payment plan. Generally, these plans are limited to three years but can take up to five years. Plans can provide for full payment of all debts or for as little as a few cents on the dollar. "Ten percent plans" are very common.

Typically, a professional Chapter 13 trustee handles thousands of cases at the same time. The trustee examines the consumer, supervises the plan, deducts a percentage as his fee, and distributes the plan payments to creditors. Not all payments have to be made through the trustee. Unlike a Chapter 7 trustee, a Chapter 13 trustee doesn't administer the estate or liquidate property.

You may have heard that some creditors look more kindly on people who file Chapter 13 than those who file Chapter 7, because under Chapter 13 the consumer is at least making an effort to pay. That's a myth perpetrated by creditors who hope that consumers choose Chapter 13 over Chapter 7. Realistically, creditors who will not give credit to Chapter 7 debtors rarely give credit to Chapter 13 debtors.

Chapter 13 offers certain consumers some important technical advantages over Chapter 7, such as:

Make past due payments over time instead of bringing them current all at once > This is particularly important if a consumer is delinquent on a mortgage or a car loan. In order to keep the property under Chapter 7, the consumer can be required to bring the delinquency current all at once. In Chapter 13, the consumer can pay the past due payments over time.

Discharge certain debts that cannot be discharged under Chapter 7 or 11 > Some debts, such as certain taxes and government-guaranteed educational loans, are dischargeable only under Chapter 13. A Chapter 7 hardly even delays creditors' efforts to collect non-dischargeable debts. A Chapter 11 can allow the debtor to pay most of these debts over time. A Chapter 13 plan can lead to the discharge of almost all debts, except debts for the support of a spouse, former spouse, or child.

Spread out legal fees > Attorneys more readily accept their fees over time for Chapter 13 cases than they do for Chapter 7 cases.

More easily protect valuable property > Because Chapter 13 arrangements are not designed to be liquidations, valuable property is not viewed as something to be liquidated. The consumer's equity in property is used primarily to gauge whether a plan provides for sufficient payments to creditors. The Code requires that creditors receive payments totalling substantially as much as they would receive under a Chapter 7 liquidation.

AUTOMATIC STAY Whenever a petition for relief under any Chapter of the Code is filed, creditors are "automatically stayed" from doing anything to collect from the consumer or from the consumer's property. The automatic stay is like an injunction, which is a court order prohibiting certain conduct. With a few technical exceptions, any collection activity committed in violation of the automatic stay is void.

The automatic stay even applies to creditors who don't know you filed. Creditors who knowingly violate the stay face severe penalties. If a creditor is about to take some sort of action against you, immediately inform the creditor of the filing. Tell the creditor, or his agent, the date the case was filed, the particular court in which it was filed, and the case number. Large creditors often ask for their account number. Although you are under no obligation to provide the account number, giving it will reduce the likelihood that the creditor will inadvertently violate the stay. Although you can inform the creditor orally, it's always wiser to have written proof you gave notice.

It helps to record a notice of the bankruptcy filing in every court where there is a lawsuit pending or a judgment against you. When you record these notices, include the case number of the state court proceedings so that it gets filed correctly.

Creditors, especially smaller landlords, often violate the stay. If that happens, don't hesitate to have the creditor summoned before the bankruptcy judge on a "rule to show cause" why the creditor should not be held in contempt of court. Among other things, you may be able to recover your attorney's fees and any damages you suffered on account of the violation.

DISCHARGE Discharge is a basic concept of the Bankruptcy Code. If a debt is discharged, it ceases to be a legal liability and cannot be enforced against the consumer. However, the law does not prohibit a consumer from VOLUNTARILY paying a discharged debt. The court order granting a discharge is a very important document. Soon after you receive a copy, go to the bankruptcy court and obtain at least a dozen certified copies. After a few years, these files go to a warehouse, and it can be troublesome to locate a copy of the discharge order.

A creditor who attempts to collect a discharged debt can be held in contempt of court, required to pay for any damages you suffer, including attorney's fees, and even be fined. However, if the creditor is unaware of the bankruptcy or you're not really damaged, pursuing the creditor can take a lot more time, effort and money than it's worth. If you're sued by a creditor whose debt has been discharged, you MUST file an appearance and a certified copy of the order granting the discharge in the court where you are being sued. If the creditor intentionally disregards the discharge or causes you actual damages, go back to the bankruptcy court and try to have the case reopened to get the creditor held in contempt of court.

General Denial of Discharge A consumer can be denied a discharge from ALL debts if the consumer:

> Has been granted a previous discharge in a case commenced within 6 years of the filing of the petition;
>
> Transfers, removes, destroys, mutilates or conceals property with intent to hinder, delay, or defraud a creditor within a year before filing the petition for relief.
>
> Transfers, removes, destroys, mutilates or conceals property with intent to hinder, delay or defraud a creditor or a trustee charged with custody of property after filing the petition for relief.
>
> Conceals, withholds, destroys, mutilates, falsifies or fails to keep records concerning the consumer's financial condition or business transactions.
>
> Knowingly and fraudulently lies concerning the filing or proceedings, makes a false claim, bribes, or accepts a bribe.
>
> Fails to give a satisfactory explanation for any loss or reduction of assets.
>
> Refuses to obey a court order.
>
> Refuses to testify for reasons other than privilege against self-incrimination.
>
> Refuses to testify after being granted immunity from criminal prosecution.

A discharge of debts will automatically be granted to the consumer, unless the trustee or a creditor formally objects. A discharge can be revoked for some of the same reasons a discharge can be originally denied. Any attempt to revoke a discharge must be made within one year after the discharge is granted or, in some instances, as late as one year after the case is closed.

Denial of Dischargeability of Particular Debts Some debts cannot be discharged in a Chapter 7 proceeding. Particular debts that are "excepted" from the general discharge include debts:

> that are not listed in the schedules with the court, unless you can prove that the creditor actually has knowledge of the proceedings;
>
> for the support of a spouse, former spouse or child;
>
> for income taxes that have not been reported, that have been fraudulently reported, that should have been reported within the last 3 years, that were reported within the last 2 years, or that were assessed within the last 240 days;
>
> for certain other taxes that usually do not apply to consumers, such as federal withholding and certain sales taxes that theoretically are held "in trust;"

for certain fines, penalties and forfeitures payable to a government agency that are not imposed as compensation for actual losses

for educational loans made, insured, guaranteed or in part funded by a government unless the loan first came due more than five years before the petition for relief is filed; or denying the discharge will impose an undue hardship on the debtor or the debtor's dependents;

for a judgment arising from the operation of a vehicle while intoxicated;

for willful injury to another person or property;

for embezzlement, larceny, or fraud;

for breach of an important duty committed by a trustee or other fiduciary;

for money, property or services obtained by false pretenses, false representations or actual fraud, or a written document that is materially false or was made with intent to deceive the creditor;

for a consumer debt to a single creditor, (a) totalling more than $500 for "luxury goods or services" incurred on or within the last 40 days; or (b) totalling more than $1,000 for cash advances obtained under an "open end credit plan" on or within the last 20 days. Most credit cards are "open end credit plans." Time is counted backwards from the day the petition is filed.

Except for family support obligations, government debts, and drunk driving judgments, a debt is automatically discharged unless the particular creditor files an "adversary proceeding" lawsuit objecting to the discharge of that PARTICULAR debt.

Debts that can't be discharged under Chapter 7 can't be discharged under Chapter 11. However, they can be paid over time under a Chapter 11 plan of reorganization. In contrast to Chapters 7 and 11, a carefully prepared Chapter 13 plan can result in the discharge of almost any kind of debt except a debt for the support of a spouse, former spouse or child.

Reaffirmation of Debts A consumer can reaffirm a debt if the court approves. Most commonly, debtors reaffirm mortgages and car loans. If a debt is reaffirmed, and the consumer later defaults, the creditor can hold the consumer personally liable.

It you need to keep the collateral, be sure to reaffirm the debt. Otherwise, on the your Declaration of Intent (a form you must file when you seek relief under Chapter 7), say you will surrender the collateral. As likely as not, the creditor will not want the collateral and will give serious consideration to a reasonable compromise. However, be prepared to surrender the property if you cannot make a deal with the creditor.

THE ESTATE When a case is filed, all of the consumer's property becomes part of the estate, which is administered under the Code. No creditor can pursue property of the estate without permission of the court. In Chapter 7 cases, the trustee administers the estate. In Chapter 11 and 13 cases, the consumer usually administers the estate.

Administration of an estate doesn't necessarily mean actual possession. Chapter 7 trustees don't go around picking up property. Actually, trustees avoid taking possession of property because they don't want to be responsible for it. Once property is exempted, ownership returns to the consumer. If a trustee files a "no asset report," and it's approved by the court, or if the trustee abandons the property, ownership returns to the consumer.

Often, consumers can seek to have liens reduced in amount and even altogether avoided.

> AVOIDING AND REDUCING LIENS UNDER THE BANKRUPTCY CODE ARE AMONG A CONSUMER'S MOST POWERFUL WEAPONS.

However, lien avoidance and reduction are complicated matters that a consumer shouldn't attempt without the help of a qualified lawyer.

BASIC PROCEDURES

A case begins with the filing of a "petition for relief" together with certain other forms, all quite short and simple. There are both voluntary and involuntary petitions. Voluntary petitions are filed by the debtors themselves; involuntary petitions are filed by one or more creditors. Involuntary petitions are very rarely filed against consumers.

SCHEDULES Within a short time, the consumer has to file a list of all liabilities and assets together with a summary of all recent financial dealings and a budget. This list, or "schedule," as well as the financial history and the budget make up the source of most, if not all, of the information that creditors and public officials will have about the consumer. Depending on the case, the manner in which this information is presented can be crucial. If your lawyer does not help you complete these forms, he is neglecting an important part of his job.

When completing these schedules, it is important to keep a few things in mind:

> Any debts that are not listed may not be discharged - It is very important to list every possible creditor and, if possible, their correct addresses. Be sure to include all potential liabilities, including any guaranties you made.
>
> Be careful about giving property values - Always state that "property values are estimated," or you may get stuck with whatever value you give. Generally, consumers want to use the lowest reasonable value so that it's more likely to be protected by an exemption. Sometimes, though, a consumer wants to give the highest reasonable value. For example, you may need to keep your car but the court may not permit you to reaffirm the auto loan unless the car is worth about as much as the unpaid balance of the loan.

Be careful about the numbers you give in any budget or "statement of income and expenses." If your income is too high or expenses too low, the creditors will want to receive more. On the other hand, if your income is too low or your expenses too high, you may have trouble convincing the court that a payment plan will be feasible.

EXAMINATION Within a few months after filing, you will be required to appear for an examination under oath. Although this is a public proceeding, the examination is usually done in the trustee's office. All creditors are invited to attend, but usually only one or two creditors, if any, appear in Chapter 7 and Chapter 13 cases.

The examination is conducted by the interim Chapter 7 trustee, or by an examiner who works for the Chapter 13 trustee, or, in most Chapter 11 cases, a representative of the U.S. Trustee. Often the person conducting the examination is not a lawyer. Frequently, the examiner makes an audio recording, but these usually are not kept for very long.

Examinations for Chapter 7 and 13 cases usually take only ten to fifteen minutes. Chapter 11 examinations can take much longer and usually attract more creditor interest. Typically, examiners do nothing more than repeat a few of the questions included on the schedules and ask for clarification of one or two points.

COURT You probably won't need to appear in court for a Chapter 7 or 13 case, unless there are special problems or you want to reaffirm a debt. Proceedings under the Code usually take place in special bankruptcy courts with bankruptcy judges. Bankruptcy judges have more power than typical state court judges. Because they are federal judges and have a wide range of powers, bankruptcy judges are rarely impeded by state lines, state laws, or state courts.

Although federal district and appellate judges outrank bankruptcy judges, they rarely know much about the Bankruptcy Code and usually defer to a bankruptcy judge's expertise. Only a handful of bankruptcy cases ever get the attention of the United States Supreme Court but, when they do, they usually cause big waves in the business world.

Most bankruptcy judges tend to be sympathetic to consumers and try to protect them. Of course, a few act as though the debtors owe them personally. Most bankruptcy judges have huge caseloads, are preoccupied with complicated business reorganizations, and have limited time to devote to consumer cases.

CONVERSION AND DISMISSAL OF CASES Cases can be converted from one Chapter to another. When this occurs, usually the case is converted from Chapter 11 or 13 to a Chapter 7 liquidation. Mostly, this happens when the consumer is unable to obtain approval of a plan, is unable to perform under a plan, or does something that convinces the court the consumer cannot be trusted to administer the estate.

A case can be dismissed for any number of reasons. Some judges use any excuse to dismiss a case just to get it off the docket. Usually, cases are dismissed for the same types of reasons that they're converted to Chapter 7. Often, though, just filing the case enables the consumer to work out arrangements with creditors causing no further need for protection under the Code. When a case is dismissed, pretty much everything goes back to where it was before the case was started.

If your case is dismissed, make sure the court order states that the dismissal is "without prejudice." This may be necessary to preserve your right to begin another case.

CLOSING CASES A case is closed when there is nothing left for the court to do. Judges love to close cases, because it gets them off their dockets. Frequently, cases are closed before plans are completed. The closing of a case usually means nothing to the consumer but sometimes can be very important. For example, the court can reconsider a creditor's claim at any time that a case remains open. Also, certain time limits for revoking a discharge do not start running until the case is closed. A case can be reopened for a number of reasons but, as a practical matter, most bankruptcy judges will resist reopening a consumer case unless it somehow helps the consumer.

IMPORTANT CONSUMER PROTECTION LAWS

CHAPTER THIRTEEN

This chapter briefly describes some of the laws intended to protect consumers and presents some of the ways a consumer can use these laws to his advantage. These laws are much more complicated and comprehensive than they appear in these summaries. Laws vary from state to state and even from court to court. Many laws that can be important in a some situations are not even mentioned here.

- **Consumer Credit Transactions**
- **Consumer Fraud and Deceptive Practices**
- **Consumer Leasing Act**
- **Defamation**
- **Door-to-Door Sales**

- **Electronic Fund Transfers**
- **Fair Credit Billing Act**
- **Equal Credit Opportunity**
- **Fair Credit Reporting Act**
- **Fair Debt Collection Practices Act**
- **Intentional Interference With Contracts**

- **Magnuson-Moss Product Warranty Act**
- **Mail Order Sales**
- **Mental Distress**
- **Motor Vehicles**
- **Privacy**
- **Retail Installment Sales**

- **Soldiers and Sailors Relief**
- **Statutes of Limitation**
- **Trespass**
- **Truth in Lending Act**
- **Uniform Commercial Code**
- **Usury**

CHAPTER 13

CONSUMER CREDIT TRANSACTIONS

The Federal Trade Commission has authority to regulate almost all creditors except banks and similar financial institutions. Depending on the political climate, the FTC can be one of the consumer's best friends.

LOAN DOCUMENTS One important FTC rule governs all consumer loan documents used by businesses other than banks. The rules prohibits any loan document from containing:

> Provisions where consumers agree to "confess judgment." These clauses allow creditors to sue consumers and have their own representatives admit liability on behalf of the consumers.
>
> Waivers of consumers' legal exemptions, except when the exempt item simultaneously is the purchased property and the security for the purchase.
>
> Automatic wage assignments, with certain exceptions.
>
> Blanket security interests in household goods and personal belongings.
>
> Charging late charges on timely payments, when the only amount not paid is the previous late payment charge (late charges on late charges).
>
> Misrepresenting the character or extent of a co-signer's liability.

HOLDER IN DUE COURSE Another important FTC rule modified what is known as the "holder in due course doctrine." The theory behind the doctrine was that an innocent person should not be punished for someone else's wrongdoing. For example, a car dealer sells you a car. You make a down payment and give the dealer a promissory note for the balance. The dealer sells your promissory note to a third party. Under the holder in due course doctrine, you would have to keep making payments to the third party even if the car were stuck together with chewing gum and fell apart a block away from the dealership.

Although you could sue the dealership, you still owed the loan payments to the holder in due course. The doctrine never applied if the holder in due course admitted knowing that you had a valid defense. But most holders in due course knew a lot more than they ever admitted. In practice, it was nearly impossible to prove that the holder in due course knew anything. The core of the FTC rule is that any defense you have against the merchant is also a defense to the promissory note itself, even if it's sold to a holder in due course.

CONSUMER FRAUD AND DECEPTIVE PRACTICES

Most states have at least one statute that prohibits merchants and creditors from defrauding consumers or using other unfair trade practices. The essence of a fraudulent practice is lying about something important. Mere opinions and puffing ("the world's best...") are not the types of lies that are prohibited. Unfair practices include such things as phony going-out-of-business sales, bait-and-switch tactics, chain-referral and pyramid schemes, and "tying" arrangements - where you can't buy something desirable unless you also buy something undesirable.

These statutes usually allow consumers to sue for actual damages, legal fees, and limited punitive damages. In most states, the office of a state's Attorney General actively helps consumers who have been victimized by fraudulent or unfair practices.

CONSUMER LEASING ACT

The Consumer Leasing Act (CLA) is very similar to the Truth in Lending Act, which is discussed later. But instead of lending, CLA covers leases of personal property used primarily for personal, family, or household purpose for a period of more than 120 days. Even when a lease is on a month-to-month basis, the creditor must meet CLA requirements if a majority of its leases run for a year or more.

CLA requires that any advertising disclose in the ad itself, the amount of down payment required, the number of monthly payments required, the amount of each payment, and the total amount of finance charges. Also, the consumer must be provided with a written agreement that clearly identifies the participants, a full description of the leased property, type, and amount of any insurance required by or provided by the creditor, and a detailed explanation of any warranty.

Creditors must provide consumers with a list of all official fees, a description of the consumer's obligation at the end of the lease, the amount of late fees and other fees not included in the monthly payment schedule, terms and penalties for early termination of the lease, the number of monthly payments required under the lease, the amount of each payment, the due date for each payment, and the total amount of all payments. Consumers have the same rights to sue for violations of CLA as for violations of TILA.

DEFAMATION

Defamation occurs when someone says (slander) or writes (libel) something untrue about another person. Usually, there is no legal remedy unless the false statement causes some damage. Damage is automatically presumed, though, if a person is falsely accused of committing a crime, being incompetent in his business or occupation, or being bankrupt.

Consumers have won lawsuits against creditors, credit-reporting agencies and former employers for damages due to defamation. For example, you want to buy a home but can't get a mortgage because some unpaid debt shows on your credit report. In fact, you have paid the debt but you can't get the report corrected in time to purchase the house, which was really a bargain. You have to wait to get the credit rating sorted out. You then buy a similar house, but at a higher price. You may have a cause of action against the merchant, and even the credit-reporting agency, to recover the difference in the costs of the two homes.

DOOR-TO-DOOR SALES

Many states have laws that protect you from door-to-door salesman. These laws give you time to rescind any sale made as a result of an unsolicited call at your home. Most of these laws provide that the specified length of time to cancel begins as soon as the salesman provides you with a written notice of your right to cancel. Also, the Federal Trade Commission has a regulation that gives consumers three days to rescind contracts signed in their homes.

ELECTRONIC FUND TRANSFERS

Electronic Fund Transfers (EFTs) are transfers of money from one place or account to another place or account that do not start with writing a check or other paper document. EFTs include transfers by wire, telephone, and automatic teller machines transfers. Federal law prohibits creditors from requiring you to pre-authorize EFTs as a condition of granting you credit.

Under Federal EFT laws, you must receive full disclosures of:

all charges;

all limitations on transfers;

the right to stop payment of pre-authorized transfers;

the name and number of a person to call to stop or correct transfers;

the right to receive documentation of all transfers;

a written summary of your rights;

the financial institution's liabilities to you;

changes of rules or practices, at least 21 days before they take affect.

You have the right to stop payment of pre-authorized EFTs either orally or in writing up to three business days prior to the scheduled transfer date. If the stop payment is oral, it should be followed-up in writing.

Your maximum liability for unauthorized EFTs is the lesser of $50 or the amount actually transferred before the bank learns that you did not or will not authorize the transfer (for example, being given notice of a lost card). If you believe an EFT is incorrect or unauthorized, notify the bank or other financial institution within 60 days after you receive documentation of the EFT. If you give notice verbally, the bank may require you to confirm it in writing within 10 days. The bank then has 10 days to investigate or up to 45 days if it gives you full use of the money pending the investigation. If the bank determines that an error occurred, it must correct the error within one business day.

If a financial institution violates this law, the consumer can sue and may recover actual damages, legal fees, and even triple damages for certain violations.

FAIR CREDIT BILLING ACT

The Fair Credit Billing Act (FCBA) applies to what is referred to as open-end credit accounts. These include credit cards, such as Visa and Mastercard, and revolving charge cards or accounts, such as department store accounts.

Under FCBA, whenever you believe a billing error has occurred, you have 60 days after receiving the bill to notify the creditor. If you call the creditor, be sure to follow-up in writing.

FCBA's definition of a billing error is quite broad. It includes charges made by an unauthorized user of your card; incorrectly identified charges; charges made for goods or services that you didn't accept; charges for goods and services delivered at times other than the times agreed on; simple arithmetic mistakes; failure to show all payments and credits; mailing to an incorrect address; and any charge that you think requires additional explanation or proof of purchase.

The creditor is then responsible for conducting a reasonable investigation to determine whether you are correct. It has up to 90 days to complete this investigation. Until the investigation is completed, the creditor can't charge interest on the disputed amount, ask for the money in dispute, report your failure to pay this disputed amount to any credit reporting agency, or close your account for failure to pay this disputed amount.

If the investigation proves that you don't owe the disputed amount, you must receive full credit, including any finance charges levied against you, for that amount. If the investigation concludes that you do owe the money, the creditor must promptly inform you of the reasons. If you still believe the amount is in error, you have 10 days to notify the creditor, in writing. The creditor can then start collection proceedings against you but, in reporting this to the credit reporting agency, your side of the story must be included.

A creditor that fails to adhere to FCBA terms waives its rights to collect the amount in dispute and any related finance charges. You also can sue the creditor and, if successful, you can be awarded damages plus twice the amount of the finance charges, plus costs, plus reasonable legal fees.

Few consumer's know it, but they can use the FCBA much like a stop payment order on a check. Actually, it can be safer to charge something on your credit card than to write a check, because you have a longer time to stop payment. If you charge a purchase on your credit card and don't receive what you expected, you can dispute the charge for up to 60 days after you receive your credit card bill.

Most merchants are very good about adjusting bills, because they don't want to lose a customer. However, credit card issuers are in a somewhat different situation. The likelihood that a credit card company will resolve a dispute in favor of the consumer depends on a number of factors. In any given credit card transaction, there are either three or four players:

the consumer;

the credit card issuer, which bills the consumer;

the credit card collector, which bills the card issuer and pays the merchant; and

the merchant, which submits charge slips directly to the credit card collector and is paid by the credit card collector.

When a disputed item is removed from the consumer's bill, the credit card issuer charges the credit card collector, who in turn charges the merchant. Consequently, the card issuer usually has little to lose by deciding in favor of the consumer. But, because one company can act as both the credit card issuer and the credit card collector, that isn't always the case. American Express (Optima card) and Sears (Discover card) are leading examples of companies that act in both capacities. With MasterCard and VISA, it is more common for the issuer and the collector to be different banks.

As a practical matter, a credit card issuer's strongest motivation is to keep its customer satisfied. If its customer is the consumer, the issuer will be more likely to find in favor of the consumer. If both the consumer and the merchant are its customers, the issuer is more likely to want to satisfy the merchant. Indeed, most Mastercard and Visa issuers usually remove disputed items from consumers' bills, then give merchants the chance to challenge the action. In contrast, American Express usually confirms with the merchant before removing a disputed item from a consumer's bill.

EQUAL CREDIT OPPORTUNITY ACT

The Equal Credit Opportunity Act (ECOA) exists to prohibit discrimination in granting credit on the basis of race, color, religion, national origin, sex, marital status, age, sources of income, or because a consumer has exercised any rights under this law. Creditors are permitted to ask about marital status, age, and sources of income for certain limited purposes.

Consumers who are victimized by violations of the act have the right to sue to recover compensatory damages punitive damages, and attorneys' fees. In addition, several government agencies have the power to investigate violations and take enforcement action.

FAIR CREDIT REPORTING ACT

The purpose of the Fair Credit Reporting Act (FCRA) is to protect consumers from credit reporting agencies that:

Distribute incorrect or out-of-date information;

fail to exercise their responsibilities in a fair and just manner; or

fail to respect the rights and confidentiality of consumers.

REQUIREMENTS FOR CREDIT-REPORTING AGENCIES

FCRA applies only to agencies that provide credit reports on consumers who seek personal credit. The law covers two types of reports generated by these agencies - the basic consumer report and an investigative report.

The basic consumer report can be either oral or written. All it must do to fall within FCRA oversight is (a) contain information about your past credit history, (b) contain information about any of your personal traits or characteristics, or (c) be intended to be used, at least in part, to determine your eligibility for personal credit, insurance or employment. The only difference between a basic report and an investigative report is that the latter involves doing personal interviews with friends, relatives, neighbors, and co-workers. Also, FCRA holds investigative reports to a higher standard of accuracy than they do basic credit reports.

Credit-reporting agencies must maintain rational and reasonable procedures for assuring they issue these reports only for legally permissible reasons. They may legally issue reports only in relation to a credit transaction in which the consumer is involved, insurance or employment purposes, certain governmental licensing purposes, or other valid business criteria.

If the creditor receiving the report denies the consumer credit at least partly as a result of that report, the creditor must notify the consumer and must supply him with the name and address of the credit-reporting agency. If credit is denied as a result of something other than the credit report, the creditor has to make that information available to the consumer, if requested, within 60 days.

Consumer-reporting agencies must keep their files up to date. They must remove all negative reports once the statute of limitations has gone by or if more than seven years have elapsed, whichever is longer. These negative items include, but are not limited to lawsuits brought against you, judgments entered against you, tax liens that you have paid; collection agency accounts, accounts that your creditor has written off, and information about arrests, indictments, and convictions.

> Bankruptcies are excepted from the seven-year time limit; they can be shown on a report for ten years. Reports for certain insurance or employment situations are also excepted from the seven-year time limit. Older adverse information can still be provided to insurance companies if the amount of the policy in question is $50,000 or more, and older information can be reported for employment purposes if the proposed job pays more than $20,000 a year.

Certain quirks in the law limit the consumer's ability to seek redress. You can't hold a store liable under FCRA for providing inaccurate information about you to a credit-reporting agency. First, the store is neither a credit-reporting agency nor a user of that information; second, what the store provides isn't a consumer report under the terms of this law. If you can prove the store was "willful" or "negligent" in providing incorrect information, you have a potential defamation suit against the store, but no recourse under the FCRA.

RIGHTS TO CORRECT A REPORT AND TO SUE FOR VIOLATIONS

When a credit report is the basis of an unfavorable decision against you, the creditor, employer, or insurer must tell you who provided the report and inform you of your rights. You have the right to see your credit file and to include your written explanation of the dispute in the report. You have 30 days to see your file at no charge to make sure your explanation has been properly placed in your file.

> For example, you may want your credit file to show that you refused to pay a particular bill because the bill was disputed. Generally, your statement will be more meaningful if you provide a specific reason for the dispute such as a defect in the product. Or, you may want the report to include a number of credit accounts that you have kept in good standing but the credit reporting agency missed.

Even if you have not been turned down for credit, you still can find out what's in your credit file, for a slight fee. First, you must give the credit-reporting agency reasonable notice that you intend to show up at its offices. You must arrive during normal business hours and have proof of your identity. To find out by phone, you must first write to them with proof of your identity and prepay any long distance or telephone toll charges. The credit-reporting agency must provide you with:

> the nature and substance of all information, other than medical information, contained in your file;
>
> the sources of all information, except those used solely for an investigative report;
>
> the names of all recipients of reports furnished during the last two years for employment purposes;

the names of all recipients of reports furnished during the last six months for any purpose other than employment; and

a trained person to explain the file to you.

You have the right to dispute the contents and tone of your file. The agency must conduct an investigation to determine the accuracy of its information and delete any information it can't verify. If you and the agency disagree about one or more items in the report, you have the right to submit a brief written statement. The agency can limit that statement to 100 words if it provides you assistance writing the statement. From then on, if the agency continues to report the disputed item, the agency must note that the item is disputed and the report must include either a copy of your statement or a clear and accurate summary of the statement. If you convince the credit-reporting agency that it reported an item inaccurately, the agency must inform all who received the inaccurate information within the previous six months, or within the two previous years, if the information was provided for employment purposes.

If a credit-reporting agency fails to adhere to the rules established by FCRA, you have the right to sue it for actual damages, costs, and legal fees. If the action was willful or negligent, you also are entitled to punitive damages. If you didn't suffer out of pocket damages, you still have the right to sue for injury to your reputation and to your ability to obtain credit.

FAIR DEBT COLLECTION PRACTICES ACT

In 1977, Congress passed the Fair Debt Collection Practices Act (FDCPA) to curb abusive tactics sometimes used by collection agencies. FDCPA is a powerful tool, but it is limited to consumer debts and to professional debt collectors - people who collect debts for other people. Debt collectors include collection agencies and collection lawyers who function like collection agencies. FDCPA does NOT apply to in-house collection efforts conducted by a creditor on its own behalf. Briefly, FDCPA:

bans many of the abusive collection practices historically used by the industry;

requires collectors to follow specific procedures; and

authorizes consumers and the FTC to sue collectors who violate this law.

PROHIBITED DEBT COLLECTION PRACTICES

CONTACTS WITH A CONSUMER The collector may not:

Use a postcard to contact the consumer or use any name or symbol on an envelope, including the collector's business name, that indicates that the communication concerns the collection of a debt.

Contact a consumer before 8:00 a.m. or after 9:00 p.m. without the consumer's consent.

Contact a consumer on the job if the collector has any reason to suspect that the consumer's employer will disapprove.

Contact a consumer if the collector knows the consumer is represented by a lawyer in connection with that debt, unless the consumer or the attorney gives consent or the attorney does not respond to communications.

Contact a consumer who has written the collector a letter saying that he refuses to pay the debt or that he no longer wants to be contacted by the collector. However, the collector still may inform the consumer that it will terminate collection efforts or take other specific action.

CONTACTS WITH THIRD PARTIES A collector may not contact any third party if he knows the consumer is represented by a lawyer. A collector may not contact any third party except for the purpose of locating the consumer or enforcing a valid judgment. The consumer's spouse, attorney, parent (if the consumer is a minor), guardian, executor, and administrator are not considered third parties.

When contacting a third party, the collector must correctly identify himself (individually - not his company) and state only that he is confirming or correcting information about the consumer's location. The collector may not:

State that the consumer owes a debt.

Communicate by postcard.

Use any language or symbol on an envelope or in a letter or telegram that indicates the writer is a debt collector or the communication relates to the collection of a debt.

Identify the collector's employer unless requested by the third party.

Contact the third party again unless the third party requests such contact or the collector has reason to believe that his initial response was incorrect or incomplete and he now has more accurate or complete information.

OTHER PROHIBITED PRACTICES

Collectors also are prohibited from:

Using or threatening to use violence to anyone's physical person, reputation or property.

Using profane or obscene language.

Publishing a list of consumers who refuse to pay debts (except to a credit-reporting agency) or advertising a debt.

Repeatedly using the telephone with intent to annoy, abuse or harass the person called.

Telephoning anyone without disclosing the caller's individual identity.

Using any false or misleading representation, including:

> falsely claiming that the collector represents the federal or a state government;
>
> falsely representing that the collector is an attorney;
>
> falsely representing that the collector works for a consumer reporting agency;
>
> using a false business name;
>
> giving a false purpose for a communication;
>
> misrepresenting the nature or amount of a debt;
>
> misrepresenting the consequences of nonpayment;
>
> misrepresenting that the consumer committed a crime;
>
> threatening any action that cannot legally be taken or that is not intended to be taken;
>
> simulating official, government or court documents;
>
> misrepresenting that papers are legal process when they are not; or
>
> communicating or threatening to communicate false credit information.

Collecting any amount greater than the debt unless authorized by contract or permitted by law.

Misusing post-dated and undated checks by:

> accepting a post-dated check without informing the consumer in advance when it will be deposited;
>
> depositing or threatening to deposit a post-dated check earlier than the date specified; or
>
> soliciting a post-dated or undated check for the purpose of threatening or instituting a criminal prosecution.

Causing a consumer to accept collect calls or pay for telegrams by concealing the purpose of the communication.

Taking or threatening any non-judicial action to take property unless there is a present right and intention to do so.

Using any other unfair or unconscionable means to collect a debt.

REQUIRED COLLECTION PROCEDURES

VERIFICATION OF THE DEBT Within five days after the initial communication, the collector must send the consumer a written statement that indicates the amount of the debt and the name of the creditor who claims the debt. The notice also must CLEARLY inform the consumer that:

> unless he disputes the debt within 30 days after receiving the notice, the collector will assume the debt is valid, and
>
> the consumer has 30 days after receiving the notice to WRITE the collector and either (a) notify him of any dispute or (b) require him to verify the debt in writing or, if the debt was assigned by the original creditor, provide the consumer with the name and address of the original creditor.

Once a consumer writes the collector, the collector cannot take any action until the consumer receives a copy of the verification or the name and address of the original creditor. A consumer's failure to exercise the right to write to a collector cannot be treated as an admission of liability by any court.

APPLICATION OF PAYMENTS If a consumer owes more than one debt that a collector is handling, the collector must apply the payments to the debt that the consumer designates. This enables consumers to decide which creditor and what debts will be paid. The law neither authorizes nor prohibits applying payments to principal rather than interest.

BRINGING LAWSUITS A debt collector who sues to recover real estate that was given as collateral for the debt, must bring suit in the county where the real estate is located. Otherwise, the suit must be brought where the contract was signed or the consumer resides at the time the suit is commenced. This prevents collectors from bringing lawsuits in courts that are in locations where it would be unreasonably difficult for a consumer to litigate. For example, most consumers who live on the East Coast would have a hard time defending a lawsuit brought in California.

SUING FOR VIOLATIONS

Any person harmed by a violation of this law can sue the debt collector up to one year after the violation occurs. Even if a consumer actually owes the debt, the debt collector still can be held liable for violating the law. The collector cannot be held liable if the violation was unintentional and the collector maintained reasonable procedures to prevent the violation.

Unfortunately, many debt collectors still violate the law. A person injured by a violation can recover any actual damages caused by the violation. Some courts have even held that actual damages can include illnesses and emotional damages resulting from a violation. In addition to actual damages, or even in the absence of actual damages, a consumer can recover statutory damages up to $1,000. The amount of statutory damages will be determined by the judge, who will consider the seriousness of the violations. The act also authorizes class action suits that can be brought on behalf of all consumers subjected to similar violations by that debt collector. If you win, you can be awarded all costs, including legal fees. But if you lose, and the judge believes you sued in bad faith or for the purpose of harassment, you can be ordered to pay the debt collector's costs and legal fees.

The United States Federal Trade Commission (FTC) is authorized to enforce FDCPA and pass rules and regulations that are almost the same as statutes. The enthusiasm that the FTC will give to enforcing FDCPA and its own rules and regulations at any particular time depends on the prevailing political climate. Nevertheless, a consumer may be able to cause endless problems for a collector by reporting a violation to the FTC which, among other things, can impose fines of up to $10,000 per violation. Just responding to an FTC investigation can cost a debt collector considerable time, energy, and legal fees.

INTENTIONAL INTERFERENCE WITH CONTRACTS

All states have laws that prohibit people from maliciously injuring another person's occupation or business. A collection agency or creditor can be sued for "intentionally interfering with contract" or for "intentionally interfering with prospective business advantage" if it violates this rule. "Prospective business advantage" is a term relating to your opportunity to make money that, although not contractual, is reasonably likely. For example, if a creditor calls your customers for the purpose of embarrassing you or putting pressure on you and you lose business, you can sue the collection agency for your lost profits. Similarly, if a creditor calls your employer for the purpose of pressuring you and you lose your job, you can sue the creditor for your lost income.

CHAPTER 13

MAGNUSON-MOSSPRODUCT WARRANTY ACT

Congress passed the Magnuson-Moss Consumer Product Warranty Act out of concern for consumers who were receiving misleading warranties and guaranties, especially from auto makers. The act forces manufacturers and merchants to disclose the terms of their warranties and guaranties prior to sale and to back up those warranties and guaranties rather than hiding behind the small print. Under this law, a full warranty includes:

> a right to repair, replacement or, if the consumer approves, a refund, within a reasonable time and without charge;
>
> all implied warranties (good title, fitness for the intended use);
>
> a requirement that any limitation on consequential damages (damages to a person or property other than the product or service being sold) be stated; and
>
> a right to a replacement or refund after a reasonable number of unsuccessful attempts to repair.

Full warranties remain in effect for the time stated. They apply to anyone who owns the product - not just the initial purchaser - unless the warranty states otherwise. Beware of the phrase "for as long as you own this product," because it limits the warranty to the initial purchaser. Full warranties benefit consumers. That's why merchants and manufacturers no longer offer many full warranties. "Limited warranties" have taken their place, but compared to full warranties and guaranties, these are pretty weak.

One problem with limited warranties is that they don't cover everything. Another is that they usually are worded to exclude problems most likely to require service or repair. Moreover, limited warranties usually limit the duration of implied warranties.

A big advantage to all warranties governed by the Act is that they cannot exclude implied warranties. Implied warranties promise that the seller is giving good title (full ownership) to the consumer and that the product or service is fit for its intended use.

Although Magnuson-Moss doesn't reduce any consumer rights, many state statutes and court decisions give consumers even more rights.

> Always get a seller to make as many promises, guaranties, and representations as possible, even if they aren't in writing. If the product or service doesn't measure up to all those promises, guaranties, and representations, you will have additional rights, defenses, and claims against the creditor.

If a merchant violates Magnuson-Moss, you can recover actual damages, legal fees, and sometimes even punitive damages.

MAIL ORDER SALES

Federal law specifically prohibits the use of the United States mail and telephone lines to defraud anyone. Consumer scams that use the mails or phones, even if it's use is incidental to the scam itself, should be reported to the office of the United States Postal Inspector or the Federal Trade Commission. It's almost impossible to imagine any transaction that doesn't use one or both.

Federal law also governs many specific mail order sales practices. Merchants are prohibited from mailing unsolicited goods to consumers. If you are sent unsolicited merchandise, it is yours to keep - for free. Also, if goods are ordered by mail, merchants are required to deliver them within the advertised time or thirty days, whichever is longer. If the merchant does not deliver within that time, the consumer may cancel the order. Finally, there are a number of FTC regulations governing sales of land through the mails. If you have purchased land through the mails, it is likely the seller did not fully comply with FTC regulations. If you are looking for a good defense to paying the debt, it's may be well worth your time to check with the FTC.

MENTAL DISTRESS

Consumers have beaten both creditors and collection agencies in court for "intentional infliction of mental distress." Often, when trying to collect debts, creditors and agencies step beyond the limits of decent behavior and the law. If that leads to real mental distress, you can sue for damages. Most states, however, require some physical symptom of the distress. Professional medical treatment is important evidence.

If you or a member of your family is physically, mentally, or emotionally ill or for some reason especially sensitive to stress, you should inform the creditor in writing and instruct the creditor to refrain from contacting that person. If the creditor continues to cause problems for that person, the creditor may end up paying substantial actual and punitive damages.

MOTOR VEHICLES

States have laws governing sales of motor vehicles, especially retail installment (credit) sales and sales of used cars. Often, dealers must give certain warranties and disclose mileage, defects, prior repairs, and other information. "Lemon Laws" often provide some additional protection from incurably defective products. Dealers, especially those operating in low income areas, frequently violate these laws in many different ways.

Federal law prohibits used-car dealers from "rolling back" mileage, but they still commonly do it, or have it done for them. Federal law holds manufacturers responsible for defects in exhaust emission control systems. Manufacturers and dealers rarely tell consumers, but repairs relating of these components should be provided free by the manufacturer. Manufacturers also are supposed to inform consumers of safety defects and remedy them. However, the law has so many loopholes that the manufacturers usually keep quiet about defects some consumer-advocate forces appropriate action.

PRIVACY

FINANCIAL

Federal law prohibits banks and other financial institutions, including credit card issuers, from disclosing your financial records to any government agency unless:

> you have given proper written authorization, which cannot be effective for longer than 3 months, or
>
> the records are disclosed in response to a summons, subpoena, or search warrant.

These limitations do not apply to routine overview of the financial institution by agencies such as the Federal Deposit Insurance Corporation. You must be notified of any disclosure demanded by a government agency unless the government obtains a court order allowing delayed notification.

Many states have similar laws prohibiting financial institutions from disclosing records to anyone without the customer's consent, unless the records are demanded by summons, subpoena, other court order, or search warrant.

INVASIONS OF PRIVACY

Over the years, a growing number of court decisions have recognized your right to be left alone, known as the right to privacy. These decisions favor any lawsuit against a creditor or collection agency that goes too far in its investigations or attempts to collect.

A collection agency has no right to pry into matters that do not directly assist the debt collection process. For example, your sexual habits are not a proper area of interest to a collection agency or creditor. Creditors have, at times, attempted to publicly embarrass consumers into paying by doing such things as running newspaper ads naming delinquent customers. Some of these creditors have been successfully sued for invasion of the consumer's privacy.

RETAIL INSTALLMENT SALES ACTS

Every state has some version of a retail installment sales act (RISA). These acts generally pertain to consumer retail transactions involving either merchandise or services. The transactions also must involve deferred or installment payments on which finance charges are added to the cash sales price. Some states have separate statutes for motor vehicles, generally similar to RISA except for their more stringent insurance provisions. Other states combine the two acts.

RISAs generally require that all contracts be put into writing and contain a provision for your getting at least a partial refund if you prepay the debt. The contract shouldn't contain any blank spaces when you sign. Make sure you get a copy of the signed contract.

State legislators enact RISA laws to force creditors to give consumers adequate information about the terms and conditions of the credit. This allows the consumer to make an intelligent decision before signing a pre-printed form. The disclosures required by RISAs generally follow along the same lines as those mentioned in the federal Truth in Lending Act. A typical RISA provides that:

> Actual cash price and finance charges must be clearly shown. You can't waive your right to a partial refund of the finance charges if you prepay. Your debt can't be accelerated unless you have been in default for at least 30 days, or you have abandoned or destroyed the merchandise, or the creditor believes you are about to leave the state.
>
> If you already carry insurance that covers such merchandise, you can't be forced to take additional insurance. If you end up buying insurance, the creditor cannot make a profit on that item. He can charge you only what he himself pays, and must reflect this charge in the retail sales contract. If you buy insurance, you must receive a written copy of the policy within one month.
>
> If you default, RISA allows the creditor to repossess its property and dispose of it according to UCC requirements. Some states modify creditors' rights under the UCC, usually by increasing consumers' rights when a certain portion of a loan is paid. Most RISAs allow consumers to redeem collateral if all defaults are cured within a certain number of days after repossession. The right to cure defaults is very important, because the consumer might otherwise be required to pay the entire debt. The difference between curing a default and paying the entire debt usually is significant. When curing a default, you only pay the amount you are behind, not the entire debt.

SOLDIERS AND SAILORS RELIEF ACT

Soldiers and Sailors Relief Act (SSRA) protects consumers in the military from previously incurred debts while they are on active duty. It offers no protection from debts incurred after you enter active duty. SSRA also gives courts the authority to extend the same protection to dependents, co-signors, and guarantors of debts of such military personnel.

> In order to secure SSRA benefits, give your creditor a letter asserting these rights. If possible, accompany this letter with documentation showing that you are in active military service.

LAWSUITS Under SSRA, a creditor cannot obtain a default judgment against you. If you don't appear in court and it's shown that your military duty impairs your defense, the court must suspend the proceedings against you. If you don't appear and there is no such showing, the court may order the appointment of a lawyer to handle your defense.

If the court does appoint a lawyer, and it is later shown that your military duty interfered with a valid defense, any judgment entered against you must be vacated. The court also may suspend execution of any judgment if your military duty interferes with your ability to comply with the judgment.

OTHER COLLECTION ACTIVITIES SSRA prohibits eviction of your family, but only if the rent does not exceed $150 per month. It also states that creditors cannot terminate contracts, foreclose mortgages, or repossess property without a court's permission.

LEASES Under SSRA, you have the right to cancel any leases of real property for dwelling, professional, business, agricultural, or similar purposes.

INTEREST SSRA limits the interest you can be charged to 6% while on active duty.

STATUTES OF LIMITATIONS

Statutes of Limitations bar non-government creditor lawsuits after the passage of time. Generally, the time specified by the statute of limitations in the state where you reside governs. However, there are exceptions. Federal law always governs lawsuits brought by the federal government.

Typically, these laws limit the time for bringing lawsuits on written contracts to ten years. For oral agreements, the limit is shorter, usually about five years. Most statutes don't begin running until default has occurred. Often, the limitations on lawsuits by the federal government are considerably shorter than comparable state laws.

Some states have no statute of limitations barring suits by the state government and many have eliminated all statutes of limitations regarding government-guaranteed educational loans. There is no time limitation on the collection of federal taxes for years a consumer files no tax return.

Statutes of limitation are not as simple as they might sound. Most such statutes can be "tolled," or temporarily suspended. For example, a statute of limitations may be deemed tolled during the period of a payment plan or while a consumer is hiding in another state. Also, the consumer can waive the statute.

> It is never a good idea to agree to waive or extend any statute of limitations. Nor is it a good idea to admit the existence of an old debt, because in some states that admission may enable the creditor to get around a statute of limitations.

TRESPASS

No one is allowed on the premises of your home without your permission. Two major exceptions are:

landlords, because written leases usually that give them the right to inspect the premises to make sure they are safe and properly maintained, and

law enforcement officials acting in response to an emergency or with the authority of a search warrant, eviction order, or other court order.

As a practical matter, though, it can be difficult to sue or prosecute a trespasser unless the property is posted with "no trespassing" signs, the trespasser is told to leave the property, or the trespasser evades or breaks down a locked door or gate.

If someone trespasses on your property, you can sue for actual damages. Most state laws assume that the mere act of trespassing causes damage. If the trespass is intentional, you can seek punitive damages.

TRUTH IN LENDING ACT

Truth in Lending Act (TILA) requires disclosure of the actual costs of consumer credit including interest rates, closing fees, and most other charges. TILA does not limit the amount a creditor can charge except to prohibit certain types of kickbacks to lenders.

Keep in mind that certain disclosures are always required. However, creditors are very good at providing the information at times and in ways that discourage most consumers from understanding the information. Sometimes they provide the information at the last minute; sometimes they bury it under more interesting literature. Also, a creditor need inform only one participating consumer, and some creditors make a point of informing the one least likely to understand or complain about the relevant credit terms.

Keep copies of all disclosure forms you receive. You may later find that the creditor did not comply with the law.

TRANSACTIONS THAT ARE COVERED BY TILA As a general rule, consumer credit means credit given to an individual or individuals primarily for personal, household, or family purposes. TILA excludes credit given primarily for business purposes. TILA protects all consumer credit transactions under $25,000. It covers consumer transactions above that amount if the credit was obtained, in whole or in part, by the consumer using his home or other personal property as collateral. TILA also covers all credit card and revolving charge card transactions. However, student loans are generally excluded.

AMOUNTS THAT MUST BE DISCLOSED TILA requires the creditor to fully disclose to the consumer the actual finance charges and the **A**nnual **P**ercentage **R**ate (APR). Remember, finance charges and the APR include not only the so-called interest rate and amount being charged, but all additional finance charges as well. What are some of these additional charges? One favorite is closing points. Another is the loan fee. Others include the application fee; a credit check fee; a finder's fee; charges for credit life, health, and property insurance; and add-on or discount interest charges. All of these charges, plus the basic interest rate, constitute the actual finance charge. All these charges must be fully disclosed to you in both dollars and APR.

There are other add-on charges the creditor is NOT required to include in its disclosure. These include late charges, prepayment penalties, overdraft charges, title insurance, title examination fees, document preparation and recording fees, and notary fees. All in all, it's still hard to know what the true finance costs are.

WHEN THE DISCLOSURES MUST BE MADE Disclosure must be given before you accept the credit. Advertisers who promote interest rates or credit terms in their ads, must disclose, in the ad itself, the amount of down payment required, the number of monthly payments required, the amount of each such payment, and the total amount of other finance charges. Many creditors, especially credit card companies, don't make many of the disclosures until they send the actual credit card to the consumer. Be sure to read everything that is sent to you at the last minute - it probably contains the most objectionable of the credit terms.

There is a special rule for loans secured by your principal residence. If you have secured the credit by your residence, you have three days after disclosure to rescind, or cancel, the transaction. This three day period doesn't begin until the disclosure is made.

> **Rescission** If, within the allowed time, you notify the creditor that you are canceling the credit transaction, the creditor has ten days to release its security interest in your property. You don't have to give the creditor a reason for your cancellation, and until the creditor has released or returned your collateral, you aren't required to return his money or property. If, for some reason, the creditor doesn't take actual possession of the returned money or property within ten days from the date you tendered it, it's yours to keep, free and clear.

VIOLATIONS OF TILA If you experience a TILA violation, you have one year to bring a lawsuit against the creditor. If you win, you can be awarded actual and punitive damages, costs, and reasonable legal fees. The law provides for fairly modest damages - up to about $1,000 per consumer - but also allows recovery of the consumer's attorney fees.

You can't offset claims for TILA violations against debts otherwise owed to the creditor unless you already have a judgment against the creditor. However, TILA violations sometimes can be raised as defenses and counterclaims to creditor lawsuits.

TILA is so extremely technical that it's difficult for a consumer to know whether a creditor has complied with the law. Generally, a consumer should inquire into a possible TILA violation if:

the creditor's advertising was misleading;

the creditor never made a formal disclosure of some sort; or

the creditor's formal disclosure was inaccurate or incomplete.

UNIFORM COMMERCIAL CODE

The Uniform Commercial Code (UCC) is a set of laws that all states have adopted. However, the code is not truly uniform, because the states haven't all passed exactly the same law. Also, court decisions interpreting the UCC vary from state to state.

The UCC covers many things, including sales of goods, checks, promissory notes, and secured loans. Two major areas not covered by the UCC are motor vehicles and most real estate transactions. This book couldn't possibly, and doesn't try, to discuss everything the UCC covers.

LAND TRUSTS Some states recognize what is known as a land trust. In a land trust, title is held in the name of a trustee, but the real owners are beneficiaries of the trust, not the trustee. Land trusts are very useful, but:

> NEVER give a creditor an Assignment of Beneficial Interest (ABI) in a land trust that holds title to your home or other real estate. ABIs are treated like personal property and can be foreclosed, like other personal property covered by the UCC. When granting an ABI to a creditor, you lose the important protection provided by mortgage foreclosure laws. Never trust a creditor who insists on obtaining an ABI. If your property is in a land trust and a creditor requests an ABI, offer to take the property out of the land trust and secure the credit with a mortgage. If your property is not in a land trust but a creditor insists that you put your property in a land trust and give it an ABI, find a different lender. This one is in the business of foreclosing, not lending.

SELLING COLLATERAL One important consumer area the UCC governs is "secured transactions." Among other things, the UCC requires that a secured creditor sell or otherwise dispose of repossessed collateral in a commercially reasonable manner. Yet, very few creditors dispose of collateral in such a manner. Most just sell collateral at liquidation auctions, the one method almost certain to bring the lowest possible price for the collateral.

> If you learn that a creditor is about to sell your collateral, mail the creditor a casual letter suggesting the best ways to sell the collateral. Include the names of any potential purchasers. If the creditor proceeds with a liquidation auction, you will have a strong defense against any claim for a deficiency. For reasons explained below, your letter should not acknowledge receipt of any notices from the creditor.

The UCC requires a secured creditor to give you notice before selling or otherwise disposing of collateral. It isn't necessary that the notice actually reach you, but the creditor must make a reasonable effort to get the notice to you.

> MANY creditors fail to give consumers reasonable notice of disposition of collateral. In some states, such failure relieves the consumer from any deficiency. In other states, such failure to give notice requires the CREDITOR to prove that the sale was commercially reasonable and that the failure to give notice did not actually harm the consumer.

The UCC requires collateral to be sold within a reasonable time period. If the creditor holds the collateral for too long, or uses the collateral for any purpose, this can be interpreted as taking the collateral in full satisfaction of the debt. This relieves the consumer of any responsibility for a deficiency. At the very least, the consumer should receive credit for interest charges that would not have run up had a collateral sale been held within a reasonable period of time.

The UCC also gives consumers the right to redeem collateral by paying off the entire debt before the collateral is sold. However, many state Retail Installment Sales Acts are even more liberal, permitting redemption merely by making all OVERDUE payments. It's easier to come up with the money for overdue payments than to come up with enough money to pay off an entire loan. If a creditor has repossessed collateral that you want to redeem, notify the creditor immediately and confirm your notice in writing.

> **Waiver** The UCC does not permit consumers to waive their notice and redemption rights BEFORE there is a default. Many creditors put language in the their loan documents that says the consumer waives those rights, but this provision is not enforceable. However, the UCC does permit you to waive your rights AFTER there has been a default.
>
> > IF YOU HAVE DEFAULTED ON A SECURED LOAN, DO **NOT** SIGN ANY PAPER WAIVING ANY NOTICE OR REDEMPTION RIGHTS UNLESS YOU ARE GIVEN A FULL AND UNCONDITIONAL RELEASE FROM LIABILITY FOR ANY DEFICIENCY.

A growing number of states are enacting what is known as Article 2**A** of the UCC. This new article covers leases and gives lessees, especially consumers, a broad range of very important legal rights. Within a few years, nearly every state will adopt some version of Article 2A, but many lessors and lawyers will not study and adjust to the changes as quickly as they should. In most respects, the old law will govern leases formed before the new law is adopted. However, the new law will govern new leases and even some old leases that incorporate amendments to existing law. If one of your problem debts is a lease it will be well worth your time and effort to check whether your state's commercial code includes Article 2A.

USURY LAWS

States limit the interest rates that lenders and creditors can charge on some loans. They almost always place limits on consumer vehicle loans and retail installment sales contracts for furniture and appliances.

Often, however, there are no limits on mortgage loans or credit cards. Very few states limit interest rates for loans made for business purposes. Sometimes, state usury laws do not apply to federally chartered financial institutions.

Penalties for violating usury laws range from the loss of the usurious interest to severe criminal penalties. Creditors are careful not to violate usury laws by charging too high a rate of interest. Sometimes, though, they inadvertently violate the law by assessing additional loan charges, such as closing points, attorneys' fees, late payment charges and prepayment penalties.

section

FIVE

SPECIFIC KINDS OF DEBTS AND ASSETS

HANDLING SPECIFIC KINDS OF DEBTS

CHAPTER FOURTEEN

SECURED DEBTS

- Household Goods
- Mortgages
- Taxes
- Vehicle Loans

UNSECURED DEBTS

- Credit Cards
- Educational
- Guaranties
- Loans, general
- Medical
- Rent
- Store Charges
- Support Obligations
- Utility Bills

SECURED DEBTS

Secured debts are secured by collateral. If the debt isn't paid, the creditor can obtain possession of the collateral and sell it. The proceeds of the sale, after deducting related costs, are applied to the debt. If the proceeds aren't sufficient to pay off the debt, there is a "deficiency." In most cases, the creditor can pursue the consumer for the amount of the deficiency. Very rarely, creditors make "non-recourse" consumer loans that limit collection rights to the collateral. As you've already discovered, creditors must follow certain procedures when they repossess and sell collateral.

A creditor with collateral is in a stronger position than one without collateral. However, once the collateral is sold, or is basically worthless, or is protected by law, the creditor, in effect, is in no better a position than an unsecured creditor.

HOUSEHOLD GOODS

Debts secured by your household goods, such as furniture or appliances, usually result from the actual purchase of those goods. Any other debts that are secured by household goods are not very well secured. In many such cases, creditors are severely restricted from taking such items by one or more state laws. In almost all such cases, the creditor's security interest can be avoided through bankruptcy proceedings.

As a practical matter, household goods are very poor collateral. They rapidly depreciate and have little resale value. Household goods are portable. Even if a creditor knows where they are located, it generally cannot legally repossess household goods without your consent or a court order. Moreover, consumers often have good defenses to debts arising from these goods. Household goods sold on credit often have defects, are not properly delivered, or are improperly installed.

When creditors secure their debt with household goods, they commonly do so as a means to apply pressure to consumers, not as a real source of collection. Consumers who refuse to surrender this type of collateral leave creditors essentially unsecured. Once these creditors understand that they are essentially unsecured, they will gladly agree to extended payment plans and, if you have a reasonable grievance, even to a favorable settlement.

MORTGAGES

Mortgage lenders are in the strongest position of all creditors. Mortgage lenders generally are assured of collecting most, if not all, of their money. The mere threat of foreclosure gets your attention.

Mortgage foreclosure laws vary from state to state. Some states permit foreclosure proceedings that can be completed in just two or three months. Other states require that creditors first go to court which can take anywhere from six months to two years. Some states even permit private Uniform Commercial Code foreclosures of beneficial interest in land trusts. If your home is in such a land trust, read the discussion of the Uniform Commercial Code in Chapter 13.

Mortgage lenders, as a general rule, have to spend considerable time and money to foreclose on a house before selling it. They would rather get paid by you and usually will agree to at least one payment plan before beginning the foreclosure proceeding. If interest rates have fallen, many mortgage lenders will even renegotiate the terms of the loan, or direct you to another lender who will make a replacement mortgage loan.

Almost every state gives you the right to redeem your property before a foreclosure auction. Usually, you must pay the entire amount of the loan, but some states give consumers a one-time right to cure all delinquencies and reinstate the loan. Usually the time to cure is shorter than the time to redeem.

If your mortgage is guaranteed by a government agency, or made under a government program (such as the VA or FHA), you have a packet of additional rights. These additional rights include a grace period, at least one payment plan, and additional opportunities to cure defaults. The creditor almost always will inform you of these rights.

From time to time, federal, state, county and local governments also offer homeowner assistance programs. They are well worth looking into. For example, the federal government has an emergency assistance plan for homeowners who lose their jobs. The plan is administered by the Department of Housing and Urban Development, and can be a great help when it has available funds. Many states, counties, and municipalities have similar programs for the unemployed, elderly, sick, and working poor.

TAXES

Although taxes never start out as secured debts, if they remain unpaid long enough, they become secured.

REAL ESTATE TAXES Real estate taxes are secured by the property on which they are assessed. Sometimes, the owner of property can be held personally liable for unpaid taxes. Usually, real estate taxes have the highest priority of any debt secured by the property. Homeowners generally have at least one or two years before they lose their property for failure to pay real estate taxes. Loss of vacant and commercial property can take much less time.

Homeowners must be given clear notice before the property is lost because of non-payment of real estate taxes. However, even if real estate taxes are simply delinquent, they can become extremely expensive because it's not uncommon for consumers to pay 20%, and even 30%, interest on delinquent real estate taxes.

INCOME AND OTHER TAXES Generally, there is very little property that a tax collector cannot encumber, and eventually seize. The IRS has broader powers than any other creditor. State and local revenue departments have far less power than does the IRS, but they still have more than most private creditors. A primary limitation on such state revenue departments is that you can simply decide to move to another state. Most state tax collectors operate, more or less, in the same way as the IRS. Tax collection activity increases just before tax returns are due and slacken just before elections.

Assessment The tax collection process begins when you file a tax return. The tax return actually constitutes a self-assessment of a tax. If the tax collector realizes that you have not filed a required return, he can file the return on your behalf. Needless to say, a return filed for you by the tax collector is likely to show a much higher tax liability than a return filed by you.

Sometimes, the tax collector determines that you have not reported enough income. Then, you receive a notice of intent to assess additional taxes. You must file a timely objection, or the proposed tax is assessed. By filing a timely objection, a number of protective procedures take place.

Collection If the proposed additional taxes are not paid, you are sent a bill. If the bill is ignored or not paid, you usually, but not always, will be sent a second bill. Eventually, you will be sent a final notice threatening that enforcement action will be taken if the bill is not paid. You will have at least 30 days, and probably much longer, before enforcement action actually commences.

Up until this time, the IRS computer has done all of the work. It will continue its work by withholding any refunds that might otherwise be due to you. Your file will be assigned to a living and breathing collection officer located near where you live. If the computer has not already done so, the collection officer will record a tax lien that encumbers everything you own within the tax collector's jurisdiction.

Collection officers have no right to enter your private property without your consent or a court order. Most will try to set up a meeting with you. Usually, it is a good idea to agree to this meeting. However, if you are concerned about the ramifications or implications of disclosing something detrimental to the collection officer, get professional advice before attending any meeting.

At the meeting, the officer will ask you for a financial statement. This financial statement will be used to determine the proper method of collection, evaluate payment plans and compromises, and, if necessary, be used as a map for enforcement action. Remember, any financial statement you submit will be checked against your tax returns. Lying to an IRS agent is extremely risky because you can be charged criminally. If you refuse to provide a financial statement, you will not be able to enter into a payment plan or compromise. You can also expect the collection officer to give your case special attention.

If this meeting doesn't produce a solution, the IRS collection officer will send you a notice of levy, or some other collection action. If that does not work, the IRS will go after your bank account. Then the collection officer will start looking for other property with value that can be easily sold. Many tax collectors have a special fondness for cars and vans.

The IRS isn't supposed to seize and sell property unless there a good chance for a substantial recovery from that seizure after expenses are deducted. But, don't bet on it; they frequently seize property anyway. Even after property is seized, the IRS may release it - if you offer to pay at least as much as the IRS could recover by selling it. There are other ways to get seized property released, but they are rather technical, and rarely offer any better options for you.

Getting Rid of the Collection Officer There are several ways to get the collection officer off your back:

> Pay the taxes - but, if you had the money, you wouldn't have this problem.
>
> Wait until the collection officer seizes and sells enough property to pay the tax or gives up trying - this can take quite a while, especially if you remain in the same location.
>
> Enter into a payment plan - this will be based on your ability to pay and will be subject to review every two years.
>
> Enter into a compromise - this will be based on the total amount the officer thinks can be collected by liquidating all non-exempt property. Compromises are hard to negotiate if you are young and healthy.

> Convince the collection officer that you are a hardship case. Usually, this requires you to show that you are ill, disabled, or have a lot of dependents and a very low income. Or, convince the collection officer that the tax is uncollectible because you don't have any assets and you are unemployed or marginally employed.
>
> Don't get your hopes up. The tax collector probably will not release any tax liens that already have been recorded. These liens will remain effective for about ten years.

Collection officers have authority to cancel penalties if you can show reasonable cause for the failure that led to the penalty. Collection officers do not have authority to cancel any of the tax or interest owed. You have a right to appeal an officer's decision to a supervisor and, in some instances, even to higher authorities within the IRS.

If the IRS is giving you an unreasonably hard time, try calling the Problem Resolution Office. Don't be surprised if this doesn't solve your problems with the IRS, but it may gain you a little time.

VEHICLE LOANS

Most lenders specializing in motor vehicle loans are just plain tough. Most of the larger ones go by the book, but many of the smaller ones do not. All of them want their money, or the vehicle, or both. However, these lenders are vulnerable to consumer defenses, because most vehicles have something wrong with them.

With these lenders, prepare your defenses early and well. As soon as you get the vehicle, be sure to complain about all deficiencies. Keep a record of everything wrong and keep copies of all written complaints.

If the loan is otherwise uncollectible from you, the lender may be willing to forgive any deficiency, if you surrender the vehicle. However, you will lose your bargaining power if the lender finds and repossesses the vehicle.

> Don't leave the vehicle in your unlocked garage or in your driveway. Don't leave the car on the street or in an unattended parking lot near your house or workplace. Repo men will even try to grab the car while it's in your church parking lot. Even if you have to store the vehicle in a friend's garage and not use it for awhile, you still will have it as a bargaining chip.

If the lender does repossess the car, and later sues you for a deficiency, be sure to look into the foreclosure sale. If you did not get notice of the sale, you have a strong defense. Even if you did get notice, there is a good chance that the car was not sold in a commercially reasonable manner, giving you almost as good a defense. Pay especially close attention to the so-called costs of sale. Often, they are exaggerated or simply faked. If the car was repossessed without your consent, while it was on your property, you can counterclaim for trespass.

CHAPTER 14

UNSECURED DEBTS

Other than child support and alimony payments, unsecured debts are only urgent if they are owed to a creditor that has something you will need in the future. Otherwise, an unsecured non-governmental creditor has no weapons to use against you except to threaten a bad credit report or a lawsuit.

CREDIT CARDS

Credit card companies are among your least dangerous creditors. For emergency purposes, it's a good idea to try to keep one credit card in good standing. All others should be just about the last debts you worry about.

> Keep in mind, though, that credit card debt is VERY EXPENSIVE. Interest rate charges on general purpose credit cards average 18.8% per year.

Once they get their piece of plastic back in their hands, most credit card companies are quite amenable to payment plans and compromises. Unless you are foolish enough to give them a financial statement, they know very little about you. Often, they don't even know whether you are still employed.

In order to enforce collection, credit card companies have to use a local collection attorney and hope you aren't judgment-proof. Often, they don't even bother to pursue collection. You are in a good position to vigorously negotiate with these creditors, and almost always will have another chance to negotiate with the collection attorney who gets your file.

EDUCATIONAL

Most educational debts are either unpaid tuition owed directly to a school or government-guaranteed loans. Don't be embarrassed to tell a school you need financial help; a lot of people do. Most not-for-profit schools will bend over backwards to help consumers work out tuition bills. Even some of the more respectable for-profit trade schools often will help out. Many schools can arrange for deferred payment plans, partial scholarships, and part-time jobs for students.

Under federal law, disabled, and otherwise impaired students, are entitled to be educated. If a local school is not able to provide the needed educational resources, it must provide the funds to obtain them elsewhere. Almost every government educational loan program offers the consumer many rights, including grace periods and reduced payments. Even after those benefits are exhausted, there are so many delinquent loans that it usually takes years before collection activity is taken against you.

Federal law, and many states, now enable government funded or guaranteed educational loan programs to confiscate your tax refunds. Keep in mind that most government educational loan programs depend on repayments to make future loans. Loans that aren't repaid deprive other students of the chance to get an education.

GUARANTIES

A guarantor, or "surety," guaranties the performance of an obligation owed by someone else, such as a borrower. For example, a father guaranties a car loan made to his child. If the child defaults, the creditor can call upon the father to pay the loan. A creditor requires a guaranty because it thinks there is a good chance the borrower will default, so guarantying a debt is always risky.

Although guaranties can themselves be secured by collateral, most guaranties are not. There are different kinds of guaranties:

> The most common is an unconditional, full guaranty, where the surety is primarily liable for the debt, just as though he had borrowed the money himself. A co-signer, who is not the borrower, is such a guarantor.
>
> There also are conditional guaranties, where the surety is not liable unless some specified event occurs, most commonly a default by the borrower.
>
> There also are limited guaranties, where the sureties' obligation cannot exceed a specified dollar amount or percentage of the loan.
>
> Finally, there is a guaranty of collectability, where the surety is not liable until the creditor has exhausted all other legal means to collect from the borrower. Of course, this is the best kind of guaranty to give, but few lenders will take it.

The law recognizes an important distinction between "gratuitous guaranties" and "guaranties given for consideration." Gratuitous guaranties are given without payment to the guarantor. Guaranties given for consideration are given in return for some sort of financial gain to the guarantor. A father who guaranties his son's car loan is a gratuitous surety. A business owner who guarantees a bank loan to his company is giving a guarantee for personal financial gain. The law will release a gratuitous guarantor much more readily than it will a guarantor who stands to personally gain from the loan being guarantied.

Guarantors have all of the protections provided to borrowers under the Uniform Commercial Code (see Chapter 13). Although creditors have the right to give priority to their own legitimate interests, they can't just ignore the guarantor's interests. Creditors often make mistakes that have the legal result of releasing a guarantor, but few consumers have enough knowledge to recognize when such a mistake has been made. These mistakes often involve a failure of the creditor to take REASONABLE steps to protect the guarantor. Sometimes, creditors are even foolish enough to damage the guarantor's interests.

The most common mistake made by creditors consists of INCREASING THE GUARANTOR'S RISK without first obtaining the guarantor's consent. This type of mistake often occurs when a consumer guaranties a debt that is secured by collateral. When the surety gives the guaranty, he assumes that the creditor can collect from the collateral. Releasing the collateral will increase the risk that the guarantor will have to put up money if the borrower defaults. If the collateral is worth enough, and the creditor releases it without the surety's consent, this may relieve the surety from all or some of his obligations under the guaranty. Creditors often make a similar error by taking no action to collect from a defaulting borrower, then years later turning to the guarantor for payment.

> As a rule of thumb, if you have any reason to believe that a creditor mishandled a loan or otherwise did not protect your interests as a surety, it is worth consulting with a lawyer to see if you have a viable defense to your guaranty.

LOANS, GENERAL

Unsecured loans are not especially pressing debts. There is little, or nothing, the creditor can do without first filing a lawsuit. However, commercial lenders are more likely than other creditors to go to court. Consumers rarely have viable legal defenses to simple unsecured loans because there are few opportunities for the lender to make a mistake. If there is a defense, it will likely arise from a violation of the Truth in Lending Act or your state's usury statute (see Chapter 13). Judgments against defaulting borrowers almost always can be obtained with a simple motion and without a trial (see the discussion of lawsuits in Chapter 10).

MEDICAL

Medical bills are important if you still need medical services and cannot get them elsewhere. If you no longer need a particular medical service, the bill is no more pressing than any other. Most medical providers will agree to reasonable payment plans.

There are many sources of help to pay medical expenses or provide medical services, including Medicaid, Medicare, school districts that sometimes offer certain types of care for impaired students, Veterans Administration, charitable foundations, and not-for-profit hospitals that are legally obligated to provide certain amounts of free care.

RENT

Unless you are prepared to move, rent is a critical debt. In most states, the landlord has to serve you with a "notice and demand" to bring your rent current before going to court to have you evicted. Usually, it will take a landlord at least 30 to 60 days to get you evicted. In many regions, courts and sheriffs will refuse to evict people during cold weather.

Even if you are behind in your rent, the law almost always prohibits landlords from locking you out of your home without a court order. If the landlord does try to lock you out, and you have a lease, you probably are within your rights to break the lock, re-enter, and sue the landlord.

Landlords sometimes try to hold your belongings as security for back rent. The law permits landlords to hold a tenant's property, but the landlord must immediately go to court and follow certain technical procedures. Landlords rarely do this, and lawyers almost always advise against doing this with consumer tenants. If a landlord tries to hold your property, and you do not shortly receive a court summons, you probably can successfully sue the landlord for the value of your property.

STORE CHARGES

Retail creditors are not much better off than credit-card companies. Unless you have no other place to shop, a debt to a retailer should be given very low priority. Many retailers won't even pursue collection of small accounts and will continue to do business with you on a cash basis. If you have expressed a legitimate complaint, most retailers will be very reluctant to sue. However, interest on retail debts often is even higher than on general purpose credit cards.

It's always worth asking a retailer if it will forgive the debt if you return the merchandise. Many retailers will agree, if the merchandise is returned in its original packaging. Make sure any such agreement is set forth in writing. If you are concerned that the retailer will be reluctant to sign a formal paper, at least make sure that the returned merchandise is accompanied by a letter setting forth the agreement. (See the discussion of settlements in Chapter 12.)

SUPPORT OBLIGATIONS

Obligations to pay child support, and to some extent alimony, are important and pressing debts. They arise from a court order, can be enforced in many different ways in every state, and are being enforced with increasing vigor by a growing number of government agencies. These obligations are not dischargeable in any bankruptcy proceedings.

If you are financially unable to make child support or alimony payments, or you believe the payments are unfairly high, go back to court and try to have the obligation modified. If you can make the payments and, for whatever reason, refuse, you have the choice between fleeing or facing numerous unpleasant experiences, such as being cited for contempt of court and having your paychecks and tax refunds grabbed by some governmental agency.

UTILITY BILLS

Utility bills are among the most important bills you have because you need their services. However, most states require utilities to offer payment plans to consumers. In some states, there are assistance programs for the elderly and those with low income. In others, utilities cannot be disconnected during cold weather.

Even if you are planning on filing for relief under Chapter 7 of the Bankruptcy Code, you may want to pay your utility bills. It may take less cash to pay the bill than to come up with the security deposit a utility may demand after its debt is discharged in bankruptcy.

PROTECTING SPECIFIC ASSETS

CHAPTER FIFTEEN

- Businesses
- Income
- Household Goods
- Insurance
- Motor Vehicles
- Personal Effects
- Real Estate
- Retirement Funds
- Savings and Checking Accounts
- Stocks and Other Securities

BUSINESSES

Corporations and partnerships are hated by consumer creditors because, if properly organized, these creditors cannot reach your business assets. Creditors love proprietorships because, legally, they are one and the same as its owners. All assets and income of proprietorships belong to the owners and can be reached by creditors.

If your business is a corporation, you have followed the proper formalities, and you have dealt with the corporation as a separate entity from yourself, then its assets and income belong to the corporation, not to you. Your only interests in those assets are indirect - as a shareholder and, probably, also as a creditor of the corporation. Your personal creditors cannot directly reach the assets or income of the corporation. Your creditors can only reach your shares of stock and rights as a creditor, if you are one.

If you are the only shareholder of a corporation, a creditor can eventually reach the assets and income of the corporation through your stock. Otherwise, your personal creditors' ability to reach the income and assets of the corporation depends on how much of the stock you own, and how your rights as a shareholder are defined. Such rights can be limited in many ways that will render the stock almost worthless to a creditor.

If your business is a general partnership, your personal creditors can reach your share of partnership assets and income, unless there is a written partnership agreement that limits your partnership rights. A partner's rights can be limited in many ways that render the partnership interest almost worthless to a creditor.

If your business is a limited partnership, and you are a general partner, you are in a the same position as you would be if the business were a general partnership. If you are a limited partner, your personal creditors will not be able to reach the income or assets of the partnership. Moreover, a limited partner's rights can be limited in many ways that will render the limited partnership interest almost worthless to a creditor.

> A KEY TO PROTECTING YOUR BUSINESS ASSETS AND INCOME IS HAVING ONE OR MORE CO-OWNERS WHO ARE NOT LIABLE TO YOUR PERSONAL CREDITORS.

Merely forming a corporation or partnership isn't particularly difficult. However, properly protecting your interests from your creditors AND co-owners requires both knowledge and planning (see the discussion of Legal Entities in Chapter 12).

> If you already have a business, or if you want to start a business, invest in a good lawyer. If you act early enough, your business assets and income can be fully protected from creditors.

INCOME

If you are employed, your creditors may be able to seize up to 25% of your take-home earnings. The IRS can take more, but avoids doing so. Some portion of any child support and alimony payments often can be reached by creditors. In some states, creditors even can reach a portion of your unemployment, workman's compensation, and public assistance payments. Social Security payments and federal retirement benefits cannot be taken by creditors. In most states, creditors cannot take distributions from spendthrift trusts established by someone else, unless the debt is for child support or alimony. Creditors cannot take payments from qualified ERISA plans but many states do not adequately protect other retirement and benefit plans. Creditors also can reach annuities you have purchased from insurance companies.

Creditors usually can take protected or exempt income, if they grab it AFTER it has been paid to you and BEFORE you spend it. You may be able to arrange additional protection for your earnings by granting a wage assignment to an essential or friendly creditor (see Chapter 12).

HOUSEHOLD GOODS

Almost every state protects a portion of your household goods from creditors. Moreover, household goods usually have little or no resale value. Creditors rarely go after household goods. Most household goods, even family heirlooms, have much less resale value than you think.

If you have antiques, silver, collections, or other identifiable personal property that are especially valuable, take measures to protect them from creditors. Property such as this is easy for you to sell or move out of state. Remember, though, that you must act to protect this property before you are served with a citation summons. Once served, you're prohibited from selling or moving your property for the purpose of evading payment to judgment creditors.

INSURANCE

Insurance policies that don't have cash value (usually term insurance) are worthless to creditors, unless and until there is a loss that pays off. Almost every state protects at least one life insurance policy and some of its cash value from creditors. Some states protect only policies that name at least one of your dependents as a beneficiary. If your state does not provide enough protection for your life insurance policies, and you can't cash them in, consider assigning the policy as collateral for a friendly or essential debt.

Most states protect a portion of the insurance proceeds payable to a consumer on account of someone else's death. Some states only protect the proceeds if the consumer was a dependent of the person who died. Generally, it's a good idea to make sure that you are not named as a beneficiary of any policy. If you are named as a beneficiary, the policy should be changed to name either someone else or a spendthrift trust, which includes you as a beneficiary of the trust, but not as a trustee.

If a creditor has a judgment against you, have all medical insurance benefits paid directly to the medical provider. The easiest way to do this is to give the provider an assignment of benefits and let the provider process the insurance claim. If the payments go through your hands, the creditor may try to grab them before you can pay the medical provider.

MOTOR VEHICLES

Most consumers buy their cars on credit, and the cars are rarely worth much more than is owed to the finance company. If you do own a motor vehicle that has equity, part of it is probably protected by a state exemption. Some courts have held that certain vehicles can be protected by exemptions covering equipment needed for a trade or occupation. Often, these trade and occupation exemptions are more generous than the motor vehicle exemptions.

If your equity in your vehicle is considerable, creditors may try to go after it. If it is financed, there is little you can do, other than make it hard for your creditors to find the vehicle. Refrain from any maintenance that enhances the vehicle's value. If the vehicle isn't financed, consider selling it to a friend and leasing it back.

Regardless of how much equity you have in a vehicle, never drive it to a citation examination. Creditors sometimes try to seize them, just to put pressure on you.

PERSONAL EFFECTS

Personal effects are partially protected by exemption and rarely are worth enough for a creditor to pursue. Most personal effects, even jewelry, have much less resale value than their owners believe. However, at a citation examination, limit your jewelry to a simple wedding band and inexpensive wristwatch. Even if the creditor does not try to take expensive jewelry during such an examination, it will prompt the creditor to investigate more thoroughly.

If you do have jewelry, furs, or other personal effects that are especially valuable and likely to interest a creditor, take measures to protect any of it that cannot be exempted. Property such as this is easy to sell or move out of the state. Remember, though, that you must act to protect the property before you are served with a citation summons that prohibits you from selling or moving your property.

REAL ESTATE

The vulnerability of real estate to unsecured creditors depends on:

The value of your equity > If there is no equity, the property is of no value to unsecured creditors. The more you owe on mortgages, the lower your equity. Often, the best way to protect real estate is to borrow as much as you possibly can against it.

Whether it's your primary residence > Your home is given much greater protection than investment and vacation property.

Whether there are any co-owners > If there are co-owners who have no liability to your creditors, their interests in the property make it more difficult for creditors.

Where the property is located > A judgment obtained in one state generally cannot be enforced against real estate in a second state, unless the judgment is registered and enforced through courts in the second state.

Whether you are in a proceeding under the Bankruptcy Code > Property located anywhere in the country can easily be sold in bankruptcy proceedings, even if there are co-owners.

RESIDENCE

In certain states, no one, other than the lender who provided the purchase price, can touch your home. In other states, you are granted a "homestead exemption" that protects some of your equity in your primary residence. In yet other states, homestead exemptions are not effective against creditors who obtained judgments before the consumer purchased the home. In a few states, homestead exemptions are effective only against claims for debts incurred after you purchased the home.

Generally, you can claim a homestead exemption only for your primary residence. Some states provide a separate homestead exemption for each adult resident who has an ownership interest in the home. In most states, it's easy for a creditor to place a lien on your interest in your home, but it's difficult for the creditor to force the sale of a home that is co-owned by a person who isn't liable to the creditor.

INVESTMENT PROPERTY

Investment and vacation property usually are not protected by any exemptions, except possibly a small catch-all exemption. If you have equity in such property, measures should be taken to protect your interests. If it isn't practical to sell your interests, then borrow against them and spend the loan proceeds, or convert the proceeds into exempt property.

FORMS OF OWNERSHIP

There are several different ways to own real estate:

"**Fee simple**" If you are the only owner, and the property is in your name, there is nothing to protect the property from your creditors, except for prior liens and any homestead exemption your state provides.

"**Tenancy by the Entirety**" Some states allow spouses to own their residences in "tenancy by the entirety." Generally, such property cannot be reached by a judgment creditor, unless both spouses are liable to the creditor. However, if the non-liable spouse dies, the ownership of the entire property shifts to the surviving spouse, and the creditor may then be able to reach the property.

"**Joint Tenancy**" Most states permit any property to be held in "joint tenancy," by any number of persons. Most homes are owned in joint tenancy with "rights of survivorship." If the non-liable owner dies, the creditor may be able to reach the property. On the other hand, if the owner who is liable to the creditor dies, the surviving joint tenants will own the property clear of creditor claims against the deceased.

It's difficult for a judgment creditor to force the sale of a house that is owned in joint tenancy, unless all of the owners are liable to the creditor. However, if it's worth it to the creditor to spend a lot of time and money, and risk owning an unusable interest in some jointly owned property, a creditor may be able to reach the property.

It's easy for a judgment creditor to place a lien on a consumer's joint tenancy interests. Even if the creditor cannot force the sale of the property, the lien will prevent the consumer from selling his interests in the property without paying the creditor.

"**Tenancy in Common**" Property is owned in "tenancy in common," is owned by two or more persons with no special rights other than as co-owners. The property is extremely vulnerable to any owner's judgment creditors. Generally, it's easier to get a court to partition and sell property owned in tenancy in common.

"**Beneficial Interests in Land Trusts**" Many states now permit title to real estate to be held in a land trust. Usually, the trustee is a bank, or similar institution, and does absolutely nothing but collect an annual fee. The real owners are "beneficiaries" of the trust who also hold power of direction. Land trusts can be very flexible, and useful, tools for holding and transferring ownership. Creditors cannot encumber the property by simply recording a judgment lien. However, some courts have held that the homestead exemption does not protect property held in a land trust.

To reach the property held in a land trust, a judgment creditor has to have the court attach the consumer's beneficial interest and sell it at auction. If there are other beneficiaries who are not liable to the creditor, the consumer's beneficial interest will not be worth much. Even if the creditor buys the consumer's interest, there may not be much the creditor can do with it. Depending on the laws of the state, and the terms of the land trust, the creditor is likely to have considerable difficulty forcing partition and sale of the property itself. However, if all the beneficiaries have given assignments of beneficial interest to a creditor, the property is extremely vulnerable to that creditor (see the discussion of the Uniform Commercial Code in Chapter 12).

"**Active Trusts**" Every state permits property to be owned in a trust actively managed by a trustee, pursuant to a trust agreement. If a trust is carefully created, and the agreement is thoughtfully drafted, almost any property can be protected from a creditor. However, almost no trust will be effective if it's funded through a "fraudulent transfer."

It's extremely difficult to form a trust that will protect property from creditors without the assistance of an experienced lawyer. Most "estate planners" do not have sufficient experience with trusts to provide adequate asset protection.

"**Community Property**" Several states provide that property acquired by spouses during their marriage is owned as "community property." Community property is a very complicated concept and the law varies a lot from state to state. Basically, though, community property can be reached by the creditors of one spouse if the other spouse authorized the expenditure or if the expenditure was for necessities. In order to protect community property from the creditors of one spouse, it is important for the other spouse to let potential creditors know in advance that expenditures will not be authorized. If you are concerned about community property, you need to consult a lawyer who is familiar with the laws of your state.

RETIREMENT FUNDS

Other than qualified ERISA plans, which are protected by federal law, private retirement funds often are not adequately protected from creditors. Even ERISA plans are vulnerable, if a consumer seeks relief under the Bankruptcy Code.

Even if you have to pay an early withdrawal tax penalty, take measures to protect all of your vulnerable retirement funds. If you cannot convert them into exempt assets, turn them into cash and spend the money. Getting the use of most of the funds is better than losing all of your funds to a creditor. Moreover, you probably will face the same early withdrawal penalty if your creditor grabs the funds.

SAVINGS AND CHECKING ACCOUNTS

Savings and checking accounts are the most vulnerable property you have. Even though a small portion usually is exempted, the entire account gets frozen. Make sure that your creditors do not know where you bank. Even better, try not to keep any accounts in your own name or social security number. Do not have funds in any account in your name, social security number, or under your control when you appear for a citation examination.

STOCKS AND OTHER SECURITIES

If you own publicly traded stock, bonds or other securities, they are almost as vulnerable as savings and checking accounts. If your investment is in a small or closely held company, then the value to a creditor will depend on your investment rights (see the discussion of Legal Entities in Chapter 12).

If you own valuable stocks, bonds, or other securities that may be of interest to a creditor, take measures to protect them. If, for some reason you cannot sell them, consider pledging them to secure an essential debt to a friendly creditor.

section SIX

HANDLING YOUR MONEY

CHECKING ACCOUNTS AND CHECKS

CHAPTER SIXTEEN

Checking accounts are a great convenience, but they're not essential.

GENERAL

Checking accounts get almost as many people into trouble as do credit cards. Many people have trouble thinking of checks as real money.

Never write checks in anticipation of depositing money. First deposit the money, and then write your checks. If there is any real chance that a check you deposit will bounce, do not count on it being good. Wait until it clears because, if it doesn't clear, you'll find your checks bouncing all over town. Your creditors are going to blame you, not the person who gave you a rubber check.

Most banks run a credit check before they allow a consumer to open an account. If you expect to have financial trouble in the near future, or plan to seek relief under the Bankruptcy Code, open a contingency account immediately. Don't keep very much money in that account unless you're sure your creditors won't learn about it. Do not pay creditors with checks drawn on that account, or with money orders or cashier's checks from that bank. But, if your social security number is on an account, the IRS can always find it through its computer tracking capability.

Jointly held accounts don't offer much protection from your creditors and can put other people's money at risk. However, you can be added as an authorized additional signer to someone else's bank account. Keep in mind, though, savvy collection lawyers ask if you have signature rights on any accounts. If you seek relief under the Bankruptcy Code, you have to disclose all accounts in which you have signature rights, or have had them at any time during the prior year.

Chapter 16

BAD CHECKS

ISSUING BAD CHECKS

JUST ABOUT THE WORST WAY TO HANDLE A DEBT IS TO ISSUE A CHECK WITHOUT HAVING SUFFICIENT FUNDS IN THE ACCOUNT.

A bad check gives a creditor enormous power over you. It's a crime to intentionally issue a bad check. Many creditors use bad checks as a way to get local police and prosecutors to serve as their collection agents. Creditors also have the right to recover costs, damages, and even attorneys' fees if they have to sue to collect on a bad check. Banks also charge a hefty fee for every bad check, and if you issue enough of them, the bank will close your account.

It's more dangerous to give a bad check in direct exchange for something of value than to use a bad check to pay an already existing debt. When someone gives up something in direct exchange for a check, he is relying on the check being good. Giving a bad check to that person is the same as lying. But, when a creditor receives a check in payment of an old debt, the creditor is not relying on the check and will not be any worse off if the check bounces.

Post-dated checks that bounce are not so bad, if you can prove two things. First, the creditor knew that the check wasn't good when it was received and second, that the creditor was aware that there was a possibility that sufficient funds wouldn't be deposited before the date of the check. A frequent problem with post-dated checks is that creditors deposit them before the agreed date. If you must give a post-dated check, near the date on the face of the check clearly write the words "POST-DATED".

If you do inadvertently bounce a check or two, don't be frightened into believing you are going directly to jail. It's very difficult to prove that someone intentionally issued a bad check, because the person can claim that he intended to make a deposit, made a computational error, forgot to enter a check, used the wrong account, or any number of other legitimate explanations. It is hard to establish intent, even when a person bounces several checks at the same time, because the same explanations can be used.

However, police and prosecutors may become very interested when creditors complain about bad checks issued at different times by the same consumer. A pattern of issuing bad checks over time can, itself, suggest criminal intent.

KITING CHECKS

"Kiting" checks is a scam that many people and companies have used. Kiting checks is criminal. It's done by opening several checking accounts, preferably in different cities or states. Bad checks from one account are covered with bad checks from another account, for as many accounts as possible. Eventually, though, the checks have to be covered or the banks get stung and start investigating. There is no legitimate explanation for kiting checks. Don't do it, unless you are prepared to face the criminal consequences.

GETTING BAD CHECKS

Sometimes consumers who have been given a check use that actual check to pay another person. This is done by writing "pay to the order of..." and signing the back of the check. When you do this, you become responsible for the check, as if you wrote it yourself. So, whenever possible, above your signature write the words "without recourse." This relieves you of responsibility if the check bounces. However, your bank won't let you do this with checks you deposit into your own account.

If you are given a bad check, don't just give up. Some of them can be collected, even if the person who issued the check doesn't have any money. Important, but little known, provisions of the Uniform Commercial Code and Federal Reserve Board require a bank to either pay or "dishonor" a check within ONE banking day after it is received. If this rule is violated, the bank is liable for honoring the check, even if the person who issued the check does not have enough money to cover it.

This rule applies to the bank on which the check is drawn; that is, the bank with its name printed on the check, not the bank that collects the check for the receiver of the check. If it seems that it took a long time before a bad check is returned to you, consider the possibility that the check was held too long.

Usually, the biggest problem for a consumer is to determine exactly how long the check was held by the bank, before it was dishonored. Sometimes, you can track a check by examining the date stamps on the back. If not, then -

> estimate the amount of time by counting the days between the date of deposit and the date of return; and
>
> subtract the maximum number of days your bank claims that it needs to process such a check.

If it appears that the dishonored check was held too long, ask your bank to submit a "protest" of the dishonor. The Federal Reserve System then collects the amount of the check for you. If your bank refuses to file a protest, call the nearest Federal Reserve office and ask for guidance.

WORKING WITH CASH

CHAPTER SEVENTEEN

Cash can be your best means of survival.

Cash is portable, easy to use, and very hard for a creditor to find. It isn't as hard to live on a cash basis as we have been taught to believe.

Bills can be paid with cashier's checks or money orders. If a bank account is crucial, it can be established in the name of a simple trust or small corporation that has its own tax identification number. Credit cards can be obtained in the name of a corporation and, if necessary, guaranteed by an individual.

Millions of Americans deal only in cash. Some of them use cash to evade income taxes, or hide other criminal activity. A large number of decent and honest people are forced to live with cash, for reasons beyond their control, or because they made a mistake that creditors won't forgive. For example:

> small businessmen who couldn't pay employee withholding taxes and are unable to settle with the IRS for a manageable amount;
>
> former students burdened by government-guaranteed education loans that can't be paid because they can't make a decent living;
>
> people who would lose government benefits, if they disclosed their marginal earnings; and
>
> immigrants who can't obtain valid "green cards."

There isn't anything illegal or immoral about dealing in cash. You aren't under any legal or moral obligation to make it easy for your creditors to find your money. There are, though, two important legal restrictions on the use of cash:

First, there are a number of laws that prohibit intentional concealment of assets from creditors, especially the IRS > If you owe money to a creditor, do not sell your property and hide the cash proceeds. Apart from being illegal, concealing large amounts of cash usually means that you don't need the money to live, and have no reasonable basis for withholding payment from legitimate creditors.

In contrast, you aren't concealing assets if you sell your property and spend the proceeds. The key difference between legitimately using cash and imporperly concealing cash is that, with the former, you no longer have the cash. As a practical matter, it's extremely expensive, time consuming, and difficult for a creditor to find cash and prove it was deliberately hidden by a particular person. Unless there are very large amounts of money involved, very few creditors, and almost no government agencies, are anxious to try to enforce these laws.

Second, perjury is illegal > Testimony given under oath requires that you give truthful answers. Failure to do so is called perjury, and is a crime. Unless you have sought formal bankruptcy relief, or have made an assignment for the benefit of creditors, you don't have to volunteer any information, including your cash balance. If you're under oath, answer honestly when asked a proper question. Testifying under oath and perjury are discussed in Chapter 22 in greater detail.

If you anticipate having financial difficulties, follow these precautions:

Open an account at a new bank where you've never done business.

Don't maintain an account at any bank that is also a creditor of yours. If you don't pay the bank, it will grab all the money in your accounts and pay itself.

Never send the IRS or any other creditor a check, cashier's check, or money order drawn on bank where you, or any member of your family, has an account.

By taking these simple precautions, your cash should be pretty well protected from seizure by creditors, including the IRS. But these precautions should be taken before a judgment creditors serves you with a citation summons and before the IRS sends you notice that it's going to commence collection activity. Your bank account is the first asset a judgment creditor will try to grab. As soon as the bank is served, your funds will, at the very least, be frozen. These funds may end up being paid to your creditor.

If a judgment creditor or the IRS is about to pursue your assets, you will find it helpful to follow a few additional precautions:

Do not deposit more money than you will IMMEDIATELY spend in any bank account under your name or social security number. You may find it less expensive to pay a currency exchange to cash your paycheck than to lose your money to a creditor who seizes of you bank account.

Don't allow anyone to keep a keep a savings, checking, money market, or trading account with you named as a joint tenant, trustee, or as custodian for a child. It could be difficult to prove the money really isn't yours.

Even if the money isn't yours, avoid personally depositing large amounts in an account owned by a member of your family. Someone may conclude the money is yours.

DEBT PAYMENTS REFINANCING AND DEBT CONSOLIDATIONS

CHAPTER EIGHTEEN

MAKING PAYMENTS

Making payments to creditors is a skill that requires thought and practice. If your debts are too high, simply writing checks, as the bills arrive, doesn't do you any good. You have to think about:

WHO TO PAY

WHEN TO PAY

HOW MUCH TO PAY

HOW TO PAY

WHO TO PAY

If you can't pay all your creditors in full, you have to select which creditors to pay in full, which to pay in part, and which not to pay at all. These choices are based on your particular circumstances, but here are a few guidelines that may help.

Don't give undue importance to your credit history > Don't worry about your credit history, if it's already bad. Taking proper steps to put your finances back in order will be the best way to restore your credit history.

Don't pay creditors who pose no immediate threat to you > Pay only those creditors who can damage you. Hoard any remaining cash. You will need it to live on, pay an attorney, or settle with one or more creditors.

Pay secured creditors before unsecured creditors > If you don't want to lose the collateral that is securing a loan, pay that secured creditor before you pay unsecured creditors. If you don't care about the collateral, think of the secured creditor as if it were unsecured.

Try not to make promises, but try to keep any you do make > If you make a specific promise to make a payment, try to keep it. Your credibility is more important now than ever.

Don't run up unnecessary late fees > If you have two creditors who impose late fees, and one debt is already overdue, pay the debt that is not overdue.

Watch for older bills > Be sensitive to creditor impatience. As a debt grows to more than 60 days overdue, it becomes an increasingly likely candidate for collection activity. If a debt is growing old, it may be useful to send some sort of a payment, even if it is not a full payment. It will show an effort to pay and may delay collection activity.

Don't pay a creditor just because it is making more noise than other creditors > Often, the creditors that make the most noise are your least important creditors, and can do the least to hurt you. Moreover, you can take steps to prevent almost any creditor from harassing you.

If you are planning a Chapter 7 liquidation, don't pay any dischargeable debts.

If you are planning to move out of the area, don't pay unsecured local creditors.

WHEN TO PAY

Pay as late as you possibly can, without breaking a promise or incurring a late charge. Payments by mail should be sent far enough in advance to make sure they get there on time. If you can, make sure that every creditor receives some payment at least once every two months.

HOW MUCH TO PAY

Of course, pay as little as possible. But if a debt is current, especially a secured debt, try to keep it current by making full payments. If a debt is already overdue, and it's not especially important or pressing, send the smallest amount you estimate will keep the creditor from taking action to collect.

HOW TO PAY

You do not want your creditors to know where you are banking. Use cashier checks or money orders from some other bank or a currency exchange. If you have moved, do not show your new address on the payment or on the envelope.

If you are delinquent, and you have agreed to pay interest on the debt, first direct application of the payment to the principal, then the interest, and then late charges. This reduces the amount of interest that will accrue. This directed payment is accomplished by writing on the back of the check, "APPLY FIRST TO PRINCIPAL, THEN TO INTEREST, AND THEN TO LATE CHARGES". If the debt already has been turned over for collection, and the creditor has the right to recover collection costs, write "APPLY FIRST TO PRINCIPAL, THEN TO COLLECTION COSTS, THEN TO INTEREST, AND THEN TO LATE CHARGES".

If the debt is to a credit-card company, send such directed payments to an address other than the address where you usually send your payments. If you have to send a directed payment to the usual address, paper clip the check to a slip of paper that repeats the directions. Make a photocopy of the two clipped together. You want to prevent the creditor from successfully arguing that the direction was ineffective because the check was automatically processed.

If you have signed an agreement authorizing the creditor to apply payments in its discretion, the creditor will have the right to return the payment without cashing it. However, if the creditor accepts the payment, the creditor must apply it in accordance with your directions.

The IRS always honors the taxpayer's directions, but will not accept directed payments if you have agreed to an installment payment plan. When making directed payments to the IRS, write on the back of the check: "APPLY FIRST TO PRINCIPAL TAX, THEN TO INTEREST, AND THEN TO PENALTIES".

REFINANCING

Never borrow new money to pay old debts, unless the borrowing is to obtain something essential, such as medical care, or unless the borrowing will provide a comprehensive and lasting solution to your financial problems. Borrowing new money to pay old creditors is particularly dangerous if the new payments will be as high as, or higher than, your current actual payments.

> The new creditor always demands interest, whereas some of the old creditors may not be entitled to interest.
>
> The new creditor may require collateral, while many of the old creditors were unsecured.
>
> The new creditor may be owed enough to pursue collection, whereas some of the old creditors may simply write-off the debt.

Be especially careful about borrowing from lenders who specialize in junior mortgages or "home equity" financing. Traditionally, loans secured by junior mortgages have been less risky than loans secured by first mortgages. Nevertheless, junior mortgage lenders charge higher interest rates, and frequently exploit the financial problems of responsible consumers.

> NEVER borrow from a lender who insists that you place your home in a land trust and grant it an assignment of the beneficial interest. The lender is trying to deprive you of the protection given by your state's mortgage foreclosure laws. At the first opportunity, such a lender will try to grab your home.

Many so-called experts suggest borrowing from family or friends. This may appears to be an easy solution, and the interest rate usually is low. However, this can lead to even bigger problems. Frequently, borrowing the money doesn't solve your financial problems, and it ends up dragging your family and friends down with you. Apart from the guilt you'll feel, you no longer have anyone on whom to fall back.

> It is NOT prudent to borrow money from family or friends to pay creditors. Reserve the resources and good will of family and friends for times when you need help to pay your vital and necessary living expenses.

Family and friends would rather help feed, house, and clothe you than contribute to a creditor's upscale lifestyle. For the same reasons, it's rarely a good idea to ask family or friends to co-sign or guaranty a loan.

Some people turn to their neighborhood loan shark. Don't - no creditor is worth that kind of trouble.

CONSOLIDATIONS

A debt consolidation lumps a bunch of separate debts into one debt. There are two ways to consolidate debt payments. You can do it through a debt consolidation loan or through a debt payment service.

DEBT CONSOLIDATION LOANS

You can consolidate your debts, and debt payments, by borrowing enough money to pay some, or all, of your creditors. This is the same as refinancing, but lenders that specialize in "debt consolidation loans" usually charge high interest rates that are disguised behind low monthly payments that go on, it seems, forever. Before you borrow to consolidate your debts, consider three things:

How your cash flow will be affected > If you cannot make the payments on the new loan, your problems will not be solved and you will be in a worse position. Don't fool yourself into believing that you can make the new monthly payment just because it is less than the old monthly payments you were supposed to be making. You weren't able to make those payments, either.

Whether a consolidation loan will cost more or less > If most of your debt comes from credit-cards, or lenders that charge comparably high interest rates, a debt consolidation loan actually may save you money. If most of your debt comes from creditors who charge relatively low interest rates, or no interest at all, then in the long run, a debt consolidation loan will cost you a lot more money. The only way to find out whether a consolidation loan will cost you money or save you money is to examine the specific numbers.

If you have to provide collateral for the consolidation loan, will you be at a greater risk of losing property that you value and care about > If you have to give the consolidation lender a lien on property that your existing creditors cannot reach and you end up defaulting on the consolidation loan, you stand to lose less now than later. In this instance, the consolidation loan significantly increases your downside risk.

DEBT PAYMENT SERVICES

There are many companies and not-for-profit organizations that handle and pay your debts for you. You pay them, and they, in turn, pay your creditors. Often, these services also negotiate payment plans with creditors. Be wary of these companies because many are scams.

But reputable, not-for-profit, organizations can be very helpful. They may charge nothing, or a small fee. Sometimes, they try to fund themselves by convincing creditors to contribute a portion of the amounts paid to them. If your financial problems can be solved simply by good cash management, budgeting, and communications with creditors, these organizations can provide exactly what you need, while relieving you of stress.

> These organizations have to maintain good relationships and credibility with creditors. This means they are not free to be as aggressive as you can be.

The businesses that offer these services range from highly professional to charlatans who do not perform as promised. They can sit on your money for a long time before forwarding it to creditors or just plain steal it. Many of these companies charge high fees that only make your problems worse.

> BE EXTREMELY CAREFUL ABOUT GIVING YOUR MONEY TO ANYONE, EVEN A *BONA-FIDE* NOT-FOR-PROFIT ORGANIZATION.

Determine precisely what assurances they can give you that your money will be promptly forwarded to your creditors. If all they say is "trust me," DON'T. Many financial consultants, accountants, lawyers, and officials of charitable organizations have stolen money entrusted to them. Demand to see evidence of a surety or fidelity bond. Make sure the bond is large enough to cover all the consumers whose money may be stolen. A bond for $1,000 will cover next to nothing; a bond for $3 million probably is more than enough.

One company that is reputed to offer an especially fine program for helping consumers budget their expenses, control payments, and re-establish their credit is FINANCIAL ALTERNATIVES, 3585 Telegraph Road, Suite B, Ventura, California 43003; (800) 237-8604.

COMPOSITIONS

A debt composition is a contractual arrangement covering all of your debts. Compositions can consist of a payment plan, a settlement, or a combination of both. In essence, you and your creditors enter into a contract.

You must promise to do certain things, including making certain payments. Often, compositions involve allowing creditors to place liens, or otherwise secure, property or income needed to implement the composition. Some compositions even make use of the appointment of a private trustee. Creditors promise to refrain from collection action, if you perform as promised. Often, creditors also agree to accept less than the full amount of the debt.

The **advantages** of compositions are:

> You can get the time and peace of mind needed to sort out your problems, sell assets in an orderly manner, and do whatever else may be needed.
>
> They can produce a much greater recovery for creditors, at a much smaller cost to you.
>
> They are private and no courts or public agencies are involved.
>
> If assets need to be sold, you can sell them yourself. Generally, you are more motivated and better able to maximize the amount recovered from the assets.
>
> They can lead to your full rehabilitation as a valued customer of the creditors.

The **disadvantages** of compositions are:

> *Compositions can be complicated and expensive* > Usually, compositions require separate negotiations with each creditor. They always have to be put into a written form, requiring the assistance of a lawyer. If there are very few creditors, the composition may be workable. When you have considerable assets and the debts are large, the composition may be complicated but the costs may be justified. Compositions usually are not economical when there are many creditors, but relatively few assets.

Compositions usually depend on the consent of all, or nearly all, the creditors > Far more often than not, you cannot obtain the approval of enough creditors. Many creditors lack the experience, self-confidence, authority, or common-sense needed to evaluate and agree to a proposed composition. It's always easier for a creditor to say no when it doesn't fully understand something than it is to make a knowledgeable and reasonable decision.

A properly formulated, *bona fide* composition is far better for the creditors than other alternatives unless:

There is reason for your creditors to believe that your disclosure of your financial affairs is unreliable.

You have made preferential payments, or transfers of valuable property, that could be voided by a state court or a bankruptcy trustee.

There is a strong possibility that you cannot, or will not, perform and the creditors could be put in a significantly worse position if the composition is not successfully completed.

Before you attempt a composition, be prepared to face a lot of frustration. Understand that it's unlikely that many of your creditors understand compositions and, therefore, will not behave in their own best interests.

section

S E V E N

SOME HELPFUL TECHNIQUES

COMMUNICATING WITH CREDITORS

CHAPTER NINETEEN

Communications with your creditors can make or break you.

GENERAL RULES

Unless you are sure of what you're doing when you communicate with a creditor, try to follow these rules:

Know what you are trying to achieve when communicating with the creditor > Always keep those goals in mind during your communication. When you have accomplished your goals, or as many of them as you think it's possible to accomplish, bring the communication to an immediate end. Continuing a communication after accomplishing your goals will achieve nothing but give your creditor a chance to change its mind.

Listen attentively and read carefully > You can learn a lot from a creditor. Often, a creditor will advise you of rights, or special procedures, that can help you. Sometimes, a creditor will inadvertently disclose a mistake, or a possible defense, you may have. Usually, the creditor will give you a good idea of what it really wants from you, and what it will really do if you don't satisfy that desire.

Never be embarrassed or defensive about owing money > It isn't a sin. Wealthy people owe more money than you do. At the same time it is dunning you, your creditor owes money to others. You aren't subordinate merely because you're in debt.

Always be courteous and polite > The person with whom you're dealing is human. Even if he is rude, it may be that his child is sick, or simply that he never learned any manners. It costs you nothing to be civil. Being courteous and polite puts you on the moral high ground, and enables you to control the dialogue. When you're rude, you give your creditor another reason to target you. You also may find your rude language, especially if it's in writing, being quoted in court.

Never admit that you owe the creditor anything > It's not your responsibility to establish that you're in debt. If you admit to owing a debt, you may be admitting to something you don't legally owe for reasons that you, yourself, may not even know.

Always repeat every imaginable grievance you have against the creditor > If you didn't get everything you were supposed to get, you don't owe the creditor everything it claims. If the creditor violated the law, you may not owe the creditor anything. If delivery was late, or the merchandise less than advertised, you probably won't have to pay all that is being asked of you.

Try to avoid giving the creditor specific data > Your social security number, address, telephone number, employer, bank, information about your relatives, and names of other creditors will be used to hurt you and your family.

FORMALITY VERSUS INFORMALITY

Usually, clear and complete agreements are far better than blurry arrangements. Such arrangements frequently lead to disputes. That is why lawyers write lengthy contracts that contain very specific language. However, use of formal language when speaking or writing, especially formal legal language, often puts people on their guard, and makes them think more carefully about a matter.

If you are trying to persuade a creditor to do something for you, informality is better than formality. If you are making an offer or confirming an agreement, then it's usually better to use precise language.

Sometimes you will not be able to obtain an agreement from a creditor, if you push for too much clarity or use too much legalese. In those instances, you'll have to decide whether pushing for a formal agreement is worth the risk of frightening off the creditor.

TELEPHONE

Never take a telephone call from a creditor. Always call the creditor first or take a message for yourself and call back. When a creditor calls you, he is mentally prepared to beat on you; when you call the creditor, he's surprised at your honesty and receptive to what you have to say.

Always assume that your telephone conversations with creditors are being recorded, or listened to by a third person. Collection supervisors frequently listen in on their staff's telephone conversations.

Whenever you have an important telephone conversation with a creditor, make a written memorandum of:

the date and time of the call;

whether you made or received the call;

if you called, the telephone number you called, and how you got the number;

the name and title of each person with whom you spoke, and how you knew who they were;

each topic of conversation; and

any exact language that seems important, especially agreements, promises and threats.

"**Telephone Tag**" is a back and forth series of calls with each person missing the other. Telephone tag can be used effectively by a consumer who wants to appear cooperative, while at the same time gaining time. While telephone tag is going on, creditors are less likely to move on to the next collection step. Telephone tag often can be managed by returning the creditor's calls when the creditor is least likely to be available. Always make sure you leave messages. Calls made a few minutes before or after business hours, or during lunch, are less likely to connect. Keep in mind that collection departments often stay open during evening hours. When you call and miss the bill collector, find out collector's working hours by asking whoever answers the phone. This makes playing the game easier.

MAIL

Papers are sent by certified or registered mail in order to prove you received them. Registered or certified mail NEVER is intended to benefit you. Never accept certified or registered mail unless you are expecting to receive valuable documents, such as stock certificates, that ordinarily are sent by certified or registered mail.

> If you are trying to keep your current address private, be wary of letters that do not have return addresses, want you to respond to some intriguing, but unclear proposal, or claim to come from some long lost friend you don't remember. Many creditors use this and similar ruses to fool consumers into disclosing their home addresses.

Whenever you write to a creditor, first decide whether you want to be informal or formal. Handwritten letters appear much less formal than typed letters. Certified and registered mail is viewed as formal, but can be very important, if you later need to prove delivery.

CHAPTER 19

MEETINGS

Face to face meetings can be the best, or the worst, mode of communications. Before you request or agree to a meeting with a creditor, try to make sure that the meeting will help you achieve your goals. If the meeting won't help you, don't request or agree to a meeting.

The **advantages** of meetings are:

Humanizing the parties > It's easier to develop feelings for a person you see than a voice over the telephone or a signature on a letter.

Judging personality, character and sincerity > You can learn a lot by seeing a creditor's body language, clothing, and place of work.

Speeding up settlements > Meetings are less likely to be interrupted or forgotten than telephone calls and letters. All topics can be covered, and the people are there to exchange any necessary papers.

The **disadvantages** of meetings are:

Creating and intensifying personal animosities > If there is a personality clash at a meeting, it's likely to last a lot longer than a disagreement over the telephone or in letters.

Revealing information > Smart creditors will use meetings to cajole consumers to disclose information. It can be hard for a consumer to find a polite way to refuse to provide information.

Speeding up collection > If a meeting is successful, the creditor will get something from the consumer, usually cash or a promise of cash. If a meeting is unsuccessful, the creditor will move on to the next step in the collection process.

Going to a meeting at your creditor's office puts you at a psychological disadvantage. On your opponent's turf, you feel less comfortable than he does. If possible, and it usually isn't, arrange the meeting at a place where you will feel comfortable or, at least, at a neutral location, such as a restaurant.

Although each person has his own style, there are a number of techniques that have proven to work well in dealing with creditors. Before you attend a meeting, consider the following suggestions:

SUGGESTIONS FOR MEETINGS WITH CREDITORS

Before a Meeting:

Make sure you know what your goals are. Think about how you intend to achieve them. Prepare a written agenda so that you, not the creditor, will control the direction of the meeting.

Know exactly what information and promises you can, and are willing, to make at the meeting. Don't end up making promises, or giving information, you'll later regret.

Prepare yourself to politely decline to provide information you want to withhold.

Going to a Meeting:

Make sure your appearance is consistent with the image you want to present. If you're pleading poverty, don't drive up in a new car, wearing a custom-tailored suit, and an expensive watch.

Bringing one well-behaved young child is almost certain to keep the meeting short and civil, while conveying an image that you are responsible. This will evoke positive feelings from your creditor. Bringing a brat, or more than one child, causes disruption and prevents accomplishing anything at the meeting.

Be on time, or even a little early. Being late undermines your credibility and reliability. If you must be late, call ahead.

Don't be surprised or upset if the creditor makes you wait for several minutes. Some creditors may actually be busy. Most make you wait in order to give themselves a psychological advantage. If you are made to wait more than 30 minutes without being given a very good reason, politely leave a message that you will call to arrange another meeting, and leave.

At a Meeting:

At all times, remember, you are there to protect YOUR interests and not the interests of your creditor.

Ask for business cards from everyone at the meeting. This will help you learn their names and keep a record of the people attending. If a person does not have business cards, he's probably a fairly low-level employee.

Relax. Keep in mind that your money probably paid for the chairs in which you all are sitting.

> If you are offered a beverage, accept it. It helps relax the atmosphere and, if you're lucky, the creditor will have to get it himself. Being served by your creditor increases your self-assurance and relative status. If you're not offered a beverage, always ask for a cup of coffee or a glass of water.
>
> Engage in a moment or two of casual conversation. Ask a few harmless questions. Talk about one of your local sport's team. This gets a creditor talking to you and equalizes your positions. It also gives you some sense of control over the meeting.

Be the one to begin the business talk and try to follow YOUR prepared written agenda.

During the course of the business talk, CASUALLY take brief notes on a small pad of paper. No responsible creditor will object, and most will be impressed with your diligence. You don't need a transcript of everything said. You do need to include:

> the name of every person at the meeting;
>
> every agreement and promise made at the meeting;
>
> the exact wording of any admissions by the creditor of wrongdoing or mistakes; and
>
> the exact wording of any threats made by the creditor.

Be accurate and don't exaggerate. You will be treated with respect if your statements are believable. Express your grievances politely, and with as little passion as possible. Ranting and raving will not be taken seriously.

Most people want to be liked and seen as cooperative, so they tend to agree more than disagree. Don't let this happen to you. Being liked is not as important as being smart in these meetings.

> Just because you can't find a polite way to disagree is no reason to agree. Delay! Say you aren't sure, or you have to think about it, or you must first talk with your spouse. Say anything that will buy you a polite way out.
>
> Take advantage of the creditor's natural tendency to want to agree by phrasing your points in the form of questions such as "Don't you agree that ... ?"

Benefit from most people's tendency to want to help. Whenever the opportunity arises, ask the creditor for suggestions and then listen. At the very least, this will be taken as a sincere compliment. At best, you will get some helpful advice, and the creditor will make a positive psychological investment in you. Much like teachers, people hope to see a person they have tried to help succeed. They want their investment to pay off.

Be very careful when using the word "you." If your statement is positive, use "you" to direct it at the person to whom you are speaking. If your statement is negative, don't use the word "you." Blame the company, not the person to whom your speaking. It doesn't help you if you insult the person to whom you are speaking.

No matter what happens, remain calm and polite. It's better to adjourn the meeting, and continue it at a future time, than to get into a heated argument. You won't win the argument, and you'll end up being targeted.

PRESERVING AND RESTORING YOUR CREDIT

CHAPTER TWENTY

A good credit history is very useful, but not essential.

CREDIT HISTORY AND CREDIT

Getting credit and having a good credit history are not always the same thing. People without a good credit history frequently have access to credit, while some people with a good credit history can't get credit.

If your credit history is already bad, or is becoming bad, expect to have trouble getting future credit, renting an apartment, opening a new checking account, or getting insurance. If you are an executive, or if you work in a job where security is a major concern, a bad credit history can make it more difficult to get a job. Without a credit card, you will not be able to rent a car, cash a check, and generally will find it more difficult to spend money. This is not always a bad thing.

However, millions of Americans live quite comfortably with bad credit histories, and many of them don't even know they have bad credit histories.

CASH IS ALWAYS FAR MORE CONVINCING THAN A GOOD CREDIT HISTORY.

PRESERVING EXISTING CREDIT

You can preserve some of the credit you already have. If you cannot satisfy all of your creditors, select your most valued sources of credit and stay current with them. Let the rest slide. For example, keep at least one credit card account current. If you are current on that account, it's unlikely that a credit card will be canceled just because you file bankruptcy or slide on your other credit cards.

A bad credit history usually does not affect credit that you already have. After initially granting credit, creditors rely on your history with them. Unless you request a larger line of credit, your creditor has no reason to check on your history with other creditors.

Moreover, a creditor often feels more secure knowing that a consumer took care of it, rather than other creditors. A creditor cares only about itself - not other creditors. A good borrower is a source of income for a creditor. Other creditors are competitors. For example, there are two equally important reasons for creditors' requiring collateral. One is to prevent a borrower from selling off the assets. The other is to protect the collateral from competing claims by the creditor's competitors - other creditors.

It's not at all uncommon for one creditor to help a borrower protect his assets and income from other creditors. A friendly creditor can help you, and itself, by accepting additional security. For example, most people feel that their mortgage payments are essential. A friendly mortgage lender can be given a wage assignment to guaranty prompt monthly payments. Since the payments would be made anyway, the consumer loses nothing, but gains protection from other creditors trying to garnish his income.

Friendly Foreclosures Creditors sometimes cooperate in "friendly" foreclosures to help consumers free their property from other liens. Creditors may do this because of loyalty to the customer, but usually the creditor is more concerned about protecting its own loan. By doing this, the participating creditor enhances the value of its collateral and makes it easier for the consumer to make payments.

> In these cases, the participating creditor forecloses on the property, then resells the property to the original borrower or a person he selects. This creditor provides, or arranges, 100% financing for the repurchase, but has to be reimbursed for its foreclosure costs at the time of closing.
>
> Sometimes, the participating lender may demand an additional down payment to reduce the principal amount of the debt. Often, the lender shortens the loan to 3 to 5 years, with a balloon payment at the end. If the consumer keeps the new account current, most cooperating lenders will then replace that balloon loan with a regular, long term mortgage loan.
>
> Friendly foreclosures are perfectly legal, and proper. But beware of the pitfalls of a friendly foreclosure. If there is a lot of equity, an unfriendly creditor, or a bargain-hunter, may decide to bid for the property. If that occurs, be prepared to bid more than the actual debt owed to the friendly participating creditor. If there aren't any junior liens against the property, any amount you bid above the actual debt must be returned to you anyway.

If there is a junior lien on the property, such as a second mortgage, judgment lien, or tax lien, any amount you bid above the actual existing debt has to be paid in cash. It's unlikely the participating creditor will lend you additional money, so you'll have to arrange, in advance, for another source of funds.

OVERCOMING A BAD CREDIT HISTORY

There are many ways to get around a bad credit history. Here are some of them:

If you need to get a credit card > A few banks issue unsecured credit cards to consumers with spotty credit histories, including some who have obtained relief under the Bankruptcy Code. Even more banks now offer any consumer, regardless of credit history, what they call a "secured credit card." This card is secured by a cash deposit. The bank is at no risk. If you default, the bank takes your cash deposit.

Some of these credit card issuers are legitimate and offer very competitive fees and interest rates. However some issuers, particularly those that charge a large fee for the initial 900 number telephone call, are sharks that impose outrageously high fees and interest rates.

BANKCARD HOLDERS OF AMERICA, 560 Herndon Parkway, Suite 120, Herndon, Virginia 22070, is reputed to be an excellent source of information about issuers of secured credit cards.

If you need to open a checking account > First, open a savings account, or buy a certificate of deposit. After you have had money deposited in the bank for awhile, apply for a checking account. Banks often don't run credit checks on existing customers.

If you need to rent a place to live > Look for an apartment or home that is owned for investment purposes and is being rented by the owner. Many of these owners do not run credit checks. If the landlord does check your credit, you can offer to make a security deposit sufficient to cover rent for any time it might take to have you evicted. Usually, three months will be enough to satisfy the landlord.

If you have trouble getting insurance > Use an independent insurance agent. There are many hungry insurance companies out there searching to write new policies. Be careful though. Many insurers are themselves faced with serious financial problems.

If your credit rating interferes with getting a job > If the employer goes to the trouble of investigating your background, you probably will be given a chance to explain your financial situation. If you haven't lied about it, the employer might be convinced to hire you when you point out that the job will solve your financial problems. This argument is especially effective if your financial problems resulted from the loss of an earlier job.

If you need a loan > Offer lots of collateral and show that you have the ability to make the payments. You are more likely to get a mortgage loan if you seek a guaranteed loan from the government, because the creditor will not be put at risk.

If you want to pay off other creditors with the new loan, demonstrate how the loan will solve all your financial problems. IF YOU CAN'T PROVE THAT THE LOAN WILL SOLVE ALL YOUR FINANCIAL PROBLEMS, BORROWING THE MONEY WILL MAKE YOUR PROBLEMS WORSE.

RESTORING YOUR "CREDIT RATING"

There really is no such thing as a consumer CREDIT RATING. Most credit reporting agencies give requesting creditors a summary of your credit history, and leave it to them to interpret the information. Different creditors view the same credit history in different ways.

For example, some creditors will not lend to persons who have gone through a recent Chapter 7 liquidation. Other creditors view a recent bankruptcy as an advantage, because a loan to the consumer can't be discharged for six years after the last bankruptcy, giving the creditor a long time to collect.

Many of the more enlightened creditors look favorably on a consumer who had financial problems, but managed to pay off all his debts. These creditors recognize that the consumer demonstrated strong character. Less insightful creditors never see past the surface view.

Some creditors are willing to consider the causes of a consumer's past financial problems. Loss of job, illness, and small business failures often are considered good excuses. Other creditors, especially the larger institutions, will refuse credit without even taking the time to learn the cause of the prior problems.

Mortgage lenders sometimes disregard a one-time problem with credit card debts, if a consumer stayed current on his previous mortgage and got rid of his credit cards. Of course, credit-card issuers usually have a different view.

Most large institutional creditors follow formulas, and will automatically refuse credit if they see any red flags. Many small merchants, finance companies, and mortgage lenders will consider the causes and details of a checkered credit history.

There are a number of things you can do to rebuild a poor credit history. Start with the credit you already have and keep it in good standing. Then, starting with small amounts, and local creditors, slowly build more credit. Here a few suggestions:

> Establish and maintain a good banking history. Stay with the same bank. Try to keep a reasonable balance. NEVER overdraw your checking account.
>
> Stay current on all remaining credit accounts.
>
> Open charge accounts at local retail stores. If necessary, offer to make an advance payment towards the account.
>
> Refrain from applying for credit that is likely to be refused and reported to a credit reporting agency. Some of the larger commercial creditors, especially credit-card issuers, inform reporting agencies when applications for credit are rejected.
>
> Ask your existing creditors to say you are a "good" or "excellent" account when they receive inquiries about you. Unless the consumer asks for help, most creditors will provide only the raw numbers from their records, because of the fear of lawsuits.

If you need assistance, consider contacting a reputable debt counselor. Names of counselors can be obtained from the NATIONAL FOUNDATION FOR CONSUMER CREDIT, 8611 Second Avenue, Suite 100, Silver Springs, Maryland 20910, (800) 388-2227. Another company, FINANCIAL ALTERNATIVES, 3585 Telegraph Road, Suite B, Ventura, California, (800) 237-8604, offers a range of services, including computer budgeting, bill paying, daily personal advice, and assistance in obtaining credit, Including secured credit cards. The company charges a relatively modest monthly fee, but does not charge for the initial consultation and evaluation. FAMILY SERVICE AMERICA, 11700 W. Lake Park Drive, Milwaukee, Wisconsin 53224, (414) 359-1040 also is reputed to offer excellent counselling services at a number of locations throughout the country.

Be patient. It took time to create a bad credit history; you won't be able to restore a good credit history overnight.

LAWS AND LAWYERS

CHAPTER TWENTY-ONE

Laws and lawyers have an enormous impact on consumers' rights and burdens.

Unfortunately, our legal system is filled with greed and callousness. It's not just the lawyers. It's also the millions of others who make their living from the enactment and enforcement of laws. The legal system has grown into one of the biggest and most profitable industries in America.

LAWS

There is no single body of statutes that embody "The Law." It simply does not exist in that form. Rather, there are many different kinds of law. There are statutes and ordinances passed by federal, state, county, and local legislatures; rules and regulations adopted by thousands of federal, state, county and local agencies; and decisions pouring out of all kinds of courts. Add to this the federal and state constitutions and thousands of international treaties, and you have an unimaginable conglomeration that constitutes "The Law."

No single person recognizes, much less understands, more than a very small number of these laws. Lawyers can't even be sure whether they have found all the pertinent laws that apply to any particular case. When asked for their opinions, sensible lawyers usually respond, "It depends." On what does it depend? It depends on the actual facts of the case, the evidence admissible in court, the relative quality and dedication of each party's attorney, the amount of money each party can afford to invest in the matter, and the version of the law the judge decides to follow.

CHAPTER 21

LAWYERS

Having a good lawyer is always a big advantage. The number of really good lawyers out there is limited, but it's better to have a marginally competent lawyer than no lawyer at all.

You can, and should, learn how to select a lawyer, and how to use a lawyer. In the process, you will learn a little about dealing with collection lawyers.

UNDERSTANDING LAWYERS

LAWYERS' GOALS Lawyers are basically like everyone else. Their goals are the same as ours: Make a good living; stay out of legal, financial and personal trouble; and do a good job.

The true nature of a lawyer surfaces when there is a conflict between these objectives. For example, we consider a lawyer "honest" when he doesn't violate his integrity for the sake of money. We consider a lawyer "dishonest" when he puts his own financial welfare above that of his client's. Most lawyers are somewhere between those two extremes.

Conflict between a lawyer's financial desires and his ethical behavior is of great importance to our society as a whole, but has little short-term meaning to you, as an individual. As someone in financial trouble, your immediate concerns are to be well-represented and treated fairly by your lawyer.

LEGAL SPECIALTIES Lawyers aren't allowed to claim specialties in any but a very few areas, such as patent law and maritime law. Lawyers get around this prohibition by advertising that their "practice is concentrated in...." Be aware, though. There are no restrictions on the use of this phrase. Any lawyer can say he "concentrates" his practice in just about anything.

Some of the fields of concentration that affect people with debt problems include:

Bankruptcy Law Until recently, bankruptcy law was practiced by a small group of lawyers. The members of this elite circle knew each other very well. Such friendships allowed quick and easy deals to be made. Not that this was always bad. Deal-making is an essential part of successful bankruptcy practice.

Now that it has become so profitable, nearly every major law firm has a bankruptcy department. Most of these lawyers switched from less busy and lucrative areas of law. They have no particular affinity for, or knowledge of, this field.

A good bankruptcy lawyer typically has experience in a number of different fields, including litigation, creditor and debtor rights, the Uniform Commercial Code, and real estate. More important, he understands that the law, and the legal system, are only the means to achieve the client's financial objectives. So, in addition to legal skills, he needs life experiences, street smarts, and an understanding of his client's financial and emotional needs.

Be wary of the lawyer who goes strictly by the book because he likely lacks the negotiating and other skills needed for the give and take of bankruptcy law. Beware of lawyers who cut corners, because they may lack an understanding of the nuances and importance of detail. Beware of the lawyer who loves a good fight because you, not he, will be the one paying the price for his gamesmanship. Moreover, many of these legal gladiators quickly lose their taste for battle when you run out of money.

Collection Law Because they work on a volume basis, most collection lawyers must operate production-line practices staffed by secretaries, clerks, and paralegal staff.

Most debt collection lawyers are businessmen who don't pretend to be high-powered litigators. Although they may be cynical, most have made peace with their careers and are decent, easy-going people. They usually don't make moral judgments about people in debt. Most of them just want to collect the money as cheaply and easily as possible.

Few collection lawyers try cases, because it's too time consuming and expensive. Their time is spent enforcing default judgments. These default judgments may account for more than 90% of the average collection lawyer's legal victories. When confronted with a litigator, collection lawyers usually agree to compromise.

Consumer and Debtor Law Many consumer lawyers work for legal assistance foundations or clinics associated with law schools. Most of the senior lawyers in these organizations do it because they believe in what they do and, subject to the limitations of their very large case loads, are extremely good at what they do.

These senior lawyers are frequently assisted by law students. Law students, with the typical zeal of the young, care about the quality of their work. It may take students several attempts to learn how to do something correctly, but they don't give up. If one of the senior attorneys can find the time to attend to your case, the odds are good that you will be very well represented. Legal assistance foundations and legal clinics are almost always subsidized. Their fees frequently based are on a sliding scale.

There also are some very fine private lawyers and firms that concentrate on representing people in debt. For a variety of reasons, mostly financial, these lawyers prefer not to work for clinics or foundations. Some of these lawyers are the very best that the profession has to offer to the consumer. Their fees are frequently reasonable, and sometimes adjusted to the consumer's ability to pay.

Unfortunately, there are lawyers out there who prey on the uneducated and naive consumer. They make vague promises that can't, and won't be kept. It's hard to tell the difference between these and the honest lawyers, so check thoroughly on a lawyer before paying any retainer. If you can't get the names of his clients, ask for the names of some opposing lawyers who will vouch for him. If you can't get references, get a different attorney.

Corporate Law No one really knows what corporate law encompasses. Basic corporate law usually doesn't involve enough to require much expertise. Most so-called corporate lawyers are general practitioners of business law. Some of them are capable of representing a consumer, others are not.

Criminal Law Many lawyers who concentrate on criminal defense work are former prosecutors who want to make more money. Many of them are among the best trial lawyers in the country. However, few of them are familiar with the relative complexities of civil litigation, with all of its pre-trial motions and discovery. All else being equal, in a civil case, a commercial litigator will run a criminal lawyer in circles. On the other hand, very few civil lawyers can handle a criminal case, with all of its strange concepts and hidden dangers.

If you are charged with a crime, retain the best criminal defense attorney you can afford, and expect to put up a lot of cash. If you can't afford to hire a criminal lawyer, the government will provide one. Some of the country's best criminal defense attorneys work as public defenders, but most have very large case loads.

General Practice Good general practitioners are the best kind of consumer lawyers. They are, however, hard to find. A good general practitioner is familiar with many different areas of law.

Most so-called general practitioners aren't very good, and they have only a minimal understanding of a few areas of law. They do little more than incorporate small businesses, handle house closings, draft simple contracts and wills, and settle a few small personal injury claims.

A good general practitioner is familiar with enough law to watch all of his client's affairs, handle all routine matters, including litigation, and recognize problems that require special expertise. When such a problem arises, he refers his client to a specialist, but continues to coordinate the case, and makes certain the specialist's activities don't conflict with his client's other matters.

A good general practitioner knows enough to recognize his own limitations, and isn't embarrassed to admit to that limitation. He will personally represent a client up to that limit, but will not endanger the client by getting in over his head.

Labor Law Labor lawyers can represent either management or unions. Many of them spend a good deal of their time negotiating labor contracts and handling matters before labor relations boards. Although, some union lawyers spend much of their time collecting dues and benefits from delinquent employers, very few of them are well versed in ordinary creditor-debtor law.

Litigators Litigators are lawyers who spend much of their time preparing for trials, including preparing pre-trial motions and discovery. Generally, litigators are less easily intimidated than are other lawyers. They know that, in law, there is no such thing as a sure thing, and that most cases can be kept floating around a courthouse for years.

Some litigators are charming, others quite gruff. Most are under severe time pressure, and they tend to be impatient. They often are preoccupied and sometimes neglect to keep their clients fully informed.

All else being equal, a good litigator has a big advantage over a lawyer who has no court experience. However, beware of litigators whose first instinct is to rush into battle. Prudent litigators know that no matter who wins, everyone but the lawyers lose. Cases should go to trial only as a last resort. A good litigator never stops trying to use the courtroom proceedings as a means to achieve a good settlement.

On the other hand, be wary of "settlers," who think only of obtaining a quick settlement. Their opponents know them for what they are, and won't take them seriously.

Real Estate Law Some real estate lawyers handle nothing but sales of residential property; others handle nothing but commercial transactions. Although they are quite familiar with mortgage laws, they may never have handled a disputed foreclosure.

Tax Law Few tax lawyers spend much time preparing tax returns. Tax returns are, most often, prepared by accountants. Rather, tax lawyers really are specialists at tax planning and handling serious tax problems. They are essential if you have a serious problem with a tax collector, but too expensive for routine consumer debt problems.

Other Areas of Concentration

- Administrative hearings
- Arbitration
- Appeals
- Banking law
- Commodities law
- Constitutional law
- Construction law
- Entertainment law
- Environmental law
- Equal rights laws
- Insurance law
- Intellectual property laws
- International laws
- Lobbying
- Maritime law
- Municipal law
- Patent law
- Personal injury
- Personal property
- Real estate taxes
- Trade laws
- Transportation laws
- Transactions
- Zoning

LEGAL FEES

Lawyers are paid in several different ways:

Hourly Fees Hourly fees range from $25 to $500 or more. Lawyers may charge different hourly rates for different kinds of services. For example, actual courtroom time is usually charged at a higher rate than is travel time.

The actual time billed depends, in part, on a lawyer's minimum billing period. Lawyers may charge a minimum of one-tenth of an hour, simply because it takes that long to write and process the time slip. Some charge a minimum of one-quarter of an hour, even if the task or conversation takes only a minute or two. You can end up paying a lot of money for only a few short telephone conversations.

Hourly fees pose some hazards for the consumer. On one hand, you want to dispose of the matter as quickly, and inexpensively, as possible. On the other hand, the lawyer makes more money only if the matter requires a lot of work, or drags on. Ethical attorneys try to subordinate their own economic interests to the client's welfare.

Phantom and padded billing are too common. Phantom billing is charging for time that was not spent on your case. This is fraud. Padded billing is more subtle. This is often accomplished by one or more of the following methods: having idle law associates do unnecessary work; conducting unnecessary meetings, especially internal ones that enable several lawyers to bill you for the same period of time; and duplicating work by sending two attorneys to court to get a continuance.

If the lawyer is not familiar with some aspect of your case, you are paying for the time he spends educating himself. If the lawyer has to travel long distances, you could end paying more than if you hired a local lawyer who charges higher hourly rates.

Sometimes, lawyers agree to limit the total number of hours for which a client will be charged. However, such limits can lead to the same hazards posed by flat fees, as discussed below. If you are going to pay hourly fees, insist on receiving regular statements that show the specific tasks performed, how long each task took, and why the tasks were needed. Don't let the lawyer get away with bills that contain little more than vague descriptions, followed by large chunks of time.

Flat Fees These are specific fees charged for handling specific matters. Flat fees often are used for house closings and simple Chapter 7 liquidations.

Flat fees also pose a hazard for the consumer. If you are paying a flat fee, you expect the attorney to continue handling your matter with diligence, even if it takes more time than originally estimated. The attorney, though, has to make a living. If the flat fee is not sufficient, he may be inclined to cut corners, push for a premature conclusion, or even put your matter aside while he works on other, more profitable, matters.

Contingency Fees These are fees that a lawyer earns only if he achieves an objective for the client. Lawyers generally are prohibited from agreeing to contingency fees in criminal and domestic relations cases.

Contingency fees are most often accepted by collection, personal injury, class action, and anti-trust lawyers. It isn't a coincidence that these attorneys earn the highest incomes and get the best results for their clients. They have to win to make a living. Most other attorneys won't agree to accept contingency fees, except in rare, especially good cases.

Contingency agreements are not supposed to cover out-of-pocket costs of a lawsuit. Lawyers are prohibited from financing litigation by assuming these costs. The client must, at least, assume ultimate responsibility for the out-of-pocket costs. Collection lawyers usually require clients to advance these costs. Personal injury lawyers usually agree to advance the costs for their clients, and rarely get around to recovering such costs from clients whose cases are lost.

Contingency fees also pose a hazard for the consumer. If you decide you want to change lawyers, the original lawyer is entitled to a fee for services already provided. If you're not careful, you can end up paying two contingency fees. Also, the first attorney may hold back parts of your file until you reimburse him for all out-of-pocket costs.

Any contingency fee agreement you sign should spell out exactly what fee the attorney will be entitled to receive if you decide to change attorneys. Also, try to get the lawyer to agree that you will be able to get your entire case file, including work papers, even if you owe fees or costs.

Blended Fees and Bonuses Except for certain prohibitions against using contingency fees, there is no limit to the ways a lawyer can structure fees. Lawyers often agree to set a limit on their hourly fees, in combination with some sort of a contingency fee. Lawyers also will accept reduced hourly or fixed fees, with the understanding that they will be paid a bonus if they achieve certain desired results. Don't hesitate to suggest a creative fee structure. At worst, the lawyer will say, "No."

Advance Payments, Deposits and Retainers Most attorneys who charge flat fees require some part of the fee be paid in advance. Often, this fee isn't refundable, unless the attorney fails to perform his job. In practice, non-refundable payments are rarely returned. You can't prove the lawyer hasn't done his job without retaining another lawyer, whose fees will be more than the first lawyer charged.

Most lawyers who charge by the hour require new clients to pay a deposit, as security for payment of fees and costs. Such deposits should be placed in a separate "escrow" account. Lawyers are prohibited from using these funds, until actual work has been performed or costs incurred. Some states even require that the client be sent a bill before the escrow money can be taken.

If you do not have enough cash, the lawyer may be willing to accept some property as security.

The word "retainer" is frequently misused. Technically, a retainer is not a deposit. It's a fee paid just to obtain the representation of an attorney and it covers absolutely no work.

Costs Clients usually are billed for all "costs." Costs traditionally meant out-of-pocket expenses for filing fees, travel, expert witnesses, long distance telephone calls, and other expenses directly attributable to a specific matter. Costs did not include the lawyer's office overhead or staff.

Recently, many lawyers have expanded the meaning of "costs" to include photocopying, computer time, postage, secretarial ("paralegal"), messenger, and even clerical services. The definition of "costs" has a major effect on the ultimate size of your bill. You have the right to know, in advance, what costs will be charged to you.

SELECTING A LAWYER

Just having a lawyer often is not enough. You need the right lawyer for you and your needs. Don't just pick a name out of the telephone book. Expend the effort to make a careful selection.

First, determine what kind of lawyer you need > Generally, the best consumer lawyer is a general practitioner, who does some litigation. A good general practitioner can adequately handle almost any consumer matter. However, if you need relief under the bankruptcy code, a general practitioner is no substitute for a good bankruptcy attorney. If you have a criminal problem, don't even consider retaining anyone other than a criminal defense lawyer.

Second, identify the lawyers who can provide what you need > Get the names of lawyers by asking friends and relatives, or from your local Bar Association. Always be skeptical of lawyers and law firms that advertise. Often, they advertise low fixed fees for a "simple this" or a "simple that." In reality, few legal matters are simple enough to be handled for the advertised price. One national telephone legal service actually charges more than some leading attorneys. But you don't immediately know this because they quote their rates on a per minute basis. When you compute their per-minute charge on an hourly basis, you discover that you are paying premium rates for off-the-rack services.

Many of these advertisements offer "quick settlements" of personal injury claims. If you have a serious injury, you don't want a quick settlement. Insurance companies rarely hand over money quickly, unless they think they are getting a very good deal. If you want the maximum recovery, you need an experienced attorney, who has successfully tried cases, and who will invest the time and resources needed to force the insurance company to pay what the case is really worth.

Third, determine if the lawyer has the type of experience you need > If a lawyer is even somewhat unfamiliar with your kind of legal problem, he is going to get an education at your expense. Don't believe a lawyer just because he advertises, or claims, he can handle your problem. Ask the lawyer how many matters of that type he has handled, and how many of those were successfully concluded.

Fourth, try to assess how good the lawyer is > Some of the qualities that make a lawyer good are familiarity with similar legal matters, courtrooms and other legal procedures. Also important are experience with life and people in general. Personal characteristics, including sincere concern for clients, diligence, loyalty, perseverance, ethics, and tolerance, strongly affect the quality of a lawyer's work. Competent lawyers have good communication skills, including writing and the ability to explain complicated concepts. Finally, a good lawyer knows his clients, the substantive law of his areas of concentration, and a variety of general academic and other information.

Experience usually is the best indicator of an attorney's qualifications, but it's not always reliable. Some attorneys have been making the same mistakes for years. For example, many clients love attorneys who take every opportunity to huff, puff, and talk tough. Although this may make the client feel good, these attorneys often antagonize their adversaries and the judge, create additional work, and diminish the chances of reaching a settlement. Many lawyers never discover their habitual errors because they are not litigators and don't have to deal with their mistakes when a dispute arises.

Don't just believe a lawyer who says he knows how to handle your problem. Ask him if he has handled similar problems. How many? And what were the results? It's never easy to assess a lawyer's past performance. One of the best ways is asking lawyers who have been his opponents and lawyers who have worked with him.

Be wary of referrals from one lawyer to another. Fee splitting arrangements are still relatively common and legal. Referral fees are not, but sometimes fee splitting is nothing more than a way of hiding an improper referral fee.

If you are paying a contingency fee, fee splitting won't cost you. However, if you are paying the second attorney an hourly fee, fee splitting may very well influence how he computes his time. Similarly, any fixed or flat fee quoted by the second attorney is likely to include the amount that he has to pay the first attorney.

Fifth, decide if you can get along with the lawyer > You don't have to like your lawyer, but you do have to trust him and get along with him. If there is a strong conflict of personalities or values, look for a different lawyer.

Sixth, determine if you can afford the lawyer > Make sure you understand the fee arrangement, how it will be computed, and at least get a rough estimate of how much the entire matter will cost. If you can't afford that much, try to negotiate a lower amount, or look for a different lawyer. It won't do you much good to retain a lawyer just to have him withdraw when you fail to pay his fees. It won't do you any good to make your financial situation worse by incurring another debt you can't pay.

Make sure that your reason for hiring the lawyer is worth the cost. It would be financial folly to pay a lawyer $2,000 to defend a $1,000 collection action. Usually, though, the decision is not so obvious, and you have to carefully weigh your legal objectives against the cost of achieving them.

It is wrongly said that "you always get what you pay for." When talking about lawyers, a more accurate statement is, "You rarely get more than you pay for."

HANDLING YOUR LAWYER

It's easy to forget that your lawyer works for you. You are the boss in this relationship. The lawyer may know a lot of things you don't, but you know yourself, your circumstances, and your goals better than any lawyer does. Lawyers are far from perfect. Don't expect your lawyer to work miracles. Do expect maximum competence and efforts from your lawyer. Here are some do's and *don't's*:

Do give your lawyer the same consideration you would give anyone else. Lawyers are human. They make mistakes, have good days and bad days, and need to earn a living.

Don't assume your lawyer is always correct. Use your common sense to evaluate your lawyer's advice and actions. If they seem wrong, ask about them. If you don't get satisfactory answers, find another lawyer.

Do tell your lawyer everything relating to your case. His ignorance of important facts will hurt you more than it will hurt him.

Don't tell your lawyer that you plan to lie, or break the law, in some way. An ethical lawyer will advise you not to do it. He may even stop representing you. An unethical lawyer will help you get into serious trouble.

Do give your lawyer all important papers and information, as soon as possible. The sooner the lawyer knows about a development, or a problem, the sooner he can deal with it.

> *Don't call your lawyer every time a question comes to mind. You'll drive him nuts, prevent him from doing other important things, and run up your own bill. Instead, make a list of your questions and save them all for the next meeting or a single telephone call.*

Do as much as you can to reduce the work the lawyer, or his staff, must do. You can help obtain needed information and compile lists. Some consumers even handle simple court appearances when both sides have agreed in advance to a continuance. By contributing work and effort to your case, you save time and money, while keeping yourself actively involved.

> *Don't dump all your unrelated problems on your lawyer. If you need someone to talk to, find a friend, instead of someone who charges you $35 every time he picks up the phone.*

Do pay your lawyer's bills, if they are proper and you have the money. Nothing can lose your case quicker than not paying your lawyer. If the bill isn't proper, or if you are short of money, discuss this with him.

> *Don't pay your lawyer's bill without checking to make sure it's reasonable. Don't hesitate to question your lawyer about a bill that seems incorrect.*

Do let your lawyer know when you appreciate something he has done. Like everyone else, lawyers like and need to be stroked.

> *Don't constantly complain about the quality of lawyering you're getting. More than a couple of complaints is counter-productive. If you don't approve of his work, find a new lawyer.*

HANDLING THE OPPOSING LAWYER

If you have your own lawyer, NEVER talk to the creditor's lawyer. The creditor's lawyer will take advantage of his superior knowledge and bargaining experience. Sometimes, though, lawyers get in the way of settling a dispute.

If you discover that your lawyer is obstructing a reasonable resolution, raise the issue with him. If your lawyer does not give you a satisfactory response, look for another lawyer. Don't try to negotiate behind your lawyer's back.

On the other hand, if the creditor's lawyer is obstructing a reasonable resolution, your attorney is not allowed to advise you to contact the creditor directly. But, if your attorney complains that the case could be settled if the creditor's attorney took a long vacation, take the initiative. Without telling your lawyer, contact the creditor and suggest that the dispute could be resolved quickly by a face to face meeting.

If you don't have an attorney, sometimes you must deal with a creditor's lawyer. Always keep in mind that he is trying to get as much of your money as possible.

> Be extremely suspicious of any questions he asks.
>
> Be extremely wary of any papers he gives you to sign. Just understanding what a document says is not be enough. Often, what a document does NOT say is more important than what it does say. Don't trust the lawyer if he explains or agrees to something, unless he is willing to include the explanation or agreement in the document itself.

Creditors' lawyers often come on very strong. Remember, however, they are almost always willing to bargain. Never simply submit to the lawyer's demands. Always try to negotiate for something in return. Never give unless you get, even if it is just a verbal promise not to take any action against you for some period of time.

About the last thing a creditor's lawyer wants is for you to defend the lawsuit "*pro se*," by yourself, without an attorney. Judges bend over backwards to make sure your rights are protected in such hearings. Grievances that a lawyer couldn't possibly raise as a legal defense are often taken seriously by a judge when raised by you in a *pro se* hearing. Until clearly shown otherwise, a judge has to assume you have a valid defense, but lack the knowledge to put your defense into proper legal form.

> Although it's safest to be represented in court by a lawyer, some skillful consumers have been able to defend the first part of a case, while getting advice from a lawyer who doesn't formally appear of record. Often, just the aggravation of dealing with a *pro se* defendant causes the creditor's attorney to all but beg for some sort of a settlement. If the creditor doesn't settle, the consumer then brings in an attorney who really handles the case.

TESTIFYING UNDER OATH

CHAPTER TWENTY-TWO

If you know how to speak, you know how to testify.

Most people are intimidated by courtrooms, judges, lawyers, and judicial proceedings in general. Unless you are somehow involved in a current or potential criminal proceeding, or you have something important to hide, you really don't need to fret about giving testimony in a civil trial or a citation examination.

GENERAL GUIDELINES

Of course, you're better off represented by a good lawyer who can help you prepare your testimony. Such a lawyer is sensitive to how questions are asked and how answers should be phrased. They also know which facts are likely to help you and which facts are likely to harm you.

> If you have a particular reason to believe that you may have committed or been involved in a crime, and you may be required to give answers that could be used against you, immediately consult with a criminal defense attorney or public defender. NEVER try to give any testimony by yourself under such circumstances.

If you are representing yourself in court, you'll have ample opportunity to make your arguments and convince the court you are a good person. You don't need to make your case while you are being questioned.

If you are giving testimony about your income and assets in a citation proceeding, your only objective is to give the creditor as little information as possible, without committing perjury or being in contempt of court.

When you are being questioned by opposing counsel, follow these basic, but important, guidelines:

Listen attentively > Listen carefully, and make sure you understand the entire question before you answer it. If you don't understand the question, or the question can have different meanings, ask for clarification.

Answer only the question you have been asked > When you have given your answer to the specific question asked, stop talking. Even though you may want to justify yourself or explain, don't.

> NEVER VOLUNTEER INFORMATION. Information is a powerful weapon, so don't arm your opponent.

If you do not know an answer, don't guess > Say you don't know.

If you do not remember something, say so > No one remembers everything. The older an event, the less likely it is that you can remember it. Few people remember specific dates, times, or amounts without referring to a calendar or other writing.

If you are unsure of your answer, say you are unsure > You can try to answer the question after you have made it clear that you are not sure whether your answer is, in fact, correct.

Don't be evasive > Everyone knows something, no one forgets everything, and no one is unsure of everything. If you are evasive, you will not be believed. Moreover, the opposing lawyer will sense that you have something important to hide, and eventually get the answer.

Keep your answers as short as possible > If you can do so, answer with a simple "yes" or a "no."

Beware of questions that assume something that isn't true > An often used lawyer's trick is to ask a question such as, "Do you still beat your wife?" The question *assumes* that you beat your spouse. Any "yes" or "no" answer admits the assumed truth of the question. If you are asked this type of question, deny the untrue fact. Simply say, "Since I never ..., the question isn't proper."

> Usually, this type of question is not quite so obvious. Instead, the attorney will play with a single word. For example, instead of asking, "When did you SELL your car to your brother?," he might ask, "When did you GIVE your car to your brother?" Your answer might be, "I never gave my car to my brother, but I did sell it to him last year."

Beware of questions that quote you or put words in your mouth > Another trick of the trade is to ask a witness, "Didn't you previously say...," and then quote something other than what you actually said. If you are asked a such question, insist that your actual words be repeated from the transcript, so that you are sure you are being quoted accurately, completely, and in context.

Pay attention if you are asked a series of routine questions that all have the same "yes" or "no" answer > Some attorneys use this technique to get you into a habit of automatically giving the same answer. They then ask you an important question, hoping you won't think about it, and just automatically give the same answer.

If you are asked questions about a document, do not answer until you are shown a copy of the document > Never assume that you have seen a document, until you are shown the entire document and you really recognize it.

Never admit to signing any document, unless you are shown the document with your signature on it > Consumers often confuse documents, or assume they must have signed an important document, even though they didn't. Creditors who fail to prepare vital documents sometimes try to cover their omission by tricking consumers into admitting that they signed non-existent papers.

Stay as relaxed as possible and never lose your temper > If you get angry, you are likely to say things you will later regret. If you feel yourself about to blow up, take a few breaths and, if necessary, ask for a bathroom break to allow time to compose yourself.

LYING UNDER OATH

Many people testifying for the first time, worry that they will be prosecuted for perjury. Perjury is lying under oath. As long as you aren't intentionally and grossly lying, it is extremely unlikely that you will ever be prosecuted for perjury. Indeed, even people who intentionally lie in court are very rarely prosecuted. It's extremely difficult to prove perjury. To do so, the prosecutor must first prove that the statement was false, and then prove that you knew it was false when you said it.

> For example, suppose a bank has a $10,000 judgment against you and you are summoned to testify about your income and assets in a citation examination. You don't have a bank account in your own name, but you keep $10,000 of your money in your brother's bank account.
>
> If you are asked, "Do you have a bank account?," and you answer, "No," you are telling the truth.
>
>> You can't be convicted of perjury for failing to volunteer information you know the opposing attorney is trying to discover, but neglects to directly ask.

However, if you are asked, "Do you have money in a bank account?," and you answer, "No," you are lying.

> If the truth is uncovered, you could be prosecuted for perjury. However, if the amount involved were relatively small, it isn't likely that a prosecutor will pursue the case. It would be hard for a prosecutor to prove that you intentionally lied, rather than merely forgot about an old account with a few dollars left in it.

In short, don't lose sleep worrying that you will be sent to jail if you make a mistake in your testimony.

AFTERWORD

Finally, we need your help.

No, we don't want you to send us money. We'll return it if you do! Consumer Credit Foundation of America exists for many purposes, including:

> helping the general public overcome their credit-created financial difficulties, and
>
> helping protect consumers from all types of frauds, both large and small, perpetrated by businesses.

The help we need from you is three-fold.

First, we want to know what you think of *GETTING OUT FROM UNDER* because this book was written to help you get your financial life back on track. Please share your thoughts with us.

Second, laws change, viewpoints change, and tactics of creditors and consumers change. As these changes occur, we intend to be back to share them with you. You can help us do just that. Write to us and share both your successful and unsuccessful experiences in the handling of your debts. Unsuccessful experiences are important learning tools, not failures.

Third, send us a description of your experiences with, and knowledge of, frauds frequently used by businesses to cheat consumers. These can be nickel and dime frauds, such as a butcher with a heavy thumb or a car dealer adding hundreds of dollars to the invoice for "dealer preparation." We want you to share these "tricks of the trades" with us, so we, in turn, can share them with other consumers.

Your identity will not be disclosed. The more detail you can give us, the better. Please send all written material to:

CONSUMER CREDIT FOUNDATION OF AMERICA
P.O. Box 578371
Chicago, IL 60657-8371

APPENDIX

WORKSHEETS FOR USE WITH SECTION TWO

GENERAL EXPLANATION OF WORKSHEETS

Don't let the worksheets intimidate you. They are easy to use and do most of the work for you.

Complete the worksheets one at a time.

Read the instructions for each worksheet.

Look at each worksheet to get a feel for how it works. Don't worry if you don't understand every last detail.

Fill out the worksheet by inserting the appropriate amounts and doing the required computations. Most of the arithmetic is simple addition and subtraction. Occasionally, you will have to multiply or divide two numbers.

The most burdensome and most important task is collecting the information about your financial situation. Try to be reasonably accurate and complete, but estimated amounts are much better than no amounts at all. Don't waste time and effort on small amounts. Round off numbers to whole dollars, or even tens.

The worksheets follow the procedure outlined in Section Two of the text. The next page lists the four steps and four sets of worksheets.

STEP ONE - Assemble Information

A - Expected Cash Income

B - Living Expenses

C - Debts

D - Assets

STEP TWO - Determine Your Alternatives

E - Sufficiency of Income

F - Reduction of Debts

G - Sufficiency to Pay Debts If Debts Are Reduced

H - Sale of Assets

I - Sufficiency of Income to Pay Debts if Assets Are Sold

J - Sufficiency of Income to Pay Debts if Debts Are Reduced and Assets Are Sold

STEP THREE - Adopt A Strategy

K - List of Goals

L - Determining Whether Non-Essential Expenses Are Consistent With Your Goals

M - List of Non-Essential Expenses Consistent With Your Goals

N - Determining Whether Non-Essential Debts Are Consistent With Your Goals

O - List of Non-Essential Debts That Help You Achieve Your Goals (after likely reductions)

P - List of Essential Debts After Likely Reductions

Q - List of Debts That Prevent You From Achieving Your Goals (after likely reductions)

R - Determining Sufficiency of Funds to Implement Your Strategy

S - Cash Flow If Your Strategy Is Implemented

STEP FOUR - Implement Your Strategy

T - Schedule of Actions Needed to Implement Your Strategy

Instructions for

WORKSHEET A
EXPECTED CASH INCOME

Make a quick guess of each type of income you received over the last year. Write your guesses in the first column of the worksheet.

Determine the actual amounts of each type of income you received over the last year. Insert these amounts in the second column. If your quick guesses are a lot different from the actual amounts, you are not at all in control of your finances.

Use last year's amounts to help you estimate your monthly and annual incomes for the next twelve months. Write those amounts in the third and fourth columns. If your income does not vary from month to month, the annual amounts should be twelve times the monthly amounts.

Try to determine how much of your income can be reached if a creditor gets a judgment against you. Read the discussions in the book about wage garnishments and attachments. You also will need to find out what your particular state laws protect. If you don't have time to find out, here a couple of general guidelines:

> Federal law limits wage attachments to 25% of an individual's disposable income. Many states limit wage attachments to even smaller amounts.
>
> Federal law protects all Social Security benefits from creditors.
>
> Federal law does not permit creditors other than the federal government itself to attach amounts owed by the federal government, such as salaries of federal employees. However, income tax refunds can be reached to satisfy a debt for a state or federally guaranteed educational loan.
>
> Almost any income can be reached to make a consumer pay alimony or child support obligations.

Total each column.

WORKSHEET A - EXPECTED CASH INCOME

SOURCE OF INCOME	CASH INCOME - LAST 12 MONTHS		CASH INCOME - ESTIMATED FUTURE		HOW MUCH OF IT IS EXEMPT FROM CREDITORS
	Quick Guess	Actual	Monthly	Year	
YOUR TAKE HOME PAY					
Salary / Wages					
Commissions / Tips					
Bonuses					
Overtime					
Second / Odd Job(s)					
SPOUSE'S TAKE HOME PAY					
Salary / Wages					
Commissions / Tips					
Bonuses					
Overtime					
Second / Odd Job(s)					
INVESTMENT INCOME					
Dividends					
Interest					
Rent					
Other					
RETIREMENT INCOME					
Social Security					
Employer Pension					
IRA / Keogh					
SUPPORT PAYMENTS					
Alimony					
Child Support					
Disability					
Unemployment					
Public Assistance					
Workers' Comp					
OTHER CASH INCOME					
Tax Refunds					
Miscellaneous					
TOTALS Item Numbers	A-1	A-2	A-3	A-4	A-5

Instructions for

WORKSHEET B
LIVING EXPENSES

This worksheet is only for expenses. DO NOT INCLUDE DEBTS SUCH AS YOUR MORTGAGE OR CAR LOANS. Debts that you have a legal obligation to keep paying are treated separately.

Make a quick guess of each type of your living expenses during the past year. Write the amounts in the first column of the worksheet.

Determine the actual amounts of each of your expenses over the last year. Use the accompanying check-list of specific expenses to help you collect as complete a list as possible. Insert these amounts in the second column. If your quick guesses are a lot different from the actual amounts, you are not at all in control of your finances.

Categorize last year's expenses by their importance:

> **Essential** - needed to survive
>
> **Important** - needed to substantially maintain your standard of living
>
> **Avoidable** - not needed to maintain your standard of living
>
> Don't spend a lot of time worrying whether a particular expense belongs in one category or another. Go with your first impression. Write these amounts in the third, fourth and fifth columns.

Use last year's amounts to help you estimate your Essential, Important and Avoidable living expenses for the next twelve months. Write those amounts in the fifth, sixth and seventh columns.

Total each column.

CHECK-LIST OF SOME SPECIFIC EXPENSES
for use with Worksheet B

ALIMONY AND CHILD SUPPORT

APPLIANCES

Purchases and repairs of:

Air Conditioner	Clothes Dryer
Clothes Washer	Dish Washer
Freezer	Furnace
Hot Water Heater	Humidifier
Oven/Stove	Refrigerator
Stereo	Television
Toaster	Video recorder

BANKING FEES

Checking Accounts
Cashier's Checks and Money Orders
Check Printing
Credit Cards
Check Cashing
Overdraft Charges

CHARITIES

CHILD CARE

Babysitting	Day Care

CLOTHING AND FURNISHINGS

Athletic, Business, Casual, Dress, and School:

Belts	Blouses
Boots	Coats
Dresses	Ear Muffs
Gloves	Hats
Purses	Scarves
Shirts	Shoes
Skirts	Slacks
Socks	Stockings
Suits	Sweaters
Ties	Umbrellas
Underwear	Wallets

EDUCATION

Books
Fees
Room and Board
Supplies
Tuition
Transportation
Uniforms

FOOD

Children's lunch money
Groceries - basic staples
Groceries - prepared
Groceries - snack foods
Groceries - sweets
Restaurants - business
Restaurants - entertainment
Restaurants - personal

HOUSEHOLD AND PERSONAL

Bathroom Supplies
Cleaning Services
Cleaning Supplies
Cosmetics
Dry cleaning
Garden Supplies
Kitchen Utensils/Dishes
Laundry Supplies
Light Bulbs
Linens, towels
Postage
Small appliances
Stationery
Tools

HOUSING

Do not include mortgage or rent payments. Treat them as debts.

Down Payment
Maintenance
Repairs
Security Deposit

INSURANCE

Auto/Vehicle
Health
Homeowner's/Renter's
Life

INVESTMENT EXPENSES

MEDICAL AND DENTAL

Clinics
Dentures
Doctors and other professionals
Eye Glasses
Hearing Aid
Hospitals
Medicine

MISCELLANEOUS

Boat
Children's Allowances
Union Dues
Vacation Home

NURSING CARE

Nursing Home
Visiting Nurse/Aide/Therapist

PROFESSIONALS

Accountant
Lawyer
Tax Preparer

RECREATION

Athletics
Club Membership Fees
Concerts
Films
Hobbies
Music
Theater
Video Tapes
Vacations

TAXES

Do not include withheld taxes.

Income, city
Income, federal
Income, state
Real Estate

TRANSPORTATION

Do not include loan or lease payments. Treat them as debts.

Airfare
Buses
Down Payment on purchase of vehicle
Gas and oil
Security deposit on lease of vehicle
Taxicabs
Trains
Vehicle Maintenance
Vehicle Repairs

UTILITIES

Coal
Electricity
Natural Gas
Propane Gas
Sewer Fees
Telephone
Trash Removal
Water

WORKSHEET B - LIVING EXPENSES

TYPE OF EXPENSE	PAST EXPENSES - LAST 12 MONTHS					FUTURE EXPENSES - ESTIMATED		
	QUICK GUESS	ACTUAL				MONTHLY		
		Total	Essential	Important	Avoidable	Essential	Important	Avoidable
ALIMONY								
APPLIANCES								
BANKING								
CHARITIES								
CHILD CARE								
CLOTHING								
EDUCATION								
FOOD								
HOUSEHOLD AND PERSONAL								
HOUSING								
INSURANCE								
INVESTMENT EXPENSES								
MEDICAL AND DENTAL								
MISCELLANEOUS								
NURSING CARE								
PROFESSIONALS								
RECREATION								
TAXES								
TRANSPORTATION								
UTILITIES								
TOTALS Item Numbers	B-1	B-2	B-3	B-4	B-5	B-6	B-7	B-8

Instructions for
WORKSHEET C - DEBTS

Make a list of all your debts. Debts include loans, leases and contracts.

Categorize your debts by their future importance to you:

> **Essential** - needed to survive
> **Important** - needed to substantially maintain your standard of living
> **Avoidable** - not needed to maintain your standard of living

Don't spend a lot of time worrying whether a particular debt belongs in one category or another. Go with your first impression.

> Page 1 of the worksheet is for your Essential Debts
> Page 2 of the worksheet is for your Important Debts
> Page 3 of the worksheet is for your Avoidable Debts

ON EACH OF THE THREE PAGES:

Write the creditors' names in the first column.

Write the total amount of the debt in the second column. For a mortgage, loan, credit card or store charge, this is the amount of principal owed. For a lease or a contract, this is the total of all payments you are obligated to make. Include all creditors whose bills are overdue.

Write the minimum monthly payment that you are allowed to make in the third column. For loans, this is the amount of the installment payment. For charge cards, this is the minimum amount shown on your bill. If the debt is an overdue bill, there is no minimum monthly payment because, technically, the entire amount is due.

If there is a charge for late payment, write this in the fifth column.

If the debt is past due, write down how many months it is past due in the sixth column.

Write the names of each person liable for the debt in the seventh column. Include any guarantors or co-signers.

If there is collateral securing the loan, list it in the eighth column.

Determine what the creditor can do if you do not pay the debt. Estimate how long will it take the creditor to act.

Is there any way the amount owed or the monthly payments can be reduced? Consider whether you can dispute the debt or persuade the creditor that partial payment is better than nothing. Note your answers in the last column.

Total the first, second and sixth columns on each of the first three pages of the worksheet.

ON THE FOURTH PAGE OF THE WORKSHEET:

Copy the three totals for your Essential Debts from Page 1 onto the first row.
Copy the three totals for your Important Debts from Page 2 onto the second row.
Copy the three totals for your Avoidable Debts from Page 3 onto the fourth row.

Total the first and second rows and write the results on the third row.
Total the third and fourth rows and write the results on the fifth row.

WORKSHEET C - DEBTS (page 1 of 4)

ESSENTIAL DEBTS

NAME OF CREDITOR	TOTAL AMOUNT OWED	MINIMUM MONTHLY PAYMENT	INTEREST RATE	HOW MUCH IS LATE CHARGE	NUMBER OF MONTHS PAST DUE	TOTAL AMOUNT PAST DUE	WHO IS LIABLE FOR DEBT	WHAT COLLATERAL SECURES DEBT	WHAT CREDITOR CAN DO IF NOT PAID and HOW LONG IT WILL TAKE	CAN DEBT BE REDUCED
TOTAL ESSENTIAL DEBTS Item Numbers	C-1	C-2				C-3				

WORKSHEET C - DEBTS (page 2 of 4)

IMPORTANT DEBTS

NAME OF CREDITOR	TOTAL AMOUNT OWED	MINIMUM MONTHLY PAYMENT	INTEREST RATE	HOW MUCH IS LATE CHARGE	NUMBER OF MONTHS PAST DUE	TOTAL AMOUNT PAST DUE	WHO IS LIABLE FOR DEBT	WHAT COLLATERAL SECURES DEBT	WHAT CREDITOR CAN DO IF NOT PAID and HOW LONG IT WILL TAKE	CAN DEBT BE REDUCED
TOTAL IMPORTANT DEBTS Item Numbers	C-4	C-5				C-6				

WORKSHEET C - DEBTS (page 3 of 4)

IMPORTANT DEBTS

NAME OF CREDITOR	TOTAL AMOUNT OWED	MINIMUM MONTHLY PAYMENT	INTEREST RATE	HOW MUCH IS LATE CHARGE	NUMBER OF MONTHS PAST DUE	TOTAL AMOUNT PAST DUE	WHO IS LIABLE FOR DEBT	WHAT COLLATERAL SECURES DEBT	WHAT CREDITOR CAN DO IF NOT PAID and HOW LONG IT WILL TAKE	CAN DEBT BE REDUCED
TOTAL AVOIDABLE DEBTS Item Numbers	C-7	C-8				C-9				

THIS PAGE INTENTIONALLY BLANK

WORKSHEET C - DEBTS (page 4 of 4)

TOTAL DEBTS

NAME OF CREDITOR	TOTAL AMOUNT OWED	MINIMUM MONTHLY PAYMENT	INTEREST RATE	HOW MUCH IS LATE CHARGE	NUMBER OF MONTHS PAST DUE	TOTAL AMOUNT PAST DUE	WHO IS LIABLE FOR DEBT	WHAT COLLATERAL SECURES DEBT	WHAT CREDITOR CAN DO IF NOT PAID and HOW LONG IT WILL TAKE	CAN DEBT BE REDUCED
TOTAL ESSENTIAL Item Numbers	C-1	C-2				C-3				
plus TOTAL IMPORTANT Item Numbers	C-4	C-5				C-6				
equals **TOTAL ESSENTIAL and TOTAL IMPORTANT** Item Numbers	C-10	C-11				C-12				
plus TOTAL AVOIDABLE Item Numbers	C-7	C-8				C-9				
equals **TOTAL DEBTS** Item Numbers	C-13	C-14				C-15				

Instructions for

WORKSHEET D
ASSETS

Make a list of everything you own that is valuable and sellable. Do not include household furniture, clothing and other garage-sale items. Use the list on the worksheet to guide you.

Consider each item and decide whether it is really important for you to keep it or whether it is something that you can live without. Make a note of your decision in the second column.

Estimate the fair market value and the liquidation value of the property. If possible, get informed estimates of value. Write those figures in the third and fourth columns.

If the property is collateral for a debt, write the total amount of the debt in the fifth column. Get the amount of the debt from Worksheet C.

Deduct the amount of the debt from the value of the property. This will tell you the quick equity (liquidation value less amount owed) and the Full Equity (fair market value less amount owed). Write these amounts in the sixth and seventh columns. If the property is not collateral, then your equity equals the value of the property.

If you have enough time, check your state laws to determine how much of your equity is protected from judgment creditors. Usually, this is a flat dollar amount but sometimes it is a percentage of the value. Usually, the protection afforded the Quick Equity is more important to the consumer than the protection afforded the Full Equity because property that is seized to enforce a judgment is typically auctioned. If the entire Quick Equity is protected, it is unlikely that the property will be seized to satisfy a judgment.

Total each column.

WORKSHEET D - ASSETS

DESCRIPTION OF PROPERTY	DO YOU NEED TO KEEP IT	VALUE		if collateral TOTAL AMOUNT OWED	QUICK EQUITY	FULL EQUITY	HOW MUCH EQUITY IS EXEMPT	
		Fair Market	Liquidation				Quick Equity	Full Equity
CASH								
BANK DEPOSITS								
Checking Accounts								
Savings Accounts								
Certificates of Deposit								
PENSION/RETIREMENT PLAN								
Employer								
IRA/Keogh								
Other								
REAL ESTATE								
Investment Property								
Residence								
Vacation Home								
INTANGIBLE PERSONALTY								
Debts Owed To You								
Deposits								
Insurance								
Lawsuits								
Other								
TANGIBLE PERSONALTY								
Antiques and Art								
Boat								
Collections								
Jewelry								
Motor Vehicles								
Other								
INVESTMENTS								
Bonds								
Mutual Funds								
Stocks								
Trading Account								
Other								
OTHER VALUABLE PROPERTY								
TOTALS FOR ALL PROPERTY Item Numbers		D-1	D-2	D-3	D-4	D-5	D-6	D-7

Instructions for

WORKSHEET E
SUFFICIENCY OF INCOME TO PAY DEBTS

If the information you collected in the earlier worksheets is accurate, Worksheet E will tell you to what extent your cash income will be sufficient to cover your future expenses and future debt payments. The worksheet also tells you how many months it will take to bring all your past due debts current at three different levels of spending.

Using the information from Worksheets A, B and C, enter the appropriate amounts for each item.

Do the required subtractions in the fourth column all the way down to Line 13. Ignore the division computations and boxes on the right.

Go back to Line 9. Divide Item E-1 into Item C-15. Write the result under Item E-4.

Go to Line 11. Divide Item E-2 into Item C-15. Write the result under Item E-5.

Go to Line 13. Divide Item E-3 into Item C-15. Write the result under Item E-6.

WORKSHEET E - SUFFICIENCY OF INCOME TO PAY DEBTS

Line	Description		Monthly Amounts: Item Number	Monthly Amounts: Amount
1	Estimated Cash Income		A-3	
2	less Essential Expenses	-	B-6	
3	equals remaining income	=		
4	less Essential Debt payments	-	C-2	
5	equals remaining income	=		
6	less Important Debt payments	-	C-5	
7	equals remaining income	=		
8	less Avoidable Debt payments	-	C-8	
9	equals remaining income	=	E-1	

		Total Past Due Debts		Months Needed To Bring All Debts Current
		Item C-15		Item E-4
E-1	divided into		=	

Line	Description		Item Number	Amount
10	less Important Expenses	-	B-7	
11	equals remaining income	=	E-2	

		Total Past Due Debts		Months Needed To Bring All Debts Current
		Item C-15		Item E-5
E-2	divided into		=	

Line	Description		Item Number	Amount
12	less Avoidable Expenses	-	B-8	
13	equals remaining income	=	E-3	

		Total Past Due Debts		Months Needed To Bring All Debts Current
		Item C-15		Item E-6
E-3	divided into		=	

Instructions for

WORKSHEET F
REDUCTION OF DEBTS
BY MEANS OTHER THAN PAYMENT

List the debts that you think you can reduce by some means other than payment. These include debts you can dispute, debts you can compromise, and monthly debt payments that can be reduced.

In the first column, write the name of the creditor.

In the second column, write the amount by which you think you can get the amount of the debt reduced. Don't write the amount of the debt that will be left after the reduction.

In the third column, write the amount by which you think you can get the monthly payments reduced. Don't write the amount of the payment that will be left after the reduction.

In the fourth column, write the amount by which you think you can get the past due amount of the debt reduced. Don't write the amount that will be left after the reduction.

In the fifth column, note the actions you will need to take to obtain the reductions.

Total the first, second and third columns.

DETERMINING AMOUNTS REMAINING AFTER REDUCTIONS:

Copy the appropriate items from Worksheet C onto the first row.

Copy Items F-1, F-2 and F-3 from above onto the next row.

Subtract this row from the row above and enter the results on the last row of the worksheet.

WORKSHEET F - REDUCTION OF DEBTS BY MEANS OTHER THAN PAYMENT OF CASH

NAME OF CREDITOR	HOW MUCH TOTAL AMOUNT OWED CAN BE REDUCED	HOW MUCH MONTHLY PAYMENT CAN BE REDUCED	HOW MUCH PAST DUE AMOUNT CAN BE REDUCED	ACTIONS NEEDED TO OBTAIN REDUCTIONS
TOTAL REDUCTIONS Item Numbers	F-1	F-2	F-3	

DETERMINING AMOUNTS REMAINING AFTER REDUCTIONS

	Debts	Payments	Past Due
TOTAL DEBTS Item Numbers	C-13	C-14	C-15
Less TOTAL REDUCTIONS Item Numbers	F-1	F-2	F-3
Equals **REMAINING DEBTS** Item Numbers	F-4	F-5	F-6

Instructions for

WORKSHEET G
SUFFICIENCY OF INCOME TO PAY DEBTS IF DEBTS ARE REDUCED

Enter the appropriate items from Worksheets A, B and F.

Do the required subtractions in the fourth column all the way down to Line 9. Ignore the division computations and boxes on the right.

Go back to Line 5. Divide Item G-1 INTO Item F-6. Write the result under Item G-4.

Go to Line 7. Divide Item G-2 INTO Item F-6. Write the result under Item G-5.

Go to Line 9. Divide Item G-3 INTO Item F-6. Write the result under Item G-6.

WORKSHEET G - SUFFICIENCY OF INCOME TO PAY DEBTS IF DEBTS ARE REDUCED

Line	Description		MONTHLY AMOUNTS Item Number	MONTHLY AMOUNTS Amount		Total Reduced Past Due Debts		Months Needed To Bring All Debts Current
						Item F-6		Item G-4
1	Estimated Cash Income		A-3					
2	less Essential Expenses	-	B-6					
3	equals remaining income	=						
4	less Reduced Debt payments	-	F-5					
5	equals remaining income	=	G-1		divided into		=	

Line	Description		Item Number	Amount		Total Past Due Debts		Months Needed To Bring All Debts Current
						Item F-6		Item G-5
6	less Important Expenses	-	B-7					
7	equals remaining income	=	G-2		divided into		=	

Line	Description		Item Number	Amount		Total Past Due Debts		Months Needed To Bring All Debts Current
						Item F-6		Item G-6
8	less Avoidable Expenses	-	B-8					
9	equals remaining income	=	G-3		divided into		=	

Instructions for

WORKSHEET H
ASSETS YOU DO NOT NEED AND CAN BE TURNED INTO CASH

Take the information from Worksheet D to complete columns the second through sixth columns of Worksheet H. Include only assets that you do not need to keep.

In the last column, make notes of the actions you need to take to turn assets into cash.

Total the fifth and sixth columns.

WORKSHEET H - ASSETS YOU DO NOT NEED AND CAN BE TURNED INTO CASH

DESCRIPTION OF PROPERTY	VALUE		if collateral TOTAL AMOUNT OWED	QUICK EQUITY	FULL EQUITY	WHAT ACTIONS NEED TO BE TAKEN
	Fair Market	Liquidation				
CASH						
BANK DEPOSITS						
Checking Accounts						
Savings Accounts						
Certificates of Deposit						
PENSION/RETIREMENT PLAN						
Employer						
IRA/Keogh						
Other						
REAL ESTATE						
Investment Property						
Residence						
Vacation Home						
INTANGIBLE PERSONALTY						
Debts Owed To You						
Deposits						
Insurance						
Lawsuits						
Other						
TANGIBLE PERSONALTY						
Antiques and Art						
Boat						
Collections						
Jewelry						
Motor Vehicles						
Other						
INVESTMENTS						
Bonds						
Mutual Funds						
Stocks						
Trading Account						
Other						
OTHER VALUABLE PROPERTY						
TOTAL CASH THAT CAN BE RAISED Item Numbers				H-1	H-2	

Instructions for

WORKSHEET I
SUFFICIENCY OF INCOME TO PAY DEBTS IF ASSETS ARE SOLD

Worksheet I is the same as Worksheet E except that Lines 2 and 3 include the cash you can raise by selling assets. On Worksheet H, you estimated the amount of cash you can raise by selling assets.

On Line 2 of Worksheet I, enter either:

> Item H-1, Quick Equity, if you will not have time to sell the asset for its fair market value; or
>
> Item H-2, the Full Equity, if you will have sufficient time to sell the asset.

WORKSHEET I - SUFFICIENCY OF INCOME TO PAY DEBTS IF ASSETS ARE SOLD

Line	Description		Monthly Amounts: Item Number	Monthly Amounts: Amount		Total Past Due Debts		Months Needed To Bring All Debts Current
1	Estimated Cash Income		A-3					
2	plus Cash from Sale of Assets	-	H-1 or H-2					
3	equals available income	=						
4	less Essential Expenses	-	B-6					
5	equals remaining income	=						
6	less Essential Debt payments	-	C-2					
7	equals remaining income	=						
8	less Important Debt payments	-	C-5					
9	equals remaining income	=						
10	less Avoidable Debt payments	-	C-8			Item C-15		Item I-4
11	equals remaining income	=	I-1		divided into		=	
12	less Important Expenses	-	B-7			Item C-15		Item I-5
13	equals remaining income	=	I-2		divided into		=	
14	less Avoidable Expenses	-	B-8			Item C-15		Item I-6
15	equals remaining income	=	I-3		divided into		=	

Instructions for

WORKSHEET J
SUFFICIENCY OF INCOME TO PAY DEBTS IF DEBTS ARE REDUCED AND ASSETS ARE SOLD

Worksheet J is the same as Worksheet G except that Lines 2 and 3 include the cash you can raise by selling property. On Worksheet H, you estimated the amount of cash you can raise by selling property.

On Line 2 of Worksheet J, enter either:

> Item H-1, Quick Equity, if you will not have time to sell the property for its fair market value; or
>
> Item H-2, the Full Equity, if you will have time.

WORKSHEET J - SUFFICIENCY OF INCOME TO PAY DEBTS IF DEBTS ARE REDUCED AND ASSETS ARE SOLD

Line	Description		MONTHLY AMOUNTS Item Number	Amount		Total Past Due Debts		Months Needed To Bring All Debts Current
1	Estimated Cash Income		A-3					
2	plus Cash from Sale of Assets	-	H-1 or H-2					
3	equals available income	=						
2	less Essential Expenses	-	B-6					
3	equals remaining income	=				Total Reduced Past Due Debts		Months Needed To Bring All Debts Current
4	less Reduced Debt payments	-	F-5			Item F-6		Item J-4
5	equals remaining income	=	J-1		divided into		=	
						Total Past Due Debts		Months Needed To Bring All Debts Current
						Item F-6		Item J-5
6	less Important Expenses	-	B-7					
7	equals remaining income	=	J-2		divided into		=	
						Total Past Due Debts		Months Needed To Bring All Debts Current
						Item F-6		Item J-6
8	less Avoidable Expenses	-	B-8					
9	equals remaining income	=	J-3		divided into		=	

Instructions for

WORKSHEET K
LIST OF IMPORTANT GOALS
THAT REQUIRE MONEY

Worksheet K helps you determine your financial priorities.

Take a blank piece of paper and write down all of your important personal goals. Choose reasonable and practical goals that you really are willing to strive to achieve. Peace on earth is too big a goal. Pruning the bushes is too narrow.

Identify the goals that REQUIRE MONEY and list them on Worksheet K. If you have more goals than fit on the worksheet, use another piece of paper.

Assign each goal a value between 1 and the number of goals you have listed. Assign the most important goal the highest number and the least important goal the value 1. Don't fret over assigning exactly the correct value. Go with your first instincts.

WORKSHEET K - LIST OF YOUR MOST IMPORTANT GOALS THAT REQUIRE MONEY

SUMMARY OF GOAL	NUMERICAL * IMPORTANCE
1	
2	
3	
4	
5	
6	
7	
8	
9	
10	
11	
12	
13	
14	
15	
16	

* Numerical Importance - number your goals 1 through the number of goals listed. Assign 1 to the least important goal and the highest number to the most important. If you have more than 16 goals, use an additional sheet of paper.

Instructions for WORKSHEET L
DETERMINING WHETHER NON-ESSENTIAL EXPENSES ARE CONSISTENT WITH YOUR GOALS

If you have properly classified your expenses, then your Essential Expenses are fixed and require no further consideration. Worksheet L helps you determine which of your non-essential expenses are consistent with your personal goals. The score itself is not important; most of the scores will be negative. The score of one expense compared to the scores of the others approximates its relative importance to you. The higher the score, the more the expense contributes to achieving your personal financial goals.

However, this approach is very simplistic and its limitations can produce some rather silly results. The numbers are just a guide - DON'T AUTOMATICALLY FOLLOW THEM WITHOUT APPLYING SOME COMMON SENSE.

The instructions for Worksheet L are shown on the form itself, but an example may help:

Assume that you have listed the following goals:

Goal	Value
Living in a house in the suburbs	4
Driving a reliable car	3
Saving money for retirement	2
Having a good remote controlled color television	1

Also assume that you could change jobs but cannot get to the new job without a car. If you examine the expense of automobile insurance you find that it:

Helps you achieve these goals:

Living in a house in the suburbs	5
Driving a reliable car	2
Total	7

Hinders you from achieving these goals:

Having a remote controlled color TV	1
Saving money for retirement	2
Total	3

Subtract the second total from the first and the score is 4. If you repeat the same process for each of the expenses associated with your hypothetical goals you might get these scores:

Type of Expense	Score
Repairing roof	-2
Buying a savings bond	-6
Buying a new television antenna	-8

Since the car insurance has the highest score -4, it contributes more to your hypothetical personal goals than the other expenses. However, if your roof is pouring water into your living room, repairing your roof may be a more pressing expense than paying your car insurance premium.

WORKSHEET L - DETERMINING WHETHER NON-ESSENTIAL EXPENSES ARE CONSISTENT WITH YOUR GOALS

DESCRIPTION OF EXPENSE -

Enter Numerical Value <assigned on Worksheet H> of each Goal this Expense helps you achieve

SUBTOTAL

Enter Numerical Value <assigned on Worksheet H> of each Goal this Expense prevents you from achieving

LESS - SUBTOTAL

EQUALS = **SCORE**

IF THE ANSWER IS GREATER THAN 0, THEN THE EXPENSE HELPS YOU TO ACHIEVE YOUR MORE THAN IT PREVENTS YOU FROM ACHIEVING YOUR GOALS.

OTHERWISE, YOU SHOULD CONSIDER REMOVING THE EXPENSE FROM YOUR BUDGET.

Instructions for

WORKSHEET M
NON-ESSENTIAL LIVING EXPENSES
CONSISTENT WITH YOUR GOALS

Worksheet M is nothing more than part of your revised budget. The other parts of the revised budget will be your Essential Expenses and your debt payments.

Worksheet M should include only the non-essential expenses that clearly contribute to achieving your financial goals. If you have doubts that an expense contributes to achieving your personal goals, do not include it. After you complete Worksheet R, you may find that you have to reduce or eliminate even more of these expenses. Use the scores on Worksheet L to help you make your selections.

WORKSHEET M - NON-ESSENTIAL LIVING EXPENSES CONSISTENT WITH YOUR GOALS

NON-ESSENTIAL EXPENSE	ESTIMATED MONTHLY AMOUNT
ALIMONY	
APPLIANCES	
BANKING	
CHARITIES	
CHILD CARE	
CLOTHING	
EDUCATION	
FOOD	
HOUSEHOLD AND PERSONAL	
HOUSING	
INSURANCE	
INVESTMENT EXPENSES	
MEDICAL AND DENTAL	
MISCELLANEOUS	
NURSING CARE	
PROFESSIONALS	
RECREATION	
TAXES	
TRANSPORTATION	
UTILITIES	
TOTAL NON-ESSENTIAL EXPENSES CONSISTENT WITH YOUR GOAL Item Number	M-1

Instructions for

WORKSHEET N
DETERMINING WHETHER NON-ESSENTIAL DEBTS ARE CONSISTENT WITH YOUR GOALS

Worksheet N operates exactly the same way as Worksheet L, except that Worksheet N evaluates your debts instead of your expenses. See the instructions for Worksheet L.

WORKSHEET N - DETERMINING WHETHER NON-ESSENTIAL DEBTS ARE CONSISTENT WITH YOUR GOALS

DESCRIPTION OF DEBT -

Enter Numerical Value <assigned on Worksheet H> of each Goal this Debt helps you achieve

SUBTOTAL

Enter Numerical Value <assigned on Worksheet H> of each Goal this Debt prevents you from achieving

LESS - SUBTOTAL

EQUALS = **SCORE**

IF THE ANSWER IS GREATER THAN 0, THEN THE DEBT HELPS YOU TO ACHIEVE YOUR MORE THAN IT PREVENTS YOU FROM ACHIEVING YOUR GOALS.

OTHERWISE, YOU SHOULD CONSIDER REMOVING THE DEBT FROM YOUR BUDGET.

Instructions for

WORKSHEET O
NON-ESSENTIAL DEBTS CONSISTENT WITH YOUR GOALS

Worksheet O is a list of the non-essential debts that you have determined to be consistent with your goals. Take the figures for the second, third and fourth columns from Worksheet F.

WORKSHEET O - NON-ESSENTIAL DEBTS CONSISTENT WITH YOUR GOALS

NAME OF CREDITOR	**TOTAL AMOUNT OWED** after likely reductions <Worksheet F>	**MINIMUM MONTHLY PAYMENT** after likely reductions <Worksheet F>	**TOTAL AMOUNT PAST DUE** after likely reductions <Worksheet F>
TOTALS Item Numbers	O-1	O-2	O-3

Instructions for

WORKSHEET P
ESSENTIAL DEBTS
AFTER LIKELY REDUCTIONS

Worksheet P is a list of your Essential Debts after deducting any reasonably likely reductions that can be achieved. Take the figures for the second, third and fourth columns from Worksheet F.

WORKSHEET P - ESSENTIAL DEBTS AFTER LIKELY REDUCTIONS

NAME OF CREDITOR	TOTAL AMOUNT OWED after likely reductions estimated on <Worksheet F>	MINIMUM MONTHLY PAYMENT after likely reductions estimated on <Worksheet F>	TOTAL AMOUNT PAST DUE after likely reductions estimated on <Worksheet F>
TOTALS Item Numbers	P-1	P-2	P-3

Instructions for

WORKSHEET Q
REMAINING DEBTS
THAT HINDER YOUR GOALS

Worksheet Q is a list of your remaining debts. Take the figures for the second, third and fourth columns from Worksheet F.

These debts are not Essential and they do not help you achieve your financial goals. Rather, they hinder you from achieving your financial goals. Debts on this list are the least important for you to pay unless they are owed to creditors who are dangerous to you. Review Worksheet C to see if any of these creditors are dangerous to you.

WORKSHEET Q - REMAINING DEBTS THAT HINDER YOUR GOALS

NAME OF CREDITOR	**TOTAL AMOUNT OWED** after likely reductions estimated on <Worksheet F>	**MINIMUM MONTHLY PAYMENT** after likely reductions estimated on <Worksheet F>	**TOTAL AMOUNT PAST DUE** after likely reductions estimated on <Worksheet F>
TOTALS Item Numbers	Q-1	Q-2	Q-3

Instructions for

WORKSHEET R
DETERMINING SUFFICIENCY OF FUNDS TO IMPLEMENT YOUR STRATEGY

Worksheet R determines whether you will have sufficient funds to implement your strategy.

Use the appropriate items from Worksheets A, B, M, O, P and Q to enter the monthly amounts in the second column. Also enter any planned increases in you income.

Multiply the amounts in the second column by 12 to get the annual amounts. Enter the annual amounts in the third column. Enter the amount of cash you expect to raise by selling property. Use H-1, the quick equity, if you are under time pressure. Otherwise enter H-2, the full equity.

Add the annual amounts and enter the subtotals in the fourth column.

Do the subtraction computations in the fourth column.

Item R-7 shows whether you will have enough cash to implement your plan. If you will not have enough cash, go back to Worksheet M and reduce your planned expenses.

WORKSHEET R - DETERMINING SUFFIENCY OF FUNDS TO IMPLEMENT STRATEGY DURING NEXT YEAR

	MONTHLY			ANNUAL				
AVAILABLE FUNDS								
Monthly Income	A-3		x 12 =	A-4				
Planned Increases in Income			x 12 =					
Cash from Planned Sales of Assets				H-1/2				
TOTAL FUNDS AVAILABLE NEXT 12 MONTHS							R-1	
less PLANNED EXPENSES								
Essential	B-6		x 12 =					
Non-Essential but Consistent with Goals	M-1		x 12 =					
Subtotal >						-	R-2	
equals REMAINING FUNDS						=		
less FUTURE MONTHLY DEBT after reductions x 12								
Essential	P-2		x 12 =					
Non-Essential but Consistent with goals	O-2		x 12 =					
Subtotal >						-	R-3	
equals REMAINING FUNDS						=		
less PAST DUE AMOUNTS after likely reductions								
ESSENTIAL	P-3		x 12 =					
NON-ESSENTIAL CONSISTENT WITH GOALS	O-3		x 12 =					
Subtotal >						-	R-4	
equals REMAINING FUNDS						=	R-5	
less DEBTS THAT HINDER YOUR GOALS after likely reductions								
FUTURE PAYMENTS	Q-2		x 12 =					
PAST DUE AMOUNTS	Q-3		x 12 -					
Subtotal >						-	R-6	
equals EXCESS (+) or DEFICIENCY (-)						=	R-7	

Instructions for

WORKSHEET S
CASH FLOW
IF YOUR STRATEGY IS IMPLEMENTED

Worksheet S is a cash flow projection. The purposes is to make sure that you will have cash at the times you will need it.

There are thirteen columns with a column for each of the next twelve months. There are fourteen rows in four groups. The first, fifth, thirteenth and fourteenth rows are the results of computations made for this Worksheet. The other rows are data taken from other Worksheets.

Enter the appropriate data from Worksheets A, H, O, P, Q and R. Also, enter the amount of cash you now have in the box that is in the first column and the first row.

Do the computations in the first column.

Copy the amount of cash remaining at the end of the first month shown in the bottom box onto the top box of the second column. Do the computations for the second column.

If there will not be any monthly variations in the cash received or cash paid, you do not need to do any more computations because the figures for the other months will be the same as the figures for the second month. If there will be variations in the cash received or the cash paid, continue the doing the computations for the remaining months.

If you have cash remaining at the end of each month, you will not have any cash flow problems. Otherwise, you will have to reconsider the timing of some of you expenses or debt payments.

WORKSHEET S - CASH FLOW IF STRATEGY IMPLEMENTED

	MONTH 1	MONTH 2	MONTH 3	MONTH 4	MONTH 5	MONTH 6	MONTH 7	MONTH 8	MONTH 9	MONTH 10	MONTH 11	MONTH 12
CASH AT BEGINNING OF MONTH = cash at end of last month												
CASH RECEIVED												
Existing Income <A-3>												
Planned Increases of Income												
Cash from Sales <H-1 / H-2>												
<u>add</u> **TOTAL CASH RECEIVED**	+	+	+	+	+	+	+	+	+	+	+	+
CASH PAID												
Living Expenses <R-2>												
Essential Debts												
Monthly Payments <P-2>												
Towards Past Due Debt <P-3>												
Debts Helping Goals												
Monthly Payments <O-2>												
Towards Past Due Debt <O-3>												
Debts Hindering Goals												
Monthly Payments <Q-2>												
Towards Past Due Debt <Q-3>												
<u>less</u> **TOTAL CASH PAID**	-	-	-	-	-	-	-	-	-	-	-	-
<u>equals</u> **CASH REMAINING AT END OF MONTH**	=	=	=	=	=	=	=	=	=	=	=	=

Instructions for

WORKSHEET T
SCHEDULE
FOR IMPLEMENTING YOUR STRATEGY

Worksheet T consists of four pages covering three months each. Under each month there are three columns.

Prepare a chronological list of all the actions needed to implement your plan. You will find it helpful to review your worksheets, especially Worksheets C, F and H.

Enter a brief description of each action in the second column.

Enter the due date of the action in the first column. If the action is a loan payment, enter a date that is at least five days before the payment is due, so you will have time to mail the payment. If the action does not have a due date, pick a reasonable target date for completing the action.

Complete the schedule for the entire time it will take you to implement your strategy, but no more than twelve months.

> Even if your plan will require more than twelve months, a schedule extending more than twelve months into the future will be subject to a lot of changes and probably will not be worth the effort. If your strategy will take longer than 12 months, prepare another 12 month schedule after six months, and periodically update your schedule until your strategy is completely implemented.

As you complete the actions, check them off in the third column.

Frequently review and update the schedule, checking to make sure you have completed all necessary actions.

WORKSHEET T - SCHEDULE FOR IMPLEMENTING STRATEGY (page 1 of 4)

CATEGORY	MONTH 1			MONTH 2			MONTH 3		
	DUE DATE	DESCRIPTION OF ACTIONS TO BE TAKEN	DONE	DUE DATE	DESCRIPTION OF ACTIONS TO BE TAKEN	DONE	DUE DATE	DESCRIPTION OF ACTIONS TO BE TAKEN	DONE
BORROW MONEY									
COMMUNICATE With Creditors With Advisors									
LEGAL PROCEEDINGS									
PAYMENTS (creditor/$) Regular Monthly Bring Past Due Current									
NEGOTIATIONS Compromises Payment Plans									
INFORMATION NEEDED									
PROTECT ASSETS									
SELL ASSETS									
OTHER									

WORKSHEET T - SCHEDULE FOR IMPLEMENTING STRATEGY (page 2 of 4)

CATEGORY	MONTH 4			MONTH 5			MONTH 6		
	DUE DATE	DESCRIPTION OF ACTIONS TO BE TAKEN	DONE	DUE DATE	DESCRIPTION OF ACTIONS TO BE TAKEN	DONE	DUE DATE	DESCRIPTION OF ACTIONS TO BE TAKEN	DONE
BORROW MONEY									
COMMUNICATE With Creditors With Advisors									
LEGAL PROCEEDINGS									
PAYMENTS (creditor/$) Regular Monthly Bring Past Due Current									
NEGOTIATIONS Compromises Payment Plans									
INFORMATION NEEDED									
PROTECT ASSETS									
SELL ASSETS									
OTHER									

WORKSHEET T - SCHEDULE FOR IMPLEMENTING STRATEGY (page 3 of 4)

CATEGORY	MONTH 7			MONTH 8			MONTH 9		
	DUE DATE	DESCRIPTION OF ACTIONS TO BE TAKEN	DONE	DUE DATE	DESCRIPTION OF ACTIONS TO BE TAKEN	DONE	DUE DATE	DESCRIPTION OF ACTIONS TO BE TAKEN	DONE
BORROW MONEY									
COMMUNICATE With Creditors With Advisors									
LEGAL PROCEEDINGS									
PAYMENTS (creditor/$) Regular Monthly Bring Past Due Current									
NEGOTIATIONS Compromises Payment Plans									
INFORMATION NEEDED									
PROTECT ASSETS									
SELL ASSETS									
OTHER									

WORKSHEET T - SCHEDULE FOR IMPLEMENTING STRATEGY (page 4 of 4)

CATEGORY	MONTH 10			MONTH 11			MONTH 12		
	DUE DATE	DESCRIPTION OF ACTIONS TO BE TAKEN	DONE	DUE DATE	DESCRIPTION OF ACTIONS TO BE TAKEN	DONE	DUE DATE	DESCRIPTION OF ACTIONS TO BE TAKEN	DONE
BORROW MONEY									
COMMUNICATE With Creditors With Advisors									
LEGAL PROCEEDINGS									
PAYMENTS (creditor/$) Regular Monthly Bring Past Due Current									
NEGOTIATIONS Compromises Payment Plans									
INFORMATION NEEDED									
PROTECT ASSETS									
SELL ASSETS									
OTHER									

INDEX

A

B

C

D

E

INDEX

M

N

O

P

Q

R

S

I N D E X

T

U

V

W